FOREWORD

The safe management of radioactive waste is an essential aspect of all nuclear power programmes. Although a general consensus has been reached in OECD countries on the use of geological repositories for the disposal of high-level radioactive waste, analysis of the long-term safety of these repositories, using performance assessment and other tools, is required prior to implementation.

The initial stage in developing a repository safety assessment is the identification of all factors that may be relevant to the long-term safety of the repository and their combination to form scenarios. This must be done in a systematic and transparent way in order to assure the regulatory authorities that nothing important has been forgotten.

Scenario development has become the general term used to describe the collection and organisation of the scientific and technical information necessary to assess the long-term performance or safety of radioactive waste disposal systems. This includes the identification of the relevant features, events and processes (FEPs), the synthesis of broad models of scientific understanding, and the selection of cases to be calculated. Scenario development provides the overall framework in which the cases and their calculated consequences can be discussed, including biases or shortcomings due to omissions or lack of knowledge.

In 1987 the NEA set up a working group on the identification and selection of scenarios for performance assessment of radioactive waste disposal. This led, in 1992, to the publication of a report entitled *Systematic Approaches to Scenario Development*. This report discussed methods but, at that time, there was not a large body of practical experience. In 1993 the NEA established a working group for the development of a database of features, events and processes relevant to the assessment of post-closure safety of radioactive waste repositories. The results are documented in a recently published report; a CD-ROM version of the database is also now available.

The NEA Workshop on Scenario Development was organised in Madrid, in May 1999, with the objective of reviewing developments in scenario methodologies and applications in safety assessments since 1992. The outcome of this workshop is the subject of this book. It is published under the responsibility of the Secretary-General of the OECD and does not in any way commit the countries of the OECD.

Acknowledgements

On behalf of all the participants, the NEA wishes to express its gratitude to the Spanish National Agency for Radioactive Waste (ENRESA) and to the Research Centre for Energy, Environment and Technology (Ciemat) for their hospitality and contribution to the organisation and success of the workshop.

The NEA is also very grateful to:

- the members of the Organising Committee for their help in setting up and running the workshop: Frits van Dorp, Chairman (Nagra, Switzerland), Trevor Sumerling (Safety Assessment Management Ltd, U.K.) and Jesus Alonso (ENRESA, Spain);

- the participants who agreed to animate the discussion groups;

- the speakers and authors of papers for their contribution; and

- all the participants for their active and constructive participation.

The analysis of the outcome of the workshop and technical summary has been prepared by Trevor Sumerling (Safety Assessment Management Ltd, U.K.). It has been reviewed by the participants.

4

TABLE OF CONTENTS

EXECUTIVE SUMMARY

Scenario development is concerned with the identification, broad description, and selection of potential futures relevant to safety assessment of radioactive waste repositories. It has also become the general term used to describe the marshalling and syntheses of the scientific and technical information necessary to assess the long-term performance or safety of radioactive waste disposal systems. This includes the identification of the relevant features, events and processes (FEPs), synthesis of broad models of scientific understanding, and selection of calculational cases to be performed. Scenario development provides the overall framework in which the cases and their calculated consequences can be discussed, including biases or shortcomings due to omissions or lack of knowledge.

The Workshop on "Scenario Development Methods and Practice" took place in Madrid on 10-12 May 1999, hosted by ENRESA/CIEMAT, Spain. The objectives of the Workshop were, in summary:

- To review the experience of application of scenario development methods since the publication of the OECD/NEA report "Safety Assessment of Radioactive Waste Repositories: Systematic Approaches to Scenario Development" in 1992.

- To provide a basis from which to prepare a report summarising the current status of scenario methodologies, identifying where sufficient methods exist and any outstanding problem areas.

The Workshop attracted nearly 40 representatives of 26 organisations from 12 NEA Member countries. This included organisations working actively in the field of scenario development for repository safety assessment and others, e.g. regulatory organisations that wished to be informed of the status, practical capabilities and implications of scenario development methods.

Discussion at the Workshop was seeded and focused by a Questionnaire that was answered by all organisations before attending the Workshop and by the presentation of papers on recent work.

This document is the final product of the Workshop. The main text is intended mainly for technical specialists and managers with tasks and responsibilities related to repository safety assessment. It summarises the current status of scenario development methods and their application based on the consensus views of participants established via responses to the Questionnaire and discussion at the Workshop. This is supported by Appendices that are mainly of interest to scenario development specialists. This includes the Questionnaire, the summary of responses and papers submitted to the Workshop.

The main conclusions from the Workshop are as follows.

- Structured approaches are necessary to marshal and synthesise the scientific and technical information concerning repository safety, and to select and present the cases to be analysed in safety assessments. These provide a framework on which to organise assessment work, promote the comprehensiveness of the analysis, and provide a basis for communication and explanation of the safety case to different audiences.

- Progress been made since 1992 in the compilation of databases of relevant features, events and processes, scenario construction methods, application of the methods and documentation.

- Some problems or challenges remain, e.g. how to ensure traceability and clarity of technical documentation, how to communicate to wider audiences, and how to treat probabilities and time dependence?

- Current methods are:

  - generally sufficient for their technical purpose within performance assessment and can be flexibly applied to different repository concepts at different stages of development;

  - only just being tested for compliance demonstration. Initial experience indicates that regulatory advice is required, e.g. to set guidance on expectations for reproducibility, scope of records and the treatment of human intrusion and other stylised scenarios;

  - not much used for wider communication, e.g. to non-technical stakeholders. More inventive thought may be required on how to marshal the available evidence to construct qualitative descriptions of performance and safety that are more convincing to wider audiences, and on how to address specific stakeholder concerns.

- There are differences between projects:

  - in the methods applied. These result from national and project-specific requirements, e.g. regulation, stage of development and nature of the disposal system. This is healthy and to be expected at the current stage of development:

  - in terminology corresponding to the different methods. Special terms must be defined and consistently used within projects and their use minimised in communication to wider audiences.

1. INTRODUCTION

Background

In 1987 the NEA Performance Assessment Advisory Group (PAAG) set up a Working Group on the Identification and Selection of Scenarios for Performance Assessment of Radioactive Waste Disposal. This led, in 1992, to the publication of an OECD/NEA report "Safety Assessment of Radioactive Waste Repositories: Systematic Approaches to Scenario Development" [1]. This report discussed scenario development methods but, at that time, there was not a large body of experience of application of the methods.

In 1993 the PAAG set up a Working Group on the Development of a Database of Features, Events and Processes Relevant to the Assessment of Post-Closure Safety of Radioactive Waste Repositories. The results are documented in "Features, Events and Processes (FEPs) for Geologic Disposal of Radioactive Waste – An International Database" [2].

The latter group recommended that a workshop should be arranged to review developments in scenario methodologies and applications in safety assessments since 1992, and that this might be the basis to prepare an overview of the status of methods and practice in this area. These recommendations were discussed on several occasions by the PAAG and, in October 1997, a proposal for a Workshop prepared by a small ad hoc Programme Committee was accepted.

The Workshop on Scenario Development took place in Madrid on 10-12 May 1999, hosted by ENRESA/CIEMAT, Spain. The Workshop was attended by 37 repository safety assessment specialists and reviewers, representing 26 organisations from 12 NEA Member countries.

The Workshop

The objectives of the Workshop, defined by the ad hoc Programme Committee, were:

- To provide a forum to review and discuss methods for scenario development and their contribution to the overall formation of a comprehensive and justifiable assessment of long-term safety.

- To examine the available methods and compare their scope, consistency and function within the overall safety assessment process, based on practical experience of applications.

- To provide a basis from which to prepare a report summarising the current status of scenario methodologies, identifying where sufficient methods exist and any outstanding problem areas.

9

The Workshop attracted organisations working actively in the field of scenario development for repository safety assessment and also others, e.g. regulatory organisations that wished to be informed of the status, practical capabilities and implications of scenario development methods.

To focus the discussions and provide an information base, a "Workshop Questionnaire" was developed by the Programme Committee and circulated to interested organisations. It sought basic information on the understanding, status and practice of scenario development as applied by various organisations and also provisional views on issues within scenario development. The responses to the Questionnaire were compiled and a summary and analysis of the responses was made. Both the raw compilation and the summary were circulated to participants before the Workshop.

All the organisations that attended the Workshop responded to the Questionnaire. In addition, each organisation was invited to submit a written paper pertinent to the themes of the Workshop. The guidance given was that the paper should describe actual experience in scenario development or related sub-topics. This could describe the advantages and disadvantages of the methods used and practical constraints, e.g. the amount of effort, need for software, time required, number and type of specialists involved. In the event, fourteen such papers were submitted from eight countries.

The Workshop was held over a three-day period with the following format.

- Plenary presentations from organisations with recent experience of developing and/or applying scenario methodologies. In most cases, these were supported by written papers.

- Plenary discussions to confirm commonly agreed principles for scenario development and also to identify key issues most worthy of further discussion. The discussion was seeded by, first, a presentation of a summary of the responses to the Questionnaire and, second, a presentation of a preliminary analysis of issues identified from the responses.

- Parallel working sessions to draft position statements on key issues, as identified above, and discuss current best practice in these areas.

- Plenary presentation and discussion of draft position statements, and an opportunity for participants to make short statements giving key messages and their overall conclusions from the Workshop.

This report

This document is the final product of the Workshop. The main text is intended mainly for technical specialists and managers with tasks and responsibilities related to repository safety assessment. This is supported by Appendices with information that is of interest mainly to scenario development specialists.

The main text of the report summarises the current status of scenario development methods and their application based on the consensus views of participants established via the Questionnaire and discussion at the Workshop.

- Chapter 2 presents commonly agreed matters based mainly on the responses to the Questionnaire.

- Chapter 3 presents the position statements on key issues developed during the Workshop.

- Chapter 4 presents a discussion and conclusions on the status of scenario development.

A list of attendees at the Workshop is given in Appendix 1. The Workshop Questionnaire is reproduced in Appendix 2. A summary of responses to the questionnaire is given in Appendix 3. Papers submitted to the Workshop are reproduced in Appendix 4.

2. SCENARIO DEVELOPMENT – AN OVERVIEW

The meaning of scenario development

The NEA Scenario Working Group report of 1992 [1] defined scenario development as "the identification, broad description, and selection of alternative futures relevant to a reliable assessment of radioactive waste repository safety". Scenarios are primarily seen as a method of dealing with uncertainty about the possible future evolution of the repository, and the report states that "a single scenario specifies one possible set of events and processes and provides a broad brush description of their characteristics and sequencing.

The contemporary view expressed in the Scenario Working Group Report [1] and in the NEA Review of Safety Assessment Methods of 1991 [19] places scenario development as the first stage in a safety assessment procedure consisting of four main stages:

- scenario development;

- model representation;

- consequence analysis; and

- comparison of results to safety criteria.

Experience over the past ten years, especially with assessments of actual proposals and potential sites, has revealed a more complex pattern of safety assessment in which data is collected, scientific understanding and models are developed, and analyses are refined, in an iterative fashion [3].

Scenario development has become the general term used to describe the marshalling and syntheses of the scientific and technical information requirements necessary to the assessment. This includes the identification of the relevant features, events and processes (FEPs), synthesis of broad models of scientific understanding, and selection of calculational cases to be performed. Scenario development provides the overall framework in which the cases and their calculated consequences can be discussed, including biases or shortcomings due to omissions or lack of knowledge.[1]

Scenario development is still often presented as the first step, or at least an early step, of performance assessment (PA). It is widely recognised, however, that the above-described roles underpin the performance and presentation of a PA and, hence, that the 'scenario development' can be expected to be updated and refined considerably during a PA.

---

1. Some projects prefer the term "scenario analysis" to describe the over-arching activity, others reserve this term to describe the calculation of the results of scenario cases. In some projects, the identification and preliminary analysis of FEPs is regarded as a separate precursor activity termed "FEP analysis".

Objectives of scenario development

The main objectives of scenario development are generally agreed to be the following:

- To demonstrate or try to ensure completeness, comprehensiveness or sufficiency in the scope of a PA, usually by seeking to identify, and possibly describe, a list of relevant features, events and processes (FEPs).

- To decide which FEPs to include in PA and how to treat them. This includes screening of less important FEPs, deciding which FEPs are to be treated in quantitative models of system performance, which FEPs can be handled by scoping calculations and which FEPs should be regarded as the key defining elements of separate scenarios.

- To demonstrate traceability from data and information to assessment scenarios, models and calculation cases.

- To provide transparency (improve the understandability) of PA results to different audiences – including to act as a communication tool between the implementer, the regulator and the public.

- To guide decisions concerning research priorities, the collection of data, and allocation of funds.

Scenario development may have other specific functions within some programmes, e.g. to define cases to study the performance of individual barriers or the robustness of the multi-barrier system.

The balance of importance between the above objectives depends on the perspective of the interested audiences. For the PA specialist, the identification of FEPs and their synthesis to models and scenarios may be most important. From the regulator's perspective, the most important role of scenario development may be the production of traceable and ordered documentation and the demonstration of comprehensiveness. For others, e.g. decision makers or non-specialists, the identification of FEPs and description of scenarios provides a starting point from which to understand and/or question the scope and completeness of the analysis, and the treatment and evaluation of various FEPs.

The objectives and overall role of scenario development may change during the development of a programme, and consequently between different programmes presently at different stages of development. At an early stage of project development, scenario development may be aimed at identifying key processes, identifying and investigating broad features of sites or repository concepts, determining preliminary scenarios to be analysed and guiding further model development and data collection. At later stages, specific design variants and more detailed alternative evolutions may be examined and scenario development becomes important in documenting the comprehensiveness of consideration and recording the basis for decisions on what to include or exclude. There will be a shift from selection of cases sufficient for illustration of performance towards assurance of sufficiency and justification of cases as satisfying scientific coherence and regulatory requirements.

As programmes develop, the methods of scenario development may also become more formal, e.g. structured FEP catalogues, various graphical techniques to identify FEPs and synthesise assessment models, audit procedures and documentation. In several programmes there is also a shift from accepting the best judgements of the engaged PA specialists towards obtaining judgements from a broader range of scientific experts, sometimes by formal elicitation procedures.

Methodologies for scenario development

The methodology for scenario development varies considerably between projects. This may be a result of regulatory requirements, stage of repository development or other factors. Some common concerns can be identified. These include:

- achieving sufficient "completeness";

- decisions on treatment of FEPs;

- organisation of model development; and

- treatment of probabilistic events.

Achieving completeness, comprehensiveness or sufficiency is the key initial concern. The NEA FEP Database [2] is an important contribution in this area. Projects also emphasise the use of experts both from within the project and wider scientific disciplines to elicit FEPs and to review the scenario development. The scope of FEP lists or catalogues within individual projects are often compared to those compiled in other projects. Systematic methodologies for organising the information, such as interaction matrices, influence diagrams and directed diagrams [4,5], can also help to identify omissions, and to provide assurance of reasonable or sufficient completeness. At a later stage, the dialogue with the regulator and other independent reviewers can help to ensure completeness.

A second function is the preliminary evaluation of individual FEPs. This can lead to the screening out of less important processes and, conversely, the selection of processes to be included in quantitative assessment. Here it is recognised that the pre-existing modelling capability is often a strong influence, especially within a single assessment iteration. The process often proceeds by comparing the available models, and their scope, against the list of FEPs. Decisions can then be made on how to treat FEPs that are not directly included in the available models, e.g. as changes in boundary conditions or by changes to the models, or whether additional model development is required. Many projects choose to distinguish between those FEPs that are included in a reference scenario, represented by a standard model chain, and those FEPs that must be represented within alternative scenarios and models, although different terminology is used to make this distinction in the various programmes.

Model development often proceeds in several stages. First, a broad conceptual model is developed incorporating the scientific understanding of the overall system. This includes the definition of barriers, subsystems and main interaction. More detailed scientific models of individual subsystems may also be formulated. Then, for the key systems, conceptual models are derived that can be represented by the available mathematical and computer models. These may be simplified compared to the overall scientific understanding but aim to capture key processes relevant to the long-term performance of the disposal system.

Various graphical and tabular techniques have been used to assist in scenario development, its communication and documentation. Several types of tool can be identified, although these have been used differently, and sometimes adapted in quite specialised ways, within different projects. These include:

- Event trees, logic diagrams, Latin squares, and related approaches that analyse alternative combinations of events and/or of resulting system states.

- Fault and/or dependency diagrams that set out in a hierarchical fashion the conditions and/or processes leading to, or contributing to, an end point of interest.

- Influence diagrams that map the dependencies or interactions between various processes, often indicating the importance of interaction, either in the real world system as understood or within the model representation.

- Interaction matrices that force a comprehensive questioning of the dependencies between selected key features or processes.

- Audit tables that force a consideration of the representation of each FEP within the available models and system representation, and evaluation of bias due to omission or simplified representation.

Several tools may used in combination. For example, influence diagrams and interaction matrices may be useful to explore and illustrate the connection between scientific understanding and the calculational models, whereas event trees and logic diagrams provide a logical structure for selection or generation of calculation cases. The reader is referred to the papers and references presented in Appendix 4 for more details.

Whatever techniques are used, the model derivation process relies on the judgement of PA modellers and scientific subject experts, trying to ensure that the scientific understanding is appropriately incorporated in the models. A key value of the graphical and tabular techniques is to aid communication within projects, enabling experts to see the significance of their knowledge within the system context, and to discuss its incorporation. The techniques can also provide a logic for comprehensive documentation of the relevant processes and their treatment in models.

An issue that causes particular concern in many projects is the treatment of events that may or may not occur, or for which the timing and/or location are uncertain. As a first stage, most projects treat such uncertainty qualitatively, e.g. screening out less likely FEPs or scenarios and including qualitative statements on likelihood when making overall judgements on acceptability. Some projects note that the probability of occurrence only needs to be considered if the consequence of occurrence exceeds a regulatory limit or target. In some countries, e.g. Canada, the UK and the USA, a systematic quantitative treatment of probability is required. This may require event tree or environmental system modelling techniques to generate a coherent set of future system realisations and their associated probabilities. Even in these countries, however, some classes of events are given special treatment, e.g. the analysis of human intrusion is usually presented separately to the undisturbed performance of the repository.

3.   KEY ISSUES IN SCENARIO DEVELOPMENT

The identification of key issues

Chapter 2 has summarised aspects of scenario development and its role that are generally accepted. An important role of the Workshop was to explore aspects that are at the edge of current developments. Four topics were identified for detailed discussion:

- What can be expected from scenario development? This is concerned with a relation between scientific understanding and its representation by models, scenarios and calculation cases in PA. In particular, is there confidence that these necessarily limited cases can provide an adequate representation?

- Completeness, comprehensiveness and sufficiency. This has been a key function of scenario development and has become more important as regulatory reviews develop. Key questions are what can be expected in terms of completeness etc., and how to ensure completeness of scenarios and transparency of the aggregation/disaggregation process?

- Scenario and model formulation. This is concerned with the various methods available to manipulate the FEP information and synthesise models and scenarios. Factors such as dealing with temporal uncertainty, elicitation of expert judgement, traceability and documentation are important.

- Regulatory perspectives. This is concerned with the regulatory requirements, and guidance. In particular, to what extent is prescriptive guidance necessary and what should a regulator expect to see in terms of treatment, level of detail and documentation?

These topics were discussed in task groups at the Workshop leading to the following position statements.[2]

What can be expected from scenario development?

When designing a radioactive waste repository, or assessing its future behaviour, inevitable questions face reviewers and decision makers about the possible future evolution of the repository system. Scenario development has become a central tool in repository programmes to give answers to such questions by the construction of scenarios that encompass possible future states of the disposal system, or parts of it. A key application is in PA, where a set of scenarios can be used to illustrate

---

2.   The four position papers were developed separately, are somewhat different in character and overlap on some points. To preserve the discussion aspects of each paper only minor editing and clarification has been carried out.

differences in the possible evolution of the repository and in the impact of possible future events. It is also used to compare design or siting alternatives and their responses to different future evolutions and events. Generally, a scenario development comprises the vehicle for presenting the main results of a PA, and considerable experience has been accumulated in this over the last few years in a wide range of assessments.

It is acknowledged that scenarios (and, indeed, any means of modelling possible futures) are not able to predict the details of the actual future evolution of a disposal system, especially biosphere aspects and the impacts of future human actions. Nevertheless, a well chosen set of scenarios, that illustrates the performance of different parts of the system in different ways and addresses the main sources of environmental change, and likely events, can be used to scope the overall performance of a repository.

How confident are we that this last assertion is true? Those who have been involved in scenario analysis over the last decade are now convinced of our ability to take the four main steps required:

- providing a comprehensive description of the repository system (the waste, the repository and the surrounding geological and natural environment);

- defining and quantifying the majority of phenomena which will affect the future behaviour of the system (the natural processes and their interactions);

- comprehensively managing the FEPs which make up the above description, so as to construct scenarios of future system evolution;

- converting these scenarios into representative models and calculation cases for consequence analysis.

We are less confident in our ability to make assumptions about the future behaviour of humans and how this may affect a repository system. Thus, the descriptions of human actions that can be constructed via scenario analysis, and also the calculated consequences, can only be regarded as illustrative and must be treated with caution by decision makers.

A second area where confidence is lower is concerning the longevity of expert consensus views. The long-term evolution of a repository system will be governed by a complex interplay of many processes. While the relevant phenomena may be studied and well understood in isolation and over laboratory timescales, expert judgement is required to identify the key processes that will determine behaviour over long time periods and to define appropriate models. As new experiments are performed and different evidence evaluated, e.g. from natural analogues, then alternative views on the importance and nature of different processes may develop. This issue of the changing understanding of the scientific basis is an issue that is faced in many other fields. In the case of repository PA, the uncertainty is usually scoped by employing alternative models, where the models are thought to cover the range of possible interpretations.

Waste management decisions have to be made on the basis of present knowledge that may be imperfect. In this respect, scenarios, with their inherent uncertainties and limitations, lie at the interface between the scientific understanding that underlies radioactive waste disposal, and the politics of using descriptions of possible futures to make important decisions. They are, effectively, the way that the science is translated into a technical basis for decision making. Thus, scenarios can be used to present the implications of waste management alternatives and choices to decision makers.

They are also useful instruments for answering question from the wider community and for facilitating discussion about overall safety and acceptability of waste disposal.

Given the uncertainties involved in illustrations of possible futures, it is important to be careful about the way that the probability or likelihood of an individual scenario is both presented and applied. Estimates of probability, especially with respect to trends and events in natural systems and the behaviour of people are, at best, only semi-quantitative judgements. They are largely based on expert views and often unstated internal models, not on statistically derived data from multiple observations or experiments (as is much other information used in PA). Given the uncertainties involved, it is important to avoid presenting quantitative information from scenario analyses with levels of precision that are spurious.

Scenarios are also simplified illustrations of possible futures. Simplification occurs at all stages of scenario construction but a key aspect is in the final presentation. Scenarios can be presented as:

- illustrations or "pictures-in-words" of possible futures of general interest or concern to various audiences;

- hypothetical cases (for example, illustrating the impacts of the hypothetical loss of the multiple barriers in a repository system) to highlight particular aspects of system performance;

- bounding scenarios which illustrate the scope of the envelope of possible futures, for example:

  - in classes, which explore all the impacts of climate change, faulting, volcanic activity etc.;

  - as "barrier impact" sets, which explore all the identified ways of affecting or disrupting a specific barrier (e.g. a waste container).

For clarity in presenting scenario sets it is preferable to keep the group small and relatively simple, while also illustrating, as far as possible, the relevant processes, events and components of the system.

The following overall observations and recommendations can be made:

- We should be clear about the nature of scenarios in terms of science and decision making. They are necessarily illustrative in nature, but nonetheless essential for assessing repository safety. It is important to involve decision makers in accepting these limitations and to engage all stakeholders in the discussion of how to apply scenarios in making informed choices.

- A better dialogue is needed to facilitate this engagement, starting at the national level between the implementer and regulatory agencies. At present the level of engagement varies from country to country. Regulatory agencies could enhance overall clarity by providing examples of what is needed and of how they might utilise the results of scenario analysis in assessing repository proposals. Such examples and discussion would also be of value at an international level.

19

- Similarly, it would be useful to improve the debate on the application of probabilities in scenario selection and presentation, and possibly, more widely in radioactive waste PA. This could be a suitable topic for a workshop.

- Similarities exist between national approaches, but terminology varies widely. The subject of scenarios can be demystified by clearer definition of terms and procedures within projects and, possibly, by explaining where terminology and methodology overlap, from one programme to another.

Completeness, comprehensiveness and sufficiency

A key source of uncertainty in repository performance assessment is that which arises from the possibility of having omitted key processes or circumstances that could significantly affect the performance or safety of the repository. In scenario development terms, this could stem from failure to identify key FEPs or scenarios. Thus, completeness, comprehensiveness and sufficiency of FEP lists and scenarios is a key concern for scenario development.

The appropriate target for scenario development must first be defined – specifically, should a scenario set be sufficient, comprehensive or complete? A complete itemisation of all possible scenarios is not possible and programmes should be careful not to imply scenario completeness. Rather, the scenarios must be sufficient (or "reasonably complete" or "sufficiently complete"). The definition of "sufficient" depends on the assessment context, including the system description, safety concept and regulatory requirements. For example, a scenario set may be sufficient if it covers a range of possible repository conditions considered to be relevant within regulatory constraints. Comprehensive is also an acceptable target, since it implies that the set of scenarios covers a substantial spectrum of possible circumstances and events, but implies somewhat less audience-dependence than "sufficiency".

Given a target for the scenarios, how does one demonstrate that one has defined a sufficient set of scenarios? In practice, the generation of scenarios is closely linked with the FEPs list, so it is important that the FEPs themselves be as comprehensive as possible. There are systematic methods available to help check that any proposed FEP list is sufficiently complete. These include review by technical experts, regulators and the public, comparison against international databases such as the NEA FEP Database [2], and organisation in formal structures such as hierarchical diagrams and interaction matrices that help to identify missing interactions or FEPs.

The development of scenarios generally starts from a list of scenarios or scenario-initiating events. These are often derived from expert judgement or by examination of the FEP list. The sufficiency of these scenarios can then be checked, by comparing the scenario list with:

- the list of relevant FEPs;

- scenario sets used in other studies;

- the system and analysis requirements;

- issues pertinent to stakeholders (e.g. specific local practices and any consequent radiation exposure pathways of interest to the local community);

- whether the scenario list adequately explores uncertainties in the performance of all the barriers (e.g. waste form, near-field and far-field).

The scenario development process should be transparent. This implies that the methods and results be traceable, open and simple. While all these are important, it is observed that simplicity is the hardest to achieve. Transparency is a more tractable task if a hierarchy of descriptions (or results) are available, so that an appropriate level of information can be provided for a given audience. A method to navigate through the process is also valuable; electronic databases and graphical techniques can be useful in this context. Finally, it should be possible to describe the methods clearly, even if the product is complex. The analogy of a wiring diagram for automobile or aeroplane may be useful – although the overall diagram is complex, the procedure (of connecting each device up to an instrument or switch) is, in principle, simple and we have confidence through experience and use that such things can be reliable.

Related to transparency is the degree of aggregation or disaggregation of the scenarios and models. Typically, there are varying levels of detail throughout the PA process, with generally higher levels of aggregation at the beginning and end.

Uncertainty is handled in part by the use of multiple scenarios. In several countries, the plan is to show the effect of uncertainties in parameter values through analysing their effect on the reference scenario in particular, while uncertainties in the future evolution are illustrated through the use of multiple scenarios.

There is a significant amount of overlap in the scenario classes being considered in the various national PAs. A useful exercise may be to compile a summary table of the scenarios considered in different assessments (i.e. without any merging into an international list), along with a brief description of the physical scope of the scenarios and explanation of any specific project terminology. At this point, it sufficient to be clear on what is being used in the various studies, and not to recommend standard terminology.

Scenario and model formation

The following main themes emerged regarding scenario and model formation within scenario development:

- Procedures and methods – how to go from FEPs to scenarios and models.

- Scenario types – the roles of "normal evolution" scenarios and "variants".

- Screening – of FEPs and scenarios, and criteria for screening.

- Representing uncertainty in sequence and timing of events – methods used.

- Traceability and decision making – the role of experts, quality assurance, documentation of decisions and the use of specific software tools.

Procedures and methods used

Different techniques are used within different programmes, many of which can be seen as complementary. Some techniques are top-down (e.g. directed diagrams) whereas others rely on the bottom-up identification and aggregation of FEPs (e.g. event trees and influence diagrams). Identified techniques currently in use include the following:

- directed diagrams [5];

- event trees, fault trees, logic diagrams and related tools;

- matrix diagrams including the Rock Engineering System (RES) method [6];

- influence diagrams illustrating both scientific processes interactions and showing assessment model connections, e.g. the SKI Process Influence Diagram (PID) and Assessment Model Flowchart (AMF) techniques [7];

- top-down approaches, e.g. independent initiating events methods [8] and the PROSA methodology [9];

- less formal methods – ad hoc expert judgement.

In addition, in the past, environmental simulation techniques had been used, e.g. [10]. This method aims to represent future uncertainty within a single time-dependent overall system model, as opposed to defining scenarios each describing different potential system evolutions that may be represented by different models or model boundary conditions.

"Normal evolution" and "variant" scenarios

Most organisations seek to identify some kind of "normal evolution" or "base case" scenario, supplemented by a number of variant scenarios, for example driven by "external FEPs" or probabilistic events. The definition of the "normal evolution" scenario varies in different programmes, e.g. continuation of present-day conditions or a scenario including the expected climate evolution. A "base case" usually implies a simplified case that is a starting point for the quantitative analysis and against which scenarios involving other factors and events are compared. In most cases, uncertainty due to parameter variation is included within the normal evolution scenario or base case. Some programmes (e.g. Nagra) use the concept of a "robust scenario", i.e. a scenario that describes a minimum perfor-mance that can be confidently expected. The choice of approach is influenced by:

- the disposal concept, e.g. host geology, waste type, engineered barrier concept;

- the regulatory requirements;

- the stage of the programme, with a tendency to focus on the normal evolution scenario in the earlier stages;

- the purpose of the PA, e.g. whether for site selection, design optimisation, licensing etc.

FEP and scenario screening

Some form of FEP and/or scenario screening is seen as essential in all programmes. Screening occurs at different stages within different programmes and also at more than one stage within a single PA. Screening occurs, primarily, at the FEP identification stage and also at the scenario formation stage. Some programmes talk in terms of subsuming, rather than screening scenarios. This implies that a scenario (or FEP) is not neglected or omitted, but its effects are included within the subsuming scenario, even if not explicitly.

In making screening decisions, it is important to consider the interactions between FEPs and, in particularly, their chain of connection to the key features and processes considered in the assessment models.

The following reasons for screening were identified:

- FEP irrelevant to the site or disposal context under consideration;

- regulations allow exclusion of certain FEPs, e.g. deliberate human intrusion is ruled out in several national regulatory guidelines;

- low consequence of FEP within the time frame of interest – this is especially relevant to countries where regulations specify a time cut-off for assessments;

- FEP has similar (but lesser) consequence to other included FEPs (in this situation some programmes refer to subsuming rather than screening);

- FEP has very low probability of occurrence – there are different approaches to screening in this instance[3].

Temporal sequences in scenarios

In most programmes, time sequence of events and uncertainty of sequence and timing are not key concerns. Typically, calculations are performed for several time-independent states, e.g. of climate, engineered barrier or geosphere condition, that are assumed to persist over the assessment timescale. Where timing of an event is important to the impact, e.g. the time of waste package failure or a human intrusion event, calculations are performed for one or several illustrative times. If only one time is investigated this is usually the most conservative, e.g. the most pessimistic time for waste package failure or human intrusion at the end of a guaranteed period of site control.

More recently, a greater understanding of the long-term climatic and tectonic processes has been invoked to develop site-specific forecasts for the impact of these processes on a repository site. Typically, a deterministic "best estimate" forecast is derived and used to provide a sequence of time-dependent boundary conditions for hydrogeological modelling and/or biosphere representation within assessment models. This approach is also applicable in principle to represent other evolutions that follow a generally predictable course, e.g. resaturation of a repository and related chemical changes. It does not, however, account for uncertainty in timing or sequence.

In the past, the UK HMIP advocated the use of environmental simulation modelling to generate coherent time sequences of changing environmental boundary conditions, taking account of uncertainty in sequence and timing, and demonstrated the approach for the case of climate-induced changes. In the US, the USDOE have used a statistical model to generate sequences of human intrusion events for the assessment of the WIPP site. This is combined with time-dependent simulation of repository processes such as salt creep and gas evolution to generate probabilistic estimates of radionuclide release for a human intrusion scenario. Within CEC's SPA project, GRS Köln treated temporal and spatial uncertainties of initiating events (e.g. time, position, and amount of brine inflow, time and position of barrier failures) using a probabilistic approach. The sampling of time and position of occurrence was combined with the transient simulation of the processes in the repository system (e.g. radioactive decay, salt creep). UK Nirex is in the early stages of testing a systematic approach for considering FEP sequences based on construction of "timelines".

---

3. For example, US regulations allow exclusion of FEPs with an annual probability less than 10-8, whereas in the Nirex approach screening/subsuming is conducted on the basis of consequence, probability is only considered for non-subsumed scenarios, using a "weight-risk diagram" to display the combined effect of probability and consequence.

Experience to date suggests that uncertainty in sequence and timing of events (or more gradual changes) appears to be important for some repository systems but may be less so in others. Among the challenges for any modelling that attempts to deal with this uncertainty is that analysis of the results is necessary to identify critical sequences and that clear presentation of the results may be problematic.

In some programmes or countries, regulations have a prescribed time cut-off, whereas others have to justify an appropriate assessment period, this may also influence the need to evaluate FEP sequences in a structured manner.

Traceability and decision making

One of the main benefits of a systematic approach to scenario development is the discipline it provides, in particular, to formally justify what has been included/excluded in an assessment, to state how each FEP is treated, and to record the various decisions made. All approaches rely upon expert judgement and it is important that this is properly managed to ensure decisions are focused on PA requirements; this requires PA expertise as well as scientific subject expertise.

Traceability of these decisions is an essential part of scenario development and is essential if the PA is to withstand regulatory review. In some programmes, electronic databases are employed to record the decisions as they are made. These may include graphical interfaces or hierarchical structures to assist in the organisation of decision making. Searchable databases are valuable tools for enabling PA specialists and technical reviewers to trace decisions for themselves. Where such databases are employed, a QA regime is required to ensure control of data entries.

Observations and recommendations

The following overall observations and recommendations are made:

- Scenario-based approaches, rather than integrated simulation, still seem to be the most common method for dealing with future uncertainties, where it is recognised that model simulations are required to analyse individual scenarios. The question is which uncertainties can be covered in the model simulation and which by considering alternative scenarios? The scenario approach seems to be particularly helpful for describing processes for which the data is lacking or intrinsically uncertain, such as future human actions and major disruptions to the repository site.

- A range of systematic, and less formal, approaches to scenario development have been used. Most give broadly similar scenarios but ad hoc approaches cannot demonstrate that a comprehensive set of representative scenarios has been identified. Systematic approaches are necessary to demonstrate the logic and sufficiency of considerations, and are preferred in terms justifying a safety case.

- The degree of structure and formalism increases the traceability of scenario development. There is, however, a danger that transparency may be lost if the presentation becomes overly complex. This can be mitigated by using a hierarchical presentation, enabling the reader to start with high-level descriptions and work down to the required level of detail. Hypertext technology offers new opportunities for such presentations.

- It is important to have a means of recording decisions that is directly linked to the decision-making process. This ensures that all decisions are properly recorded and traceable. Some programmes use specially developed software tools, e.g. CASCADE (JNC), FANFARE (Nirex), SPARTA (SKI), to handle decision recording.

- Specialised tools are useful but not essential. For example, standard spreadsheet software can be used to develop matrix diagrams and standard flow-charting programmes can be used to develop influence diagrams. Custom-designed scenario development software may be required to link together different presentation methods and text data.

- Expert judgement is central to the scenario development process. It is essential to involve PA expertise alongside scientific and technical subject specialists, to ensure that decisions are made in the context of their impact on PA and to help give consistency of approach.

- There may be different degrees of confidence in expert decisions (depending on the numbers of experts involved and their own confidence in their decisions) and this should be documented. Review of more general work on group decision making may be helpful in ascertaining the degree of confidence in such decisions.

- The structured development of FEP sequences and the explicit treatment of time-dependency within scenario development is in its early stages but is a promising approach worthy of further exploration.

Regulatory perspectives on scenario development

Regulatory requirements are unique for each nation, and it is inappropriate to attempt to influence regulatory policies already in place in the member nations. Nevertheless, it is possible to offer general observations and recommendations that are applicable to most programmes. Several topical areas were identified in which useful comments could be made about the relationship between scenario development work and the regulatory framework within which repositories are licensed. These are discussed in each of the following sections.

Background to regulation

Fundamental principles for the safe management and disposal of radioactive waste and spent nuclear fuel have been established by several international organisations. Relevant documents include the IAEA Safety Fundamentals [11], ICRP Publications 77 and 81 [12,13], and the NEA Collective Opinion of 1995 [14].

This international guidance does not address scenario development explicitly but gives a starting point for more detailed guidance and for the development of national regulations. For example, international guidance indicates that both human health and the environment should be given an adequate level of protection and, also, that the impact on the health of future generations should not be greater than accepted today.

The international guidance is more or less incorporated into most national legal frameworks, or has been used as a basis when developing such frameworks. An overview of national regulations can be found in the proceedings from the NEA workshop on long-term safety of disposal [15].

Guidance (compulsory vs. optional)

Regulations governing radioactive waste disposal should not only contain requirements to be fulfilled by the applicant, but also give guidance on how compliance with the requirements could be demonstrated. Therefore, regulations generally comprise both compulsory and optional parts. In the context of repository PA and the related scenario development, minimum regulatory guidance could indicate that:

- post-operational safety evaluation should include an estimate of long-term performance of the disposal system; and that

- consideration of potential developments at the site should be required, including due consideration of disruptive events and the effects of future human actions.

Regulatory guidance is particularly needed regarding the treatment of possible changes that are not amenable to rigorous analysis. Inevitable uncertainty about future developments should be acknowledged in the regulations and they should offer guidance to limit arbitrary speculation. Regulations may accept simplifying assumptions, for example, that future people are physiologically like those of today (i.e. that ICRP dosimetric models and risk factors apply), rather than leaving it to the applicant to investigate whether metabolism or sensitivity to radiation may change. Further examples are given in the following sections, especially in the one on stylisation.

Level of detail and prescription

The regulator should expect the applicant to provide the level of technical detail needed to support the findings of the safety case. With regard to the use of scenarios, it should not be the regulator's task to propose lists of specific scenarios that must be considered for a particular repository site or geologic setting. Regulations should be flexible and afford the applicant a significant degree of latitude both to consider relevant FEPs, to define appropriate scenarios and to choose the manner in which the scenarios are incorporated into the PA models. The applicant will, however, need to respond to any omissions detected during the review process.

The regulator should not require that the applicant consult any particular recognised FEP database to ensure comprehensiveness. Rather, the regulator should promulgate a general requirement that the applicant provide convincing arguments that relevant physical phenomena have been considered in an appropriately comprehensive manner (see the section below on comprehensiveness). In those cases where the regulator and applicant have engaged in protracted pre-licensing discussions, it may be appropriate for the regulator to be more prescriptive regarding the specific FEPs and scenarios that must be addressed. This additional guidance need not be incorporated into the regulations, but could, for example, be provided to the applicant as additional notes on expectations for compliance demonstration.

Probability versus qualitative likelihood

Consideration of the likelihood of scenarios is necessary to put potentially large consequences of very unlikely scenarios into perspective. This perspective can be achieved by structuring regulations by various means so that greater weight is given in licensing decisions to the consequences of more likely scenarios.

Approaches to achieving this perspective differ between countries. Regulators may, in some nations, require the applicant to estimate quantitative probabilities for all scenarios and to weight the consequences accordingly before combining them into a single performance measure. In other nations, regulators require separate consequence analyses for different scenarios and then take their likelihood into account in making the licensing decision. Regardless of the approach taken, the goal should be to achieve reasonable weighting of the risks posed by high-consequence, low probability scenarios relative to the risks posed by the more likely behaviour of the disposal system. Uncertainties inherent in estimates of the probability of unlikely events should be acknowledged.

Different regulations for different scenarios

In current or proposed regulations in various countries, scenarios have been classified according to expected probability, time of consequence and other criteria (e.g. natural processes or human intrusion). In some countries, different criteria apply based on such a classification.

The recent ICRP Publication 81 [13] recommends that different criteria are applied to the assessment of natural processes or human intrusion. Assessed doses and risks from natural processes should be compared with a dose constraint or its risk equivalent but, for human intrusion, the consequence of one or more plausible stylised scenario should be considered in order to evaluate the resilience of the repository to such events. Where human intrusion could lead to doses to those living around the site sufficiently high that on current criteria intervention would be justified, reasonable efforts should be taken to reduce the probability of intrusion or to limit its consequences. This is because there is lack of scientific basis for predicting the nature or probability of future human actions and because an intrusion event bypasses some or all of the barriers that are in place as a result of the optimisation of radiation protection.

More generally, it may be reasonable that different criteria or constraints (rather than limits) may be applied to scenarios distinguished by other factors. For example, scenarios generated by events that themselves have significant negative impacts, such as a large meteorite impact, might be neglected or, at least, not expected to conform to normal dose and risk targets. Similarly, events that can give rise to impacts only at very long times in the future may be less rigorously analysed. Most such decisions to set different standards for analysis or criteria for endpoints are, however, likely to be taken nationally.

The case of human intrusion is one in which it is especially appropriate for regulators to offer guidance on the approach to assessment. This could include guidance on

- the consequences to be considered, e.g. immediate and/or longer-term consequences, intruder and/or others;

- the modes of intrusion to be considered, e.g. to limit undue speculation;

- assumptions on the effectiveness of mitigating measures, including site control, e.g. assumptions concerning longevity of institutional control arrangements or effectiveness of records and markers.

Restrictions of scope

The regulator will generally expect the applicant to demonstrate that the safety assessment has considered every plausible situation, including unlikely but credible circumstances. The long time span and the range of possible evolutions associated with a geological disposal facility are likely to generate a very large number of issues to be considered. It is important, then, to understand which issues are most relevant for judging the safety and, therefore, need the most detailed consideration.

The regulator may decide to explicitly limit the scope of the situations to be considered by the applicant. Possible limitation of scope can include time cut-offs, minimum levels of probability for situations that deserve specific consideration, or direct exclusion of types of scenarios.

Examples of time cut-off values exist in the United States and Canada, where the quantitative performance standards may be limited to 10 000 years following closure, and in Finland and Sweden, where no quantitative analyses are required beyond one million years. In the United States, a quantitative lower bound to the probability of occurrence of the situations to be assessed is proposed – at a value of 10^{-4} in 10 000 years. In France, no consideration of human intrusion is required during the first 500 years. In the United States high-level waste programme, human intrusion is excluded from the general scenario development and treated instead in a prescribed scenario.

These restrictions are useful in focusing the scope of analysis. They should only be proposed, however, when sufficient confidence exists that no important or relevant contribution to overall risk will be overlooked by their application.

Stylisation

In the NEA IPAG-1 report [16], stylised treatment of FEPs in PA is defined as: "A stylised presentation refers to a situation where a part of the disposal system is treated in performance assessment in a standardised or simplified way. The need for stylised presentations occurs if there is a general lack of experimental evidence such that decisions on treatment and parameter values put into performance assessment is highly judgmental." The IPAG-2 report [17] agreed with this definition, and commented that "Stylised approaches are typically used for situations where there is inherent and irreducible uncertainty, to illustrate system performance and to aid communication".

The task group agrees with the above and further notes that:

- In PA, some FEPs and issues (e.g. human intrusion into a deep repository, and some aspects of the biosphere) can only be treated by means of stylised scenarios.

- International or regional, host-rock or disposal-concept specific stylised scenarios would facilitate communication and contribute to confidence building.

- Stylised scenarios are useful only if they are considered appropriate by the regulator. Therefore, regulators need to take the lead in developing of international stylised scenarios.

Comprehensiveness

Both regulators and applicants working in the area of scenario development should recognise that absolute completeness in scenario development is neither achievable nor necessary for regulatory decision making. Rather, what is needed is a demonstration that the consideration of future scenarios has been thorough and sufficient, given the context of the specific disposal system and the applicable regulations.

Mathematical proofs that the future has been described completely are not possible, and comprehensiveness can only be demonstrated qualitatively. Tests of comprehensiveness are generally negative, that is: scenario development work is not comprehensive if reviewers can identify relevant questions that have been overlooked. The burden of defending the comprehensiveness of the analysis must fall to the applicant because there is no single test that the regulator, or the public, can apply to establish comprehensiveness. Thus, the applicant must be prepared to answer any and all "did you think of this" questions in the context of its scenario development work.

Comparison to scenario development work performed by other programmes, for example as documented in the NEA International FEP Database [2], can be a useful tool for demonstrating a sufficiently comprehensive analysis. Iterative and thorough peer review is also useful, because the observation that successive independent reviews of the work have failed to identify major new findings can provide support for the assertion that the analysis is comprehensive.

Needs for review purposes

The adoption of a step-wise repository development approach implies an iterative refinement of the safety case and also periodic review by the regulator and others. The objectives of the safety case developed in each stage will influence the depth, the level of detail and the comprehensiveness to be achieved in scenario development. A clear specification of the scope and limitations of the scenario development made in each assessment with a reference to this wider context can help to set the expectations of the review process.

During this process the regulator must be convinced that a systematic and well-structured approach to scenario development and selection has been used, that a sound methodology has been applied and that the analysis has been subjected to quality assurance procedures. No matter how complex the scenario development method applied may be, the line of reasoning followed must be well defined, coherent and founded in technically defensible arguments. A continuing dialogue between the regulator and the applicant is essential to provide a progressive and common understanding of the methods used to describe and combine safety-relevant features, events and processes in scenarios, and the basis for assumptions regarding data and models.

Simplicity and transparency are of the utmost importance in both the description of the methodology and the presentation of the results. Particular care must be taken to ensure that the whole process of scenario development be reconstructable and traceable. This requires having means of recording technical decisions that directly link to the decision-making process, which is an element of quality assurance. A hierarchical organisation of the documentation can help to achieve the balance between completeness and traceability on one side and transparency and simplicity on the other side.

Documentation and communication

One of the areas in which progress has been made is the formal documentation of the scenario analysis. Taking advantage of computer technology, a large body of information, including the documentation of all technical decisions made during the analysis and the reasons for those decisions, can be made easily accessible. Documentation of this kind has the potential to greatly assist regulators in their review task, although it should not be seen as a replacement for a two-way communication between regulator and implementer.

The documentation should include records of all items of the scenario analysis (FEPs, scenarios, etc.) that at some point in the analysis have be excluded from further consideration, explaining the reason for doing so.

Each audience, be it regulators, the technical community, politicians or the public, has its own requirements as regards the content and the form of the information given. Communicating effectively with the public requires clarity and easy accessibility of further documentation. Transparency and traceability can often be enhanced by implementing a layered documentation structure, where the highest level document is aimed at a clear and concise exposition and the finer details and background information are contained in the lower level documents.

In future, the World Wide Web and the associated linking techniques may provide a vehicle to present PA information to the public. In particular, immediate public access to the technical documents can be offered and at the same time a layered structure implemented in a convenient and attractive way to encourage the interest of a wider audience.

Scenario development is an intricate activity that usually does not necessarily follow a standard scheme, although common elements are observed in overall approaches. Therefore, an ongoing communication between regulator and implementer is necessary in order to avoid or correct possible misunderstandings as regards the analysis. Furthermore, structured and documented communication can be a valuable means to complement other formal guidance both regarding scenario analysis and more generally.

Observations and conclusions

The main observations and conclusions fall into three categories:

- the scope and purpose of scenario development in repository licensing;

- the roles and responsibilities of the applicant and regulator; and

- the need for clear communication.

With respect to its scope and purpose in the licensing process, scenario development should support the broad goals of establishing adequate protection for future human health and the environment. Scenario development should be a tool for demonstrating the thorough and comprehensive consideration of possible future states of the disposal system, while acknowledging that complete identification of all future events is not possible. Scenario development should allow decision makers to focus on the most likely behaviour of the repository, appropriately weighting the consequences of unlikely scenarios. Stylised scenarios are a valuable, and necessary, way to consider the consequences of future human actions and other aspects of the far future for which scientific assessments are unattainable. Alternative regulatory standards may be appropriate for human intrusion or other stylised scenarios, and the regulator may chose to limit the scope of the assessment to avoid undue emphasis on scenarios of lesser importance.

Compulsory regulatory requirements regarding scenario development can be generalised, to allow flexibility for both the applicant and the regulator in the licensing process. Guidance from the regulator is particularly valuable concerning the treatment of largely irreducible uncertainties such as those related to future human actions. In this case stylised scenarios may be specified to be used in the analysis.

Regardless of the degree of guidance provided by the regulator, the responsibility for defending the assertion that the scenario development has been sufficiently comprehensive lies with the applicant. The applicant's documentation should provide the basis for responding to criticisms of the completeness of the analysis, and should justify the representativeness of the scenarios chosen for analysis. The applicant should also be responsible for demonstrating that the work has been done in a sound and traceable manner.

Clear communication between the applicant and the regulator, and with other audiences, is essential to the success of a scenario development effort. Iterative analysis and review allows early recognition of potential points of disagreement regarding the approach. Documentation must be thorough, and must allow reviewers to reconstruct the process. Complete documentation must be provided of all scenarios (or features, events, and processes) that have been excluded from the quantitative assessment, as well as of those that have been included. Documentation must also be transparent, and allow effective communication with multiple audiences ranging from the general public to the technical review community. Transparency may be achieved through a layered documentation structure, in which the highest level of documents are aimed at a clear and concise exposition and the finer details and background information are contained in the lower level documents.

4.   CONCLUDING DISCUSSION AND REMARKS

In the Introduction to this report a primary objective of the Workshop is given as:

"To provide a basis from which to prepare a report summarising the current status of scenario methodologies, identifying where sufficient methods exist and any outstanding problem areas."

The preceding chapters have summarised the current consensus on scenario development methodologies and discussed issues of concern.

An overall statement on the current status of scenario development methods and practice can be based on answering the following questions that were posed during the final discussion session of the Workshop.

- Has progress been made since the publication of the NEA scenario Working Group Report in 1992 and in what areas?

- What problem areas or challenges remain?

- Are we satisfied that current methods are sufficient

  - to support technical analysis?

  - to support compliance demonstration?

  - to communicate to wider audiences?

- Are the differences in approach between projects and countries important, e.g. in terms of the methods, level of formality and terminology?

Progress since 1992

Since the publication of the NEA Scenario Working Group report [1], progress has been made in the development of scenario techniques and especially in their practice.

Comprehensive lists of relevant features, events and processes have been developed in many projects. In several projects, these are supported by detailed descriptions of the FEPs. Electronic databases have proved a useful means to record and iterate on this information.

The methods of FEP analysis that are described in theory in reference [1], have now been applied in practice. The interaction matrix technique is recognised as particularly valuable in checking the comprehensiveness of the FEP list and organising it systematically. Influence diagram techniques, such as the SKI Process Influence Diagram, form an important link between the scientific understanding and the scenario and model representation used in performance assessment. Hierachical approaches, such as event trees and directed diagrams, provide a framework to structure and present

33

assessment cases. Directed diagrams may also encourage the comprehensiveness of consideration and the systematic organisation of FEPs.

Comprehensive documentation of FEPs, and also the arguments and decisions related to their treatment or non-treatment in the assessment has been an important element of compliance demonstration in some projects.

Remaining problems or challenges

Some problems remain. Or, at least, questions can be asked about whether further efforts need to be made.

As generally in performance assessment, it is challenging to provide full traceability of information and judgements while also maintaining transparency in scenario development. It has been stated that different levels of documentation are necessary to achieve this, but it has not been clearly demonstrated that results of detailed technical analysis and complex scenario development can be accurately and traceably reduced to simplified forms. It may be that simplified presentations, where required, might be based on more simplified or qualitative safety arguments, i.e. alternative lines of reasoning. Scenario development could play a greater role in this area.

In the current generation of PA documents and scenario developments the focus has been on recording the technical arguments in support of the various decisions, and these are mainly aimed at the PA specialist or technical reviewer. In practice, especially PA the context of iterative assessments performed under time constraints, operational and resource reasons often play a significant part in the decisions on treatment etc. It is less clear that these limitations are acknowledged or recorded, although they are relevant especially to a regulatory reviewer.

In some countries, reproducibility or reconstructability of assessment results may be required to satisfy regulatory review. Whereas the technology is in place in most advanced projects to recall data sets and codes so that calculations can be reproduced, fewer projects record all FEP and scenario management decisions so assiduously, e.g. stating by who, when and on what basis a decision was made. Experience in projects where such records are kept show that significant resources are required to institute and fully maintain such a system. This is an area where regulatory advice on the expectation for different stages of a project is necessary taking account of the level of concern or other national factors.

The treatment of probability in scenario development and presentation of results is a concern in several countries.

It is difficult to justify the assignment of probabilities to objects such as scenarios that are rather broadly defined and are not necessarily independent. Subjective, order of magnitude, estimates of likelihood may be assigned to illustrate and compare the relative importance of different more or less likely scenarios. If an integrated estimate of overall performance is needed then more formal methods of estimating probability are required. Event tree, time line or environmental simulation approaches may be used to generate possible scenarios and their associated probabilities. The problem is compounded if timing and/or sequence of events has a large influence on the calculated impact. In this case, any single time sequence can only have a low degree of representativeness (or assigned probability). This will tend to lead towards the use of probabilistic techniques to generate multiple realisations each of which must be investigated.

This issue has, in the past, been thought to be mainly of concern to programmes in which a risk-based or probabilistic-release target applies. It should be a concern, however, for the assessment of any disposal system where the calculated impact is liable to vary as a result of environmental changes or human activities the timing of which is uncertain. In this case, multiple realisations need to be generated to explore the different possibilities and to identify critical sequences and timing. The assignment and presentation of probabilities in scenario development is an area where further international exchange of experience and views may be valuable.

Sufficiency of the current methods

It is concluded that current methods of scenario developments are generally sufficient to fulfil their technical function within PA. This is based on experience in a large number of recent projects. The use of graphical tools, tables and databases provides a firmer, more rigorous and defensible platform for the scenario development activities than the earlier ad hoc methods. It is observed, however, that the quality of a scenario development depends very heavily on the judgement of PA specialists and technical subject specialists in involved. As such it is important that sufficient time and resources are allowed within PA projects to ensure that the appropriate scientific and technical subject expertise is incorporated into the scenario development and its review. The necessary experience usually resides within the various project-specific and international research programmes, and it is important that this experience is fully mobilised within a structured framework guided by the scenario development or PA specialists.

Formal methods of scenario development have only recently been exposed to regulatory and independent review, for example, during the certification of the WIPP disposal facility in the USA. Requirements of scenario development for compliance may vary considerably between nations and programmes. This is an area in which it will be helpful for national regulators to set down the technical requirements or expectations. International co-operation is valuable in helping to define basic common assumptions that can be accepted in PA and scenario development and, also, the circumstances in which stylised scenarios are acceptable. In some cases, it may also be possible to specify the nature or even recommended parameter values of some specific stylised scenarios, e.g. as is currently being investigated for the biosphere within the IAEA BIOMASS project [18].

In the past, and in this report, it has been stated that scenarios and scenario development should be a tool to communicate to wider audiences of non-technical decision makers and the interested public. For example, scenario development may be a basis to explain the scope of assessment and also to explain the performance of a disposal system and its sensitivity to various possible future conditions or evolutions. This has not occurred much in practice. The reason for this may be, as alluded to above, that it is difficult to reduce a complex, technical and specific demonstration of safety to a more general assurance of safety that is transparent and palatable to a more general audience. The challenge to scenario development is to produce these more qualitative lines of argument for safety in parallel and consistent with the lines of the detailed analysis. Scenario development specialists may be well placed to do this having a general understanding of the key process and balance of performance within a disposal system. They will, however, have to think more inventively about using the various evidences from material science, chemistry, natural analogues and environmental systems, and how to marshal this in effective qualitative descriptions of performance and safety.

Differences in approach

There is a large measure of common ground regarding the role of scenario development and its general elements as discussed in Chapter 2 of this report.

There are large differences in the actual application, e.g. tools used and level of formality. This results from national and programme-specific differences, e.g. regulation, stage of repository development and nature of the disposal system. Most programmes at an earlier stage of development indicate that they are likely to move towards using more formal methods in the future. Thus, the differences in level of formality can be partly attributed to the stage of programme development. Additional formality and more complex methodology comes at a cost, however, and therefore the decisions on scope, method and formality of scenario development (and for PA), must remain a matter for individual implementer and regulator organisations, to be discussed and decided at a national level.

For different geological disposal concepts, the timescale and nature of the processes that may lead to the release of radionuclides and contamination of the human environment are different, and different endpoints may be calculated to satisfy different national regulations. It is seems that, among the various scenario development methods, some methods are more suited to evaluation of some concepts or endpoints than others. In particular, the relative importance to repository performance of longer-term gradual process against events appears to have been a determinant of preferred method in several cases.

We conclude that there are large differences in the application of scenario development methods and we expect this situation to persist for the foreseeable future. We also expect that new methods may be developed and existing methods will be adapted. This difference is both natural and healthy in an area of analysis that is still developing and given the different circumstances in which it is applied.

Consistent with the different methods, there are large differences in terminology used. Terminologies have developed organically and independently within individual programmes. Given that the prime requirement is clear communication between project staff and to technical reviewers the responsibility for clear and consistent use of terminology rests within each project. The different terminologies certainly cause confusion when communicating between projects and, to this end, each project should be aware of the special terminology it uses and ensure that it is clearly defined within their documentation and presentations. It is possible that, over time, there will be a convergence of terminology.

In presenting to wider audiences, e.g. non-technical decision makers and other scientists, the use of special terms should be minimised and where special terms are used they must be carefully defined. The term "scenario" is itself widely used in politics, business and the dramatic arts, and has a general dictionary meaning – *an account or synopsis of a projected, planned or anticipated course of action or events*. If it has a more specialist meaning in a project then this should be made clear.

Overall conclusions

Overall, we conclude as follows:

- Structured approaches are necessary to marshal and synthesise the scientific and technical information concerning repository safety, and to select and present the cases to be analysed in safety assessments. These provide a framework on which to organise assessment work, promote the comprehensiveness of the analysis, and provide a basis for communication and explanation of the safety case to different audiences.

- Progress been made since 1992 in the compilation of FEP databases, scenario construction methods, application of the methods and documentation.

- Some problems or challenges remain, e.g. how to ensure traceability and clarity of technical documentation, how to communicate to wider audiences, and how to treat of probabilities and time dependence?

- Current methods are:

    - generally sufficient for their technical purpose within performance assessment and can be flexibly applied to different repository concepts at different stages of development;

    - only just being tested for compliance demonstration. Initial experience indicates that regulatory advice is required, e.g. to set guidance on expectations for reproducibility, the scope of records and the treatment of human intrusion and other stylised scenarios;

    - not much used for wider communication, e.g. to non-technical stakeholders. More inventive thought may be required on how to marshal the available evidence to construct qualitative descriptions of performance and safety that are more convincing to wider audiences, and on addressing specific stakeholder concerns.

- There are differences between projects:

    - in the methods applied. These result from national and project-specific requirements, e.g. regulation, stage of development and nature of the disposal system. This is healthy and to be expected at the current stage of developments;

    - in terminology corresponding to the different methods. Special terms must be defined and consistently used within projects and their use minimised in communication to wider audiences.

5. REFERENCES

1.   *Safety Assessment of Radioactive Waste Repositories: Systematic Approaches to Scenario Development*, Nuclear Energy Agency, OECD, Paris, 1992.

2.   *Features, Events and Processes (FEPs) for Geologic Disposal of Radioactive Waste – An International Database*, Nuclear Energy Agency, OECD, Paris, 2000. (A CD-ROM containing a stand-alone version of the database and the report in pdf format is also available as NEA-OECD publication, under the same reference with the mention: "2000 Edition").

3.   *Confidence in the Long-term Safety of Deep Geological Repositories: Its Development and Communication*, Nuclear Energy Agency, OECD, Paris, 1999.

4.   Eng T., Hudson J., Stephansson O., Skagius K. and Wiborgh M., Scenario Development Methodologies, SKB Technical Report 94-28, Stockholm, 1994.

5.   Nirex, Conceptual Basis of the Master Directed Diagram, Nirex report S/98/010, 1998.

6.   Hudson J.A., Rock Engineering Systems: Theory and Practice. Ellis Horwood series in Civil Engineering, New York, London, Toronto 1992.

7.   Chapman N.A. *et al.*, Systems Analysis, Scenario Construction and Consequence Analysis Definition for SITE-94, SKI Report 95:26, Stockholm, 1995.

8.   Gomit J.M., Marivoet J., P. Raimbault P. and F. Recreo F., EVEREST, Vol. 1: Common Aspects of the Study, EC Report EUR 17449/1 EN, Luxembourg, 1997.

9.   PROSA PRObabilistic Safety Assessment: Final Report, OPLA-1, ECN-RIVM-RGD, Petten, Netherlands, 1993.

10.   Sumerling T.J. (ed.), Dry Run 3: A Trial Assessment of Underground Disposal of Radioactive Waste Based on Probabilistic Risk Analysis: Overview, UK Department of the Environment Report DoE/HMIP/RR/92.039, 1992.

11.   The Principles of Radioactive Waste Management, IAEA Safety Series No. 111-F, Vienna (1995).

12.   Radiological Protection Policy for the Disposal of Radioactive Waste, ICRP Publication 77, Pergamon, Elsevier, Amsterdam and New York, 1998.

13.   Radiation Protection Recommendations as Applied to the Disposal of Long-lived Solid Radioactive Waste, ICRP Publication 81, Pergamon, Elsevier, Amsterdam and New York, 2000.

14.   *The Environmental and Ethical Basis of Geological Disposal*: A Collective Opinion of the NEA Radioactive Waste Management Committee, Nuclear Energy Agency, OECD, Paris 1995.

15.   Proceeding from a NEA Workshop on "Regulating the Long-term Safety of Radioactive Waste Disposal", Cordoba, Spain, Published Nuclear Energy Agency, OECD, Paris, 1997.

16. *Lessons Learnt from Ten Performance Assessment Studies*, Nuclear Energy Agency, OECD, Paris, 1997.

17. *Regulatory Reviews of Assessments of Deep Geologic Repositories*, Nuclear Energy Agency, OECD, Paris, 2000.

18. Long-term Releases from Solid Waste Disposal Facilities: The Reference Biosphere Concept, BIOMASS Theme 1, Working Document No. 1, April 1998, available from IAEA, Vienna.

19. *Disposal of Radioactive Waste: Review of Safety Assessment Methodologies.* A report of the Performance Assessment Advisory Group of the Radioactive Waste Management Committee, Nuclear Energy Agency, OECD, Paris, 1991.

LIST OF WORKSHOP PARTICIPANTS

Madrid, 10-12 May 1999

BELGIUM

Mr. Jan MARIVOET   Tel: +32 (14) 33 32 42
Centre d'étude de l'énergie   Fax: +32 (14) 32 35 53
nucléaire (CEN/SCK)   Eml: jmarivoe@sckcen.be
Boeretang 200
2400 Mol

CANADA

Mr. Paul GIERSZEWSKI   Tel: +1 416 592 2346
Ontario Power Generation   Fax: +1 416 592 7336
Long-Term Waste Management   Eml: paul.gierszewski@
Technology Department   ontariopowergeneration.com
700 University Avenue
H16 E26 Toronto M5G IX6

FINLAND

Mr. Risto PALTEMAA   Tel: +358 9 759 88 313
Radiation and Nuclear Safety   Fax: +358 9 759 88 670
Authority (STUK)   Eml: risto.paltemaa@stuk.fi
P.O. Box 14
00881 Helsinki

Mr. Timo VIENO   Tel: +358 9 456 5066
VTT ENERGY   Fax: +358 9 456 5000
P.O. Box 1604   Eml: timo.vieno@vtt.fi
02044 VTT

Mr. Juhani VIRA   Tel: +358 9 2280 3740
Manager   Fax: +358 9 2280 3719
Posiva Oy   Eml: juhani.vira@posiva.fi
Mikonkatu 15 A
00100 Helsinki

FRANCE

Ms. Anne DUTFOY
EDF – Direction des Études et Recherches
1, avenue du général de Gaulle
92140 Clamart

Tel: +33 1 47 65 47 27
Fax: +33 1 47 65 51 73
Eml: anne.dutfoy@edfgdf.fr

Mr Didier GAY
IPSN – DES
77-83, avenue du Général de Gaulle
92140 Clamart

Tel: +33 (0) 1 4654 9158
Fax: +33 (0) 1 4654 7727
Eml: didier.gay@ipsn.fr

Ms. Sandrine PIERLOT
Agence nationale pour la gestion
des déchets radioactifs (ANDRA/DSU)
Parc de la Croix Blanche
1-7 rue Jean Monnet
92298 Chatenay-Malabry Cedex

Tel: +33 1 46 11 83 56
Fax: +33 1 46 11 80 13
Eml: sandrine.pierlot@andra.fr

Ms. Sylvie VOINIS*
Agence nationale pour la gestion
des déchets radioactifs (ANDRA/DSU)
Parc de la Croix Blanche
1-7 rue Jean Monnet
92298 Chatenay-Malabry Cedex

Tel: +33 (1) 46 11 81 10
Fax: +33 (1) 46 11 80 13
Eml: sylvie.voinis@andra.fr
*Presently at NEA

GERMANY

Mr. Rolf-Peter HIRSEKORN
Gesellschaft für Anlagen- und
Reaktorsicherheit (GRS) mbH
Theodor-Heuss-Str.4
38122 Braunschweig

Tel: +49 531 8012 288
Fax: +49 531 8012 200
Eml: his@grs.de

Mr. Siegfried KELLER
Fed. Inst. for Geosciences
and Natural Resources
Stilleweg 2
30655 Hannover

Tel: +49 (511) 643 2397
Fax: +49 (511) 643 3662
Eml: siegfried.Keller@bgr.de

Mr. Alexander NIES
Head of Division of RW Disposal
Federal Ministry for the Environment,
Nature Conservation and Nuclear Safety
(BRS III 6(A), Postfach 120629
53048 Bonn

Tel: +49 (228) 305 2959
Fax: +49 (228) 305 2296
Eml: nies.alexander@bmu.de

Mr. Klaus-Juergen ROEHLIG　　　　　　Tel:　+49 221 2068 796
Gesellschaft für Anlagen- und　　　　　　Fax:　+49 221 2068 939
Reaktorsicherheit (GRS) mbH　　　　　　Eml:　rkj@grs.de
Schwertnergasse 1
50667 Köln

Mr. Jürgen WOLLRATH　　　　　　　　Tel:　+49 5341 885 642
Bundesamt für Strahlenschutz　　　　　　Fax:　+49 5341 885 605 or 885
BfS　　　Eml:　jwollrath@bfs.de
Postfach 10 01 49
38201 Salzgitter

Mr. Bruno BALTES (absent)　　　　　　Tel:　 +49 221 2068 795
Gesellschaft für Anlagen- und　　　　　　Fax:　+49 221 2068 939
Reaktorsicherheit (GRS) mbH　　　　　　Eml:　bat@grs.de
Schwertnergasse 1
50667 Köln

JAPAN

Mr. Hitoshi MAKINO　　　　　　　　　Tel:　+81 3 8220 3316
Japan Nuclear Cycle　　　　　　　　　　Fax:　+81 3 8220 3372
Development Institute　　　　　　　　　Eml:　macky@hq.jnc.go.jp
1-2, 1-chome, Marunouchi
Chiyoda-ku
100-8245 Tokyo

NETHERLANDS

Mr. Jacques GRUPA　　　　　　　　　Tel:　+31 (224) 56 4333
NRG　　　　　　　　　　　　　　　　Fax:　+31 225 56 3490
P.O. Box 25　　　　　　　　　　　　　Eml:　grupa@nrg-nl.com
1755 ZG Petten

SPAIN

Mr. Jesus ALONSO DIAZ-TERAN　　　　Tel:
ENRESA　　　　　　　　　　　　　　Fax:
C/Emilio Vargas 7　　　　　　　　　　Eml:　jald@enresa.es
28043 Madrid

Mr. Emiliano GONZALEZ　　　　　　　Tel:　+34 91 519 4436
INITEC　　　　　　　　　　　　　　Fax:　+34 91 519 4644
C/ Padilla, 17　　　　　　　　　　　　Eml:　egoh@enresa.es
28006 Madrid

Mr. Javier RODRIGUEZ AREVALO　　　Tel:　+34 91 346 02 82
CSN　　　　　　　　　　　　　　　Fax:　+34 91 346 05 88
C/Justo Dorado 11　　　　　　　　　Eml:　jra@csn.es
28040 Madrid

Mme. Carmen RUIZ LOPEZ
Chef du Service de Déchets de
Haute Activité
Consejo de Seguridad Nuclear
Justo Dorado 11
28040 Madrid

Tel: +34 91 346 01 43
Fax: +34 91 346 05 88
Eml: mcrl@csn.es

Mrs. Celsa RUIZ RIVAS
CIEMAT
DIAE
22 Avenida Complutense
28040 Madrid

Tel: +34 91 346 6157
Fax: +34 91 346 6005
Eml: celsa.ruiz@ciemat.es

Ms. Eva SALAS SANCHEZ
Consejo de Seguridad Nuclear (CSN)
Justo Dorado, No 11
28040 Madrid

Tel: +34 91 346 0182
Fax: +34 91 346 0588
Eml: ess@csn.es

SWEDEN

Ms. Christina LILJA
Swedish Nuclear Power Insp.
SKI
Klarabergsviadukten 90
106 58 Stockholm

Tel: +46 8 698 84 55
Fax: +46 8 661 90 86
Eml: lilja@ski.se

Mrs. L. MOREN
Swedish Nuclear Fuel and Waste
Management Co. (SKB)
Box 5864
102 40 Stockholm

Tel: +46 (8) 665 2800
Fax: +46 (8) 661 5719
Eml: skblm@skb.se

Mr. Magnus WESTERLIND
Swedish Nuclear Power Insp.
SKI
Klarabergsviadukten 90
106 58 Stockholm

Tel: +46 8 698 8684
Fax: +46 8 661 9086
Eml: magnus@ski.se

SWITZERLAND

Mr. Frits VAN DORP
NAGRA
Hardstrasse 73   Eml:
5430 Wettingen

Tel: +41 (56)4371111
Fax: +41 (56)4371207
vandorp@nagra.ch

Mr. Johannes O. VIGFUSSON
Waste Management Section
HSK – Swiss Federal Nuclear Safety
Inspectorate
5232 Villigen HSK

Tel: +41 (56) 310 39 74
Fax: +41 (56) 310 39 07
Eml: vigfusson@hsk.psi.ch

UNITED KINGDOM

Mrs. Lucy BAILEY
UK Nirex Ltd
Curie Avenue
Harwell, Didcot
Oxfordshire OX11 ORH

Tel: +44 1235 825 357
Fax: +44 1235 820 560
Eml: lucy.bailey@nirex.co.uk

Mr. Neil A. CHAPMAN
QuantiSci Limited
47, Burton Street
Melton Mowbray
Leicestershire LE13 1AF

Tel: +44 (1664) 411 445
Fax: +44 (1664) 411 402
Eml: nchapman@quantisci.co.uk

Ms. Linda CLEMENTS
British Nuclear Fuels (BNFL)
Environmental Modelling
R002 Rutherford House
Risley, Warrington, WA3 6AS

Tel: +44 1925 832 048
Fax: +44 1925 832 016
Eml: Linda.Clements@bnfl.com

Mr. Len WATTS
British Nuclear Fuels (BNFL)
Environmental Modelling
R002 Rutherford House
Risley, Warrington, WA3 6AS

Tel: +44 1925 834 344
Fax: +44 1925 832 016
Eml: Len.Watts@bnfl.com

UNITED STATES OF AMERICA

Mr. D.R. ANDERSON
Sandia National Laboratories
P.O. Box 5800, MS1328
Department 6849
Albuquerque, NM 87185

Tel: +1 (505) 284 4600
Fax: +1 (505) 848 0705
Eml: drander@sandia.gov

Mr. G. BASABILVAZO
Department of Energy
Carlsbad Area Office
P.O. Box 3090
Carlsbad, New Mexico 88221

Tel: +1 (505) 234 7488
Fax: +1 (505) 234 7008
Eml: basabig@wipp.carlsbad.nm.us

Mr. Peter N. SWIFT
Mail Stop 0778
Sandia National Laboratories
P.O. Box 5800
Albuquerque, NM 87185-0778

Tel: +1 505 284 4817
Fax: +1 505 284 3964
Eml: pnswift@sandia.gov

Mr. Gordon Wittmeyer
Center for Nuclear Waste
Regulatory Analyses
Southwest Research Institute
6220 Culebra Road
San Antonio, Texas 78255-0510

Tel: +1 210 522 5082
Fax: +1 210 522 5155
Eml: gwitt@swri.org

CONSULTANT

Mr. Trevor SUMERLING
Safety Assessment Mngt. Ltd
Beech Tree House
Hardwick Road
Whitchurch-on-Thames
Reading, RG8 7HW
United Kingdom

Tel: +44 1189 844 410
Fax: +44 1189 841 440
Eml: trevor@sam-ltd.demon.co.uk

NEA SECRETARIAT

Mr. Bertrand RÜEGGER
Radiation Protection and
Waste Management Division
OECD Nuclear Energy Agency
12, boulevard des Iles
92130 Issy-les-Moulineaux
France

Tel.: +33 1 45 24 10 44
Fax: +33 1 45 24 11 10
Eml: ruegger@nea.fr

Appendix 2

THE WORKSHOP QUESTIONNAIRE

The Workshop Questionnaire lists a number of questions, the answers to which should provide important information for the preparation of the workshop.

1.   Position and tasks of "scenario development", theory and practice

1.1   What would you consider to be the appropriate position, or task of "scenario development" within performance assessment or safety analysis for radioactive waste repositories?

For example:

- the position might be:

  – the first step in performance assessment;

  – the first step in performance assessment;

  – the last step in performance assessment before finalising the documentation;

- its tasks might be:

  – to ensure completeness, comprehensiveness, or sufficiency of scope in a performance assessment;

  – to help confidence building;

  – to make decisions of what to include and what not to include in a performance assessment traceable;

  – to demonstrate traceability from data or information to assessment scenarios, models and calculation cases;

  – to guide decisions concerning research priorities (allocation of funds);

  – to provide transparency of a performance assessment and its results to different audiences in documents and presentations for e.g. regulators, non-technical groups?

1.2   Is "scenario development" required or guided by regulations or authorities in your country?

1.3   What is, in reality, the position of "scenario development" in the performance assessments or safety analyses carried out by/for your organisation?

For example:

- is "scenario development" carried out as first step in a performance assessment?
- is "scenario development" the last step before documentation, e.g. to demonstrate comprehensiveness?
- is "scenario development" carried out between two iterations of performance assessments, e.g. to improve the next iteration?

1.4 Does this position depend on the purpose of the performance assessment?
(e.g. concept development, licensing for site selection, construction, operation, closure)

1.5 Does the level of formalism or the depth of the scenario development depend on the purpose of the performance assessment?
(e.g. concept development, licensing for site selection, construction, operation, closure)

2. Definitions

2.1 What are your definitions (if used) of:

- a scenario;
- a FEP (feature, event and process);
- different (hierarchical) levels of FEPs;
- any other concept used in scenario development?
  (e.g. "umbrella", conservative or robust scenarios)

3. Specific use of "scenario development"

3.1 Is there any restriction in your methodology and/or practical application of "scenario development" in areas such as

- normal evolution scenarios;
- disruptive or abnormal scenarios;
- consideration of subsystems;
  (e.g. engineered barrier system, geology, biosphere, future human actions)
- time cut-offs?

If so for what reasons?

- regulatory requirements;
- stage of the programme;
- lack of information/knowledge;
- not considered necessary?

3.2   How do you structure scenarios? How do you rank scenarios?

For example:

- do you divide scenarios in "normal evolution scenarios" and others (what others)?

- do you have a category "disruptive events"? how is it defined?

- do you distinguish reference or base case scenarios? how are these defined?

- do you have a category "what if" scenarios?

- how do you deal with the factor time?
  (e.g. time of occurrence, variability with time, sequence or simultaneousness of FEPs)

3.3   What is your opinion on the use of stylised scenarios?
(e.g. for the biosphere or future human action)

- What process or method do you use to formulate such stylised scenarios?

3.4   What role do these methods play to achieve the tasks defined in Question 1.1?

4.   Methodologies

4.1   How do you assure completeness, comprehensiveness or sufficiency of scope?
(both concerning the FEPs and the scenarios to be considered)

- Do you use generic FEP lists (e.g. from NEA, BIOMOVS)?

4.2   How do you proceed from lists of FEPs to scenarios and conceptual models?

- How do you assure consistency and traceability?

- When (in the assessment process) do you define scenarios quantitatively?

4.3   What methods do you use in "scenario development"? For example:

- expert judgement;

- event tree analysis;

- fault tree analysis;

- influence diagrams;

- interaction matrices;
  (e.g. Rock Engineering System (RES) approach)

- directed diagrams?

4.4   How do you take into account the probability or likelihood of occurrence of scenarios?

4.5   Do you treat all scenarios quantitatively or some only qualitatively?

4.6   Do you use software in "scenario development"?

- Which software?

- Do you produce a database of FEPs?

- Is this available in electronic form?

4.7   How do you treat "probabilistic" FEPs?
(probability of occurrence, variability, uncertainty)

4.8   Could you provide a summary of recent or scheduled work relevant to the development and application of scenario development methodologies (with references)?

Appendix 3

SUMMARY OF RESPONSES TO THE QUESTIONNAIRE

Contents

Introduction

Introduction

This Appendix summarises responses to the questionnaire on scenario development circulated prior to the Workshop, see Appendix 2. The summary follows the structure established in the questionnaire.

Nineteen responses were received from 12 countries, see below:

Belgium	SCK
Canada	Ontario Power Generation (OPG)
Finland	VTT
France	ANDRA
	IPSN
Germany	GRS, Köln
	GRS, Braunschweig
	BGR
	BfS
Japan	JNC
Netherlands	NRG (ECN)
Spain	ENRESA
Sweden	SKB
	SKI
Switzerland	NAGRA
UK	NIREX
	BNFL
USA	USDOE, WIPP
	USDOE, YMP

The summary attempts to identify majority or consensus views where these exist. Special attention is drawn to responses that give significantly different or additional answers, although this is not a criticism or an endorsement of the responses. For brevity, and also so that several responses can be encompassed, responses are often paraphrased, rather than direct quotes. For traceability, organisation names are usually attached to direct quotes.

Further comments by the compiler are given in *italics*.

There is some potential for bias in analysing the responses in that more responses were received from some countries than others (4 from Germany, 2 from France, Sweden the UK and USA and one from other countries). Where this appears to be significant, e.g. on regulatory matters, responses are analysed according to country.

1.   The Position and Tasks of Scenario Development: Theory and Practice

1.1.1   *The position of scenario development*

About half the respondents place scenario development as the first step in performance assessment (PA). Several of these respondents also indicate that an initial scenario development would be iterated on and updated during the course of PA, e.g. "It should be the first step, along with FEPs analysis, with follow-up audits later during Safety Assessment including prior to release of documents" (OPG) and "the first step; as well as the last step (performance assessment results will require an update of the original scenario development exercise) and often between iterations of performance assessments" (Nagra).

Three organisations place scenario development as a second step in their methodology after a first step such as: definition of assessment basis, FEP analysis or definition of safety case context. *It may be, however, that other organisations include such activities within the scope of scenario development.* Two organisations also mention system description or definition as a prior step.

Three respondents focus on its position within an integrated and iterative PA process. For example: "the scenario development should be an integrated part of performance and safety assessment" (SKB) and ".... scenario development work must continue throughout the life of the project, identifying how PA will treat FEPs based on information developed by site characterisation and other sources" (USDOE).

The divergence in responses seems to arise because:

(a) *some respondents interpret scenario development as a broader or narrower activity than others.*

(b) some respondents replied with respect to the role of scenario development in a single phase of PA activity whereas others replied with respect to the role over the life of a project.

1.1.2   *The tasks of scenario development*

The majority of respondents mention the following tasks for scenario development, although there is some variation in words used:

- To ensure, demonstrate or try to ensure completeness, comprehensiveness or sufficiency in the scope of a PA.

- To decide what to include (and what not to include) in PA – including to reduce the set of FEPs, identify scenarios to be included in quantitative modelling and to go from exhaustive lists of events to the selection of a representative few to be studied.

- To demonstrate traceability from data/information to assessment scenarios, models and calculation cases.

- To provide transparency (improve understandability) of PA results to different audiences – including to act as a communication tool between implementer, regulator and the public.

- To guide decisions concerning research priorities, the collection of data, and allocation of funds.

In addition, many respondents mention

- to help confidence building (internally and in wider audiences),

although no specific explanation or expansion of this is given. This is a topic that may deserve attention in future, especially in view of the RWMC/PAAG document on confidence building [1].

Other tasks, each mentioned by only one or two respondents are:

- to cover the potential future conditions of the disposal system;
- to give the performance of engineered barriers and study robustness of barriers;
- to provide a starting set of assumptions (since the entire set of initial and boundary conditions cannot be known;
- to decide how FEPs have to be included in PA, e.g. by quantitative or qualitative methods;
- to define the scope and context of PA;
- to clarify the status of technical and scientific understanding;
- to define scenarios that can represent a whole group of scenarios, and indication of the scenarios covered by an assessment;
- to generate documentation on the treatment of FEPs.

The USDOE respondent noted that the most important tasks or goals of scenario development are different from regulator, implementer and external stakeholder's perspective, and also that the role of scenario development is likely to change during the life of a project. Thus, in the case of the WIPP Project:

- from the regulator perspective, the most important purpose was perhaps the documentation of FEPs;
- from the PA teams perspective, scenario development served an important role in identifying scenarios (combinations of FEPs) that were included in the quantitative modelling;
- from the external stakeholder's perspective, scenario development and the documentation of the FEP process served as an entry point into the analysis of controversial issues that had been excluded.

In the case of the Yucca Mountain Project it was noted:

- early in the project, scenario development was important in determining the important scenarios for analysis, e.g. identification of disruptive events;
- in the licensing phase, it will have an increasingly important role in documenting the comprehensiveness of the analysis and, also, the basis for decisions on what to include or exclude.

1.2   *Regulatory requirements or guidance related to scenario development*

The regulatory requirements and guidance related to scenario development are summarised below (according to the responses given).

Box 1. Regulatory requirements or guidance related to scenario development	
Belgium	Requirements not yet formulated. It is expected that scenario development will be required.
Canada	Required to estimate radiological risk as the sum over "all important scenarios", although there is no specific guidance on "important scenarios". Draft regulatory documents suggest using a "structured approach that results in a number of scenarios that represent a broad spectrum of possibilities".
Finland	Required by regulation. A background memorandum includes some examples of scenarios to be included. No detailed guidance on methods.
France	Basic Safety Rule n° 111.2.f. details the framework for assessment. Concerning scenarios, main guidelines are: • the definition of an initial period of 500 years associated with a low likelihood for human intrusion; • the definition of a reference situation and the mention of the events to which it should be associated; • the definition of a minimum list of events to be considered for the selection of hypothetical situations. The process of scenario selection (or scenario development) recommended includes: • a step of identification of the events liable to occur; • a step of classification of the events on the basis of their probability or origin; • a step of screening the events using criteria such as likelihood or expected level of radiological impact; • a step of combination of events to form scenarios; • a step of sorting of the scenarios.
Germany	The German Safety Criteria for the Final Disposal of Radioactive Waste in a Mine require the development of scenarios as a basis for site-specific safety analysis. They are set up by the Federal Government as a guideline, not as legal act or ordinance. Systematic scenario development is not required explicitly, but the chosen scenarios are to be substantiated and their boundary conditions have to be determined.
Japan	Regulations not in place. Guidelines from the Advisory Committee on Nuclear Fuel Cycle Back-end Policy of the Atomic Energy Agency require scenario development in the generic sense as one of the key parts of safety assessment.

Netherlands	Guidelines for safety analysis of geological disposal have not yet been developed. One possibility is that guidelines similar to those in place for reactor safety might be developed. These are not specific, but there is consensus that two types of scenarios should be used (1) scenarios from "Design Based Accidents" which are prescribed, and (2) scenarios from probabilistic systems analysis.
Spain	Technical regulations on safety analysis of geological disposal have not yet been developed.
Sweden	Scenario development is not required by regulations but there is consensus that a systematic approach is advisable. SKI is currently developing regulations which will given general guidance on the development and grouping of scenarios.
Switzerland	The HSK Guideline HSK-R-21/e requires safety analyses based on models predicting the future behaviour of the repository. A detailed analysis of processes and events that could affect the repository system over time is required, potential evolution scenarios are to be derived.
UK	Scenario development is not explicitly required, but regulatory guidance states that the assessed radiological risk should be summed over all situations that could give rise to exposure.
USA	Regulations are developed on facility-specific basis and may set detailed requirements on PA methodology. Regulations applicable to the WIPP require the identification of events and processes that may have a significant effect on performance. Regulations limit the time period (10 000 years) and provide screening criteria, e.g. FEPs need not be considered if the probability of occurrence is less that 1/10 000 in 10 000 years. Regulations for Yucca Mountain are, as yet, incomplete. They are likely to expect the applicant to follow a scenario development approach similar to that proposed by Cranwell *et al.* (1990).[4]

In summary:

- Regulations and guidance applying to safety analysis of geological disposal are not yet fully in place in several countries (Belgium, Japan, Netherlands, Spain, Sweden) but will, or is likely to, include advice to use systematic methods to identify cases to be considered in PA.

- Scenario development is required and quite specific guidance (on the scenarios to be treated and/or methods of analysis) is given in France and the USA, with somewhat less specific guidance being given in Finnish regulations and Swedish regulations currently under development. Scenario development is required, but only rather general guidance is given, by Canadian and Swiss regulations.

- UK regulations do not require scenario development but the requirements indicate the need to systematically identify and justify the cases to be considered.

---

4. Cranwell, R.M. *et al.*, Risk Methodology for Geologic Disposal of Radioactive Waste: Scenario Selection Procedure. NUREG/CR-1667, SAND80-1429, December 1982, revised April 1990.

1.3   The actual position of scenario development

The answers given are consistent with those given to the first part of Question 1.1 (see Section 1.1.1), but most respondents gave more prominence to the importance of scenario development within the iterative development of their safety assessments. Some state that FEP analysis and/or scenario development studies were carried out between formal PA exercises, while others note the importance of iteration between scenario development and quantitative analysis activities within a single phase of PA. One respondent notes that, in one study, scenario development was carried out during the model development stage, and resulted in modest changes to some models.

Several respondents note that past and current PAs have not been based on formal scenario development, or considered only a base scenario or a more informally chosen set of illustrative scenarios. These respondents also note that more formal application of scenario development methods is expected in future assessments.

1.4   Position in relation to the purpose of PA

The majority of respondents state that the position of scenario development does not change according to the purpose of the assessment, e.g. "the position is considered a natural one, irrespective of the status of the programme" (ENRESA). Some of these participants note however, that the care and depth of study will change.

Four responses indicate that the focus, role, or the way scenario development is implemented, will change, e.g.:

- "At the step of site selection and characterisation, the identification of relevant features of the site, e.g. related to stability and also hydraulic and geochemical confinement, is the main objective. At the step of repository design, the features of the site identified in the previous step are the main basis; design should take advantage of the benefits and mitigate the weak points of the site. The need for exhaustivity can be restricted at site selection, and design stages but becomes a priority for PA." (IPSN).

- "The role of scenario development changed through time, focusing first on scenario selection, and later on the documentation of FEP treatment for completeness." (USDOE).

1.5   Level of formalism in relation to the purpose of PA

The majority of respondents state that the level of formalism will change, increasing as more detailed PAs are performed, e.g. "in the phase of concept development it is sufficient that a small number of relevant scenarios are selected and analysed; in more formal phases, such as for licensing, it is important that the completeness of the assessment can be shown." (SCK-CEN).

Several of these respondents note, however, that the change is due to the increased data/information and/or maturity of the analysis, and expectation of the regulator, rather than fundamentally linked to the purpose of the assessment.

At least three respondents state that the formalism will remain the same but depth of study would change. One respondent related the changes to quality assurance requirements. Another respondent remarks: "Even for concept development, no "show-stoppers" can be missed so there is a need for completeness regardless of the purpose. But having identified the scenarios, not all have to be analysed at each stage or to the same depth of detail." (OPG).

2. Definitions

2.1 Scenarios

Two respondents indicate that no special terminology, or formal definition of scenario, is used within their projects, although both gave a practical indication their use of the term. All other respondents gave a definition, and representative examples are reproduced in Box 2.1. Only one respondent referred to the definition given in the NEA Scenario Working Group Report [2], which is included for completeness.

Of the definitions given, that used by SKI in the SITE-94 project is the most formal or technical and relies on the definition of other elements used in the methodology. All the other definitions are more general. In all projects the term scenario includes the idea of a possible future evolution of the disposal system. Several refer to scenario as an imaginary or hypothetical evolution, or note that it is for the purpose of illustrating performance of the system. Several also refer to a scenario as being composed or resulting from a specified set or combination of FEPs or factors (which can include evolutionary factors, e.g. glaciation).

Box 2.1. Representative definitions of "scenario"

- A description of a possible evolution of a waste disposal system. (SCK-CEN)

- A set of factors that could affect the performance of the disposal facility to immobilize and isolate nuclear fuel waste. (OPG)

- A scenario describes the possible evolution of the repository system (biosphere, geosphere, repository) specified by FEPs that characterise the system. (BGR, BfS, GRS Köln and Braunschweig)

- Scenarios are defined as sequences of FEPs which describe the hypothetical but credible future evolution of the repository for the purpose of illustrating the safety performance of the system. (JNC)

- A scenario is any potential future development of the disposal facility. Scenarios that eventually cause exposure of individuals to the materials disposed of in the facility are relevant for performance assessments. (NRG)

- Any of the plausible future evolutions of a repository system (or of its boundary conditions), not necessarily predicted, which are useful for the purpose of assessing the long term safety. (Enresa)

- One, or a set of, EFEPs (FEPs external to the Process System) acting on the Process System and its consequential development. (The Process System is a conceptual description of all the FEPs and influences, which directly or indirectly may influence the release and transport of radionuclides from the repository to the environment and to man. (SKI, SITE-94)

... future evolutions ..., each of them being a hypothetical, but physically possible, sequence of processes and events that influence the release and transport of release of radionuclides from the repository to the biosphere and the exposure to humans. The set of scenarios defined for a particular repository and which will be considered in the performance assessment should form an envelope within which the future evolution of the repository is expected to lie. (Nagra)

- A broad description of the disposal facility and its surroundings at the time of site closure, and of the evolution of the facility and its surroundings with time as a result of natural, waste-related and engineering-related processes and human activities. (BNFL)

- A scenario is a subset of the set of all possible futures of the system that contains similar future occurrences. (WIPP)

- A single scenario specifies one possible set of events and processes and provides a broad brush description of their characteristics and sequencing. (NEA SWG 1992, ref. [2])

2.2 *Feature, event and process (FEP)*

Three respondents indicate no formal definition of FEP with another respondent stating that the terms feature, event and process are used with common dictionary meanings.

Of the other respondents, nine choose to define FEP while five give separate definitions for feature, event and process. The definitions in Box 2.2 are representative. All the definitions of FEP referred to relevance to disposal system performance or construction of scenarios. Several respondents define or mention specific types of FEP with special meaning within their methodology, e.g.:

- included FEPs, reserve FEPs and open questions (Nagra);

- system FEP, probabilistic FEP and scenario-defining FEP (Nirex);

- internal FEP and external FEP (BNFL).

Box 2.2. Representative definitions of:

(a) "FEP"

- any feature, event or process that has the potential to influence the repository system. (SCK•CEN)

- FEP or factor (both terms are considered as synonymous) are any feature, process or event with a potential to influence directly or indirectly the performance of the repository system. (Enresa)

- Phenomena that will lead to changes in the disposal system and/or natural environment such as to initiate or modify radionuclide release and transport. (BNFL)

(b) "feature", "event" and "process"

OPG:

Feature – A characteristic of a component of the disposal system, such as the material used to construct the containers, fractures in the rock that pass near the disposal vault and a garden used by the critical group that may be exposed to contaminated water.

Event – An incident, generally of short duration, that could affect the system, such as a nearby earthquake, a failure in the containers caused by fabrication defects, and the drilling of exploration boreholes that intersect the vault.

Process – A natural phenomenon occurring in the disposal system, such as the dissolution of the nuclear fuel waste in groundwater, the movement of groundwater in the geosphere by hydraulic gradients, and the transfer of contaminants in the soil rooting zone to the edible parts of a plant.

GRS, Köln:[5]

Feature – is an aspect or condition of the disposal system that influences the release and/or transport of contaminants.

Event – is a natural anthropogenic phenomenon that occurs over a small portion of the time frame of interest, in other words, a "short-term" phenomenon.

Process – is a natural or anthropogenic phenomenon that occurs over a significant portion of the time frame of interest, in other words, a "long-term" phenomenon.

Nirex:

Features are general characteristics of the repository or the surrounding environment.

Events are processes that operate on a timescale that is short compared with the assessment period.

Processes are phenomena that affect the safety performance of the system and operate on a timescale that is significant relative to the assessment period.

With regard to different levels of FEPs, only three respondents indicate they used hierarchical schemes, although several others mentioned that classification schemes, e.g. natural, waste and repository-induced and human-initiated FEPs, are used to structure FEP lists. Two respondents mention different levels of detail within the application of scenario tools, i.e. within matrix diagrams and process influence diagrams.

2.3   Other concepts used in scenario development

Several respondents give the definitions of specific types of scenario used in their method such as umbrella, central, conservative, main, less likely, residual, base and variant scenarios. Representative definitions are given in Box 2.3.

---

5. From Rechard, R.P., An Introduction to the Mechanics of Performance Assessment Using Examples of Calculations Done for the Waste Isolation Pilot Plant Between 1990 and 1992. SAND93-1378.

Box 2.3. Representative definitions of types of scenarios

Central scenario – A collection of closely related scenarios that include the most probable scenarios (i.e. their summed probability approaches unity), usually that can be modelled within one (probabilistic) analysis. (OPG)

Umbrella scenario – used to reduce the number of scenarios to be considered in an analysis. It is the most constraining scenario in terms of consequences in the same family. (ANDRA)

Reference scenario – pessimistic assumptions of near field degradation, constant geology based upon understanding of present day conditions, conservative present day biosphere. (Nagra)

Main scenario – based on the likely evolution of the external conditions and realistic assumptions on the internal conditions (initial state/properties of the engineered barrier system). The main scenario should thereby include expected climate changes and reasonable assumptions … (it) should form the basis for evaluation of different types of uncertainty and for the compliance evaluation. (SKI)

Less likely scenarios – including alternative assumptions on, e.g. the sequence of climate evolution, tectonic events and initial properties of the engineered barrier system, future human action except intrusion etc. (SKI)

Residual scenarios and what-if calculations – including human intrusion and effects of other disruptive FEPs (which are analysed irrespective of probability of occurrence) to illustrate the importance of individual barriers or barrier functions. (SKI)

Base scenario – The base scenario provides a broad and reasonable representation of the "natural" evolution of the system and its surrounding environment. The "natural" evolution may be perturbed, but not redirected, by certain man-made characteristics. The base scenario contains all system FEPs and those probabilistic FEPs which are judged more likely than not to occur and which have a significant impact on radiological risk and can be included without introducing unacceptable bias. (Nirex)

Variant scenario – may be considered as the base scenario with the inclusion of one or more additional scenario-defining FEPs and their associated scenario FEPs. Variant scenarios are referred to as either single-FEP or multi-FEP variants. (Nirex)

In Germany, an agreement has been reached between institutions working in this area to distinguish between likely, less likely, and unlikely scenarios, and unintentional human intrusion. The definition of these terms is given in B. Baltes, K.J. Röhlig and A. Nies, *Development of Scenarios for Radioactive Waste Repositories from a Regulatory Point of View: Status of Discussion in Germany*, see Appendix 4, Papers Submitted to the Workshop.

Two respondents give information on scenario methodology. In particular, methods based on barrier state (NRG) and on "THMC-diagrams" (SKB) are described. In the latter, each subsystem is analysed in terms of thermal, hydrogeological, mechanical and chemical processes occurring within the subsystem and between the system and its surroundings.

One respondent mentions robust concepts, whereas another questions the meaning of robust, identifying this as a topic requiring attention at the Workshop. *Possibly, this topic is connected to confidence building, see 1.1.2.*

3. Use of Scenario Development

3.1 *Restrictions and practical application*

All respondents indicate that both "normal" and "disruptive" or "abnormal" scenarios are treated, although some mention that treatment of some abnormal scenarios can be avoided if the probability of occurrence is low. One respondent indicates that the expected evolution of the disposal system under consideration is that no release will occur, and that all release and transport calculations are therefore for "what if" situations.

A few respondents mention that the time period of concern is limited by regulatory guidance: up to 10 000 years in Canada and the USA, up to 100 000 years in France, and up to 1 000 000 years in Sweden.

Several respondents mention that the treatment of future human actions is limited, e.g. disruptive actions cannot occur before 500 years after closure (France), present day lifestyle and technology should be assumed and a scenario prescribed by regulation is treated (YMP). Several respondents also note that the treatment of biosphere must be limited, e.g. to be consistent with present-day conditions or human behaviour.

3.2 *Structuring and ranking of scenarios*

Several of the respondents make a primary distinction between scenarios caused by natural processes (including degradation processes within the repository) and scenarios related to future human actions. In addition, scenarios caused by natural processes are further subdivided according to likelihood (e.g. normal or probable scenarios versus less probable or unexpected scenarios) or according to cause (e.g. scenarios related to construction of the repository, climate change and tectonics).

Various terminologies are applied such as:

- normal evolution and altered evolution scenarios;
- base case, reference scenarios, sensitivity or what-if calculations;
- normal reference scenario and hypothetical scenarios,
- normal evolution scenario and disruptive events;
- representative scenarios;
- reference and alternative scenarios and robust safety demonstration;
- base scenario, initial defect canister scenario and variant scenarios;
- disturbed and undisturbed performance.

These may be clearly defined within individual methodologies, but there is scope for confusion when communicating between projects and also for wider audiences. This is an area where some international standardisation of terminology might be valuable. It must be recognised, however, that terminology that is established in national regulatory documents must be respected in some projects, and also that differences may arise because of actual differences in methodology and the significance attached to various types of scenarios.

3.3   Use of stylised scenarios

Several respondents note that the use of stylised scenarios (or assumptions) is the only way to deal with FEPs or scenarios that are speculative. A majority note that stylisation can be useful in respect of human behaviour and actions and also the biosphere, and several note that use of stylised scenarios in unavoidable in PA. Some note that internationally accepted stylised scenarios would be used if available.

A detailed rationale behind the definition of stylised scenarios was given by one respondent (IPSN), thus:

- The assumptions adopted must rely first on what is known for sure and on what is observed and understood; where there is insufficient understanding to back a reasonable prediction or draw general trends, the absence of evolution is assumed.

- The stylised scenario must aim at giving a meaningful and robust indication of the impact for the situation considered; it should be acknowledged as representative of the situation and take into consideration as well as possible the major characteristics of the expected impact. Reference biospheres built on the basis of multiple exposure pathways are good illustration of this concern.

- The stylised scenario must search for a reasonable conservatism; it must represent a simplified description of the situation but must be likely to lead to a relative over-estimate of the impact.

Two respondents made the connection to the requirement for regulatory guidance, or at least agreement between regulator and implementer, thus:

"Stylised scenarios are unavoidable in performance assessment, and should be acknowledged as such. For consideration of fundamentally unknowable things, like the probability and mechanism of future human intrusion, stylised scenarios are essential, and, if designed sensibly, can add greatly to the clarity of the analysis. Given that the regulator must accept the stylisation, major decisions such as the treatment of the receptor group or human intrusion are most useful if they are codified directly in the regulations." (USDOE)

"(stylisation) is only practical if the regulator or other stakeholder agrees to the scenario characteristics". (OPG)

Stylisation and standardisation (i.e. internationally agreed stylisation) has also been discussed by IPAG-1 [3] and IPAG-2 [4], wherein discussion was generally negative to the idea of internationally agreed stylisation except in specific areas, e.g. dosimetric models, human behaviour and, possibly, biosphere. This topic could be revisited, however.

3.4 Role of the above methods to achieve scenario development tasks

This question was insufficiently defined so that responses are brief and cover a number of issues.

Four responses stress the importance of systematic approaches to achieve comprehensiveness, in one case, referring especially to stakeholder confidence in comprehensiveness. Two responses refer particularly to the use of stylised scenarios: one noting this might limit the number of FEPs and interactions to be considered and another noting that stylisation of the biosphere can help to de couple biosphere uncertainties from those related to the performance of the engineered barriers and geosphere.

Two responses note that a primary goal of scenario development must be to satisfy prescriptive regulatory requirements.

4. Methodologies

4.1 Completeness, comprehensiveness or sufficiency of scope

A majority of respondents refer to the NEA International FEP Database [5], and in one case the FEP list given in the NEA Scenario Working Group report [2], as useful either as a check on project FEP lists or a starting point for future assessments. About half the respondents refer to features of their scenario methodology as helping to generate comprehensiveness, such as interaction (RES) matrices, influence diagrams, master directed diagrams (MDD) and categorisation of FEPs.

Respondents also mention one or more of the following:

- creating a large list of FEPs by brainstorming within a group of experts (although within the technical waste community);

- use of external experts to assist in compiling lists of relevant processes;

- comparison with other projects, especially of similar concepts;

- learning from workshops on key aspects of the system;

- peer review by external experts;

- audit against international or other project lists;

- seeking input from the wider community, including technical and non-technical stakeholders.

Several respondents mention that it is not possible to ensure completeness, although one of these thought it was possible to demonstrate comprehensiveness.

Surprisingly, no respondent cites dialogue between the implementer and regulator with regard to comprehensiveness or sufficiency here, although this clearly occurs in several projects and was mentioned with respect to completeness in response to other questions.

4.2   From FEP lists to scenarios and models

In answer to this question, most respondents give a brief summary of their method, although at least one admitted this was a difficult link to make, and another noted the process is not strictly objective.

Several respondents refer to a gradual selection and/or screening process and several refer to a stage of describing how each FEP is treated (or not) in the PA which is carried out after scenario and model definition.

Several describe a process in which FEPs were assigned to categories with different functions in the scenario development, such as:

- secondary and primary FEPs;

- groundwater scenario and isolation failure scenario;

- process (or reference) system and external FEPs;

- system and probabilistic FEPs.

For the most part, these methods seem to distinguish FEPs that can be included in a reference groundwater scenario, from FEPs that have the potential to disrupt one or more barrier, cause significant changes in the reference scenario or initiate other release mechanisms. Scenarios are then generated by the second class of FEPs (above) or combinations of these FEPs.

Several respondents note that the iterative nature of the process in which, for example, models or scenarios may be modified.

With regard to consistency and traceability, few respondents answer this directly but those that do refer to their method and/or sound practices such as careful documentation, peer review and adherence to procedures.

4.3   Methods used in scenario development

A majority of respondents mention expert judgements as important (or crucial) to scenario development, with one responding: "we use the common sense, imagination and creativity of experts in combination with systematic organisation of information" (SKB). Three other respondents also refer to the importance of systematics.

Six respondents mention interaction or RES matrices and five mentioned influence diagrams including the PID/AMF method (SKI); two mention top-down classification methods. Specific methods such as initiating event methodology, THMC diagrams, master-directed diagrams (MDD) and the USNRC/Sandia method are also mentioned.

4.4   Accounting for probability or likelihood of occurrence

The majority of respondents indicate a purely qualitative or only semi-quantitative approach to accounting for probability or likelihood of occurrence, e.g. "Almost all evolutional processes relevant to safety are assumed to occur. Some scenarios caused by disruptive events are discussed and their likelihood of occurrence is estimated by expert opinion or assigning probability based on historical data." (JNC).

Several respondents mention that low probability or likelihood is used mainly to screen out FEPs or scenarios that need not be treated in PA. Several respondents mention that the base or reference scenario was assumed to have a probability of one, although one respondent noted that "all our cases of consequence analysis are basically "what if" in nature" (VTT).

One respondent notes that "Likelihood is an element of judgement that is combined with other aspects of the impact to give an opinion on its overall acceptability" (IPSN). Three other respondents explain that the probability of a scenario only needs to be considered if the consequences, e.g. in terms of individual dose, are large, e.g. "less likely scenarios are assessed against a dose limit as though they occur, low probability would only be considered if the dose limit is exceeded" (Nagra).

Four respondents, from Canada, the UK and USA, indicate that a systematic quantitative treatment of scenario probabilities is required; this is related to the regulatory requirements in these countries.

4.5 *Quantitative versus qualitative treatment of scenarios*

Most participants recognise a need for qualitative evaluation of some scenarios, e.g. "we make a qualitative analysis (evaluation?) of all scenarios (including likelihood). Then, for the most probable or representative, we quantify the consequences" (ANDRA). Several indicate that a reference or base scenario is evaluated by detailed quantitative analysis, with other representative or illustrative scenarios analysed quantitatively but in less depth, and yet others discussed only qualitatively. As one respondent explains: "Qualitative treatment and scoping calculations can be used to provide the necessary breadth to an assessment, while quantitative treatment provides depth in areas identified for focus" (BNFL).

Two respondents state that all scenarios considered are analysed quantitatively, although one of these indicates their identification of scenarios is as yet incomplete. Two respondents argue there is a continuum of treatments between qualitative and quantitative, e.g. "sometimes quantification can be semi-qualitative (or semi-quantitative) for example less/more, faster, warmer etc." (SKB). Another notes that "Some scenarios were eliminated because scoping analysis and expert opinion indicated that their probability or consequences were sufficiently low that they could not contribute significantly to the radiological risk" (OPG).

Several respondents note that qualitative arguments can be used to focus or limit detailed quantitative analysis, e.g. "Where consequences of some scenarios can be shown qualitatively to be bounded by other scenarios, full calculation of a quantitative performance measure may not be necessary." (USDOE YMP).

4.6 *Use of software*

Eight respondents note they have used or intend to use the NEA International FEP Database, which is implemented on FileMaker Pro. An additional two respondents use Microsoft Access to manage FEP databases. One respondent had used Business Modeller to create influence diagrams and another used Excel to generate matrix diagrams. Two respondents mention they use graphical or specialist software without specifying what packages are used.

Six respondents state that no specialist software, or only word processing software, is used. One respondent noted that: "because of the large amount of expert judgement involved it is practically impossible to computerise this work." (NRG).

Three participants mention specially-developed FEP management and/or graphical programmes. These are:

- CASCADE (Computer Assisted Scenario Controlling and Development) system – developed to manage FEP databases and to generate influence diagrams (JNC).

- SPARTA – now under development to prepare as well as present scenario work (SKI).

- FANFARE – to assist in the development of MDD diagrams and record information in an underlying database.

4.7   *Treatment of probabilistic FEPs*

Respondents' answers here are consistent with those to Question 4.4.

Many respondents mention stochastic or probabilistic analyses to deal with uncertainties, in which probabilities or probability density functions are assigned. Several mention sensitivity analysis on the time or magnitude of an uncertain event. Several repeat (see Section 4.4) that probability is considered in the decision whether or not to treat a FEP or scenario.

4.8   *Recent and scheduled work*

Different information and levels of detail are given by respondents to this question. The reader is referred to the papers reproduced in Appendix 4, several of which summarise recent and scheduled work and refer to other published work by the various organisations.

5.   References

1.   *Confidence in the Long-term Safety of Deep Geological Repositories: Its Development and Communication*, Nuclear Energy Agency, OECD, Paris, 1999.

2.   *Safety Assessment of Radioactive Waste Repositories: Systematic Approaches to Scenario Development*, Nuclear Energy Agency, OECD, Paris, 1992.

3.   *Lessons Learnt from Ten Performance Assessment Studies*, Nuclear Energy Agency, OECD, Paris, 1997.

4.   *Regulatory Reviews of Assessments of Deep Geologic Repositories: Lessons Learnt*, Nuclear Energy Agency, OECD, Paris, 2000.

5.   *Features, Events and Processes (FEPs) for Geologic Disposal of Radioactive Waste – An International Database*, Nuclear Energy Agency, OECD, Paris, 2000. (A CD-ROM containing a stand-alone version of the database and the report in pdf format is also available as NEA-OECD publication, under the same reference with the mention: "2000 Edition").

Appendix 4

PAPERS SUBMITTED TO THE WORKSHOP

Contents

5b. **Development of a comprehensive performance assessment systems analysis methodology and supporting tools, and their application in scenario evaluation**

Neil A Chapman[1], Peter Robinson[1], Jonathan Jack[1], Mike Stenhouse[1], Bill Miller[1], Björn Dverstorp[2], Christina Lilja[2] and Benny Sundström[2].
[1]QuantiSci; Melton Mowbray, UK & USA;
[2] SKI; Swedish Nuclear Power Inspectorate, Sweden

6. **Development of Scenarios within a Systematic Assessment Framework for the Drigg Post-Closure Safety Case**

Len Watts[1], Linda Clements[1], Mike Egan[2], Neil Chapman[2], Paul Kane[3] and Mike Thorne[4]
[1]British Nuclear Fuels plc (BNFL), Risley, UK
[2]QuantiSci Limited
[3]Kanvil Earth Sciences
[4]AEA Technology plc

7. **Systematic Approach to Scenario Development using FEP Analysis**

L.E.F. Bailey[1] and D.A. Lever[2]
[1]United Kingdom Nirex Limited
[2]AEA Technology plc

8. **Scenario Development for the Waste Isolation Pilot Plant Compliance Certification Application**

D.A. Galson[1], P.N. Swift[2], D.R. Anderson[2], D.G. Bennett[1], M.B. Crawford[1], T.W. Hicks[1], R.D. Wilmot[1], and George Basabilvazo[3]
[1]Galson Sciences Limited, UK
[2]Sandia National Laboratories, USA
[3]United States Department of Energy, USA

9. **Feature, Event, and Process Screening and Scenario Development for The Yucca Mountain Total System Performance Assessment**

SAND98-2831C

P. Swift[1], G. Barr[1], R. Barnard[1], R. Rechard[1], A. Schenker[2], G. Freeze[3] and P. Burck[3]
[1]Sandia National Laboratories
[2]Los Alamos Technical Associates
[3]Duke Engineering and Services

10. **Scenario Development for Safety Assessment of Radioactive Waste Repositories in Switzerland**

Trevor Sumerling[1] and Frits von Dorp[2]
[1] Safety Assessment Management Ltd., Reading, UK.
[2] Nagra, Wettingen, Switzerland.

11. **Scenario Development and Analysis in JNC's Second Progress Report**

H. Umeki, H. Makino, K. Miyahara and M. Naito
Japan Nuclear Cycle Development Institute (JNC)

THE BELGIAN EXPERIENCE WITH SCENARIO DEVELOPMENT IN PERFORMANCE ASSESSMENTS

Jan Marivoet
SCK•CEN, Mol, Belgium

Peter De Preter
NIRAS/ONDRAF, Brussels, Belgium

Abstract

In early assessments of geological disposal in the Boom Clay layer at the Mol site, the scenario selection was based on fault tree analysis and expert judgement.

In more recent assessments a systematic approach to scenario identification and selection was applied following the recommendation of the NEA report on scenario development of 1991. Starting from the NEA FEP list of 1991, to which a few FEPs specific for disposal in clay were added, a catalogue of FEPs relevant for geological disposal in the Boom Clay formation at the Mol site was drawn up. The considered FEPs were screened by applying a number of elimination criteria. The retained FEPs were than partitioned into two groups: those that are certain or about certain to occur are considered within the "normal evolution scenario", the remaining less probable FEPs can lead to an "altered evolution scenario". The FEPs of the second group are than classified according to the state of the repository system to which they belong by considering which component of the repository system is affected by the FEP. This allows to take some FEPs together within one altered evolution scenario. Finally eight altered evolution scenario are identified for further analysis within the PA.

Introduction

A scenario study based on the application of the fault tree analysis (d'Alessandro and Bonne, 1981) was already carried out in 1979-1980 in a collaboration between SCK•CEN and the Joint Research Centre (JRC) at Ispra. The method had the advantage of offering a strong methodological framework for the scenario selection. A strong limitation on the applicability of the method appeared to be the estimation of the occurrence probability of the various primary events that can lead to failure of the disposal system and the fact that many of the considered processes do not cause an abrupt failure of a component but a slow degradation.

The selection of the scenarios that were analysed in our first series of performance assessments, e.g. for the PAGIS assessment (Marivoet and Bonne, 1989), was based on expert judgement. The selected altered evolution scenarios focused on scenarios having the potential to disrupt the host clay barrier, such as the occurrence of a tectonic fault and subglacial erosion reaching the depth of the repository.

After the publication of the NEA report on scenario development (NEA, 1992) it was decided to work out a systematic scenario study (Marivoet, 1994) starting from a catalogue of features, events and processes (FEPs) for the case of geological disposal of radioactive waste in the Boom Clay layer at the Mol site. The results of this scenario study together with results obtained from more recent complementary studies are given hereafter.

Identification of relevant FEPS

For the preparation of the catalogue of FEPs relevant for geological disposal in the Boom Clay formation at the Mol site (Bronders *et al.*, 1994), we started from the FEP list of the NEA (1991) report. This list was complemented with a few FEPs specific for the case of disposal in clay:

- decrease of the plasticity of the clay;
- oxidation of the host rock during construction and operation;
- excavation effects.

The catalogue gives a short description of each FEP and discusses its relevance for the case of disposal in the Boom Clay at the Mol site.

The considered FEPs were screened by applying the following elimination criteria:

- probability lower than 10-8;
- negligible consequences;
- not relevant for the considered waste types;
- not relevant for the considered repository design;
- not relevant for a clay formation;
- not relevant for the Mol site;
- responsibility of future generations;
- multiple entries or similar effects.

The FEPs that only have impact on the biosphere are considered in the development of the reference biosphere and have not to be taken into account for the scenario development of the repository system.

The FEP catalogue considered 134 FEPs, 58 were eliminated as irrelevant and 16 only effected the biosphere. We thus retained 60 FEPs for treatment in the scenario development.

Classifiction of FEPS according to their occurrence probability

In the case of geological disposal in clay formations, ground water will penetrate into the near field of the repository after a relatively short period and the migration of radionuclides is expected to start immediately after the perforation of the overpacks or canisters.

We introduced here the normal evolution scenario, or reference scenario, as the scenario that considers the expected evolution of the repository system. It should take into consideration all the FEPs that are certain or about certain to occur and that have the potential to significantly influence the performance of the essential repository components.

We classified the retained FEPs on the basis of their probability of occurrence into normal evolution FEPs and altered evolution FEPs.

For a number of FEPs, e.g. glaciation and gas mediated transport, this classification depends on the severity or magnitude of the considered FEP. Glaciations comparable to the three most recent glaciations of Quaternary are expected to occur on the basis of Milankovitch's orbital theory. However, the occurrence of a very severe glaciation, i.e. the ice-cap reaching the Mol area, cannot be completely excluded in this phase of the scenario development. In the case of disposal of vitrified high-level waste, the amount of metals or other materials that can contribute to the generation of gas is limited. An analysis of gas effects has shown that it can be expected that the generated gas can be evacuated by diffusion in the interstitial clay water. In this case gas mediated transport will only occur if the gas generation is higher or the evacuation rate lower than expected. On the other hand in the case of disposal of, e.g. medium-level waste, the gas generation rate is so high that gas disruptions from the disposal gallery into the clay formation will occur.

Of the 60 retained FEPs 45 were treated within the normal evolution scenario and 17 were considered for the identification of the altered evolution scenarios.

Classification of FEPS according to the sate of repository system

We applied a top-down approach, called the PROSA methodology, which has been developed by Prij (1992) at ECN for the case of disposal in salt. The PROSA methodology can be considered as a variant of the SKI/SKB top-down approach (Andersson *et al.*, 1989). The repository system is partitioned into three compartments: the near field, the host clay layer and the aquifer system. As indicated above, the biosphere is treated separately. Each component can be in two possible states: intact or by-passed. The repository system can thus be in 8 possible states (cf. Table 1).

Table 1. **Definition of the possible states of the repository system**
(i: intact component; b: by-passed component)

State number	Near field	Clay barrier	Hydrogeology
1	i	i	i
2	i	i	b
3	i	b	i
4	i	b	b
5	b	i	i
6	b	i	b
7	b	b	i
8	b	b	b

The altered evolution FEPs were classified according to the state of the repository system to which they lead. FEPs that affect the same component could in many cases be treated together or could be considered as variants within one group of scenarios.

Identifies scenarios

The normal evolution scenario corresponds to state 1. The description and, as a consequence, the analysis of this scenario are strongly simplified by the introduction of the robust repository concept (NAGRA, 1994). One or more essential safety functions are attributed to a limited number of components of the repository system.

The following altered evolution scenarios were identified:

- exploitation drilling (state 2): this scenario considers the drilling of a water well in the aquifer underlying the host formation; the drilling of a well in the overlying aquifer is already considered in the analysis of the normal evolution scenario;

- green-house effect (state 2): this scenario takes into account the possible effect of the global heating on the aquifer system and, of course, on the biosphere;

- poor sealing of the access shafts and main galleries (state 3): it is assumed that, owing to a human error, the access shafts and main galleries have not been successfully sealed and this might create a preferential pathway for the migration of radionuclides through the clay layer;

- fault activation (states 3 and 7): it is assumed that an active tectonic fault crosses the repository affecting the confinement provided by the host clay layer;

- severe glaciation (states 4 and 8): this might lead to the occurrence of an ice-cap in the Mol area; subglacial erosion can reach depths up to 400 m, and, as a consequence, seriously affect the clay barrier and, as an extreme case, bring remnants of the disposed waste to the surface;

- early failure of the engineered barriers (state 5): many variants can be considered in this group of scenarios; however their consequences are strongly limited by the presence of the intact host clay barrier; one of the more severe variants is an early failure of the overpack in the case of heat generating high-level waste: this will lead to migration of radionuclides while considerable thermal gradients exists in the near field; various coupled thermo-hydro-mechanic transport phenomena might occur;

- gas driven transport (states 3 and 7): if the gas production rate is higher than the gas evacuation rate a gas bulb will be formed in the near field and pressure builds up; when the gas pressure exceeds the effective stress of the host formation a disruption of gas into the clay layer will occur; the expelled gas bulbs can contain radioactive gases and they might also convey a fraction of the near field ground water, containing dissolved radionuclides, into the host clay layer;

- exploration drilling (state 8): it is assumed that a borehole is drilled through the waste repository; three variants of this group of scenarios are analysed: (1) the examination of a core containing radioactive waste by a geologist (cf. scenario described by Smith *et al.*, 1987); (2) the borehole cuttings contain fragments of the disposed radioactive waste and are dumped on the surface in the neighbourhood of the drilling; (3) the walls of the borehole are left open and ground water is flowing through the borehole, where it comes in contact with the disposed waste.

Discussion

A comparison of the outcome of different approaches to systematic scenario development (Gomit *et al.*, 1997), was carried out in the framework of the EVEREST project of the European Commission. The French organisations ANDRA and IPSN applied the independent initiating events methodology, while SCK•CEN applied the approach described above. It appeared that both approaches led to the identification of very similar scenarios for the case of disposal in clay formation. This conclusion strengthened the confidence that the most relevant scenarios have been identified.

Conclusion

The above described scenario development approach has shown that it allows to reach the main objectives of systematic scenario development: it is documented and traceable and it identifies the most relevant scenarios. An additional advantage is that it leads to a manageable number of scenarios to be considered in the consequence analyses.

References

Andersson J., T. Carlsson, T. Eng, F. Kautsky, E. Söderman and S. Wingefors (1989), The joint SKI/SKB scenario development project. SKB, Stockholm, technical report 89-35.

Bronders J., J. Patyn, I. Wemaere and J. Marivoet (1994), Catalogue of events, features and processes potentially relevant to radioactive waste disposal in the Boom clay layer at the Mol site. SCK•CEN, Mol, report R-2987-A.

d'Alessandro M. and A. Bonne (1981), Radioactive waste disposal into a plastic clay formation: A site specific exercise of probabilistic assessment of geological containment. Harwood Academic Publishers, Chur.

Gomit J.M., J. Marivoet, P. Raimbault and F. Recreo (1997), EVEREST, Vol. 1: Common aspects of the study. EC, Luxembourg, report EUR 17449/1 EN.

Marivoet J. (1994), Selection of scenarios to be considered in a performance assessment for the Mol site. SCK•CEN, Mol, report R-2987.

Marivoet J. and A. Bonne (1989), PAGIS : Performance Assessment of Geological Isolation Systems, Clay Option. EC, Luxembourg, report EUR 11776 EN.

NAGRA (1994), Kristallin-I safety assessment report. NAGRA, Wettingen, technical report 93-22.

NEA (1992), Systematic approaches to scenario development. OECD/NEA, Paris.

Prij J. (1993), PROSA: Probabilistic safety assessment (final report). ECN, Petten, report OPLA-1A.

Smith G.M., H.S. Fearn, C.E. Delow, G. Lawson and J.P. Davis (1987), Calculation of the radiological impact of disposal of unit activity of selected radionuclides. NRPB, Chilton, report NRPB-R205.

DEVELOPMENT OF SCENARIOS FOR RADIOACTIVE WASTE REPOSITORIES FROM A REGULATORY POINT OF VIEW: STATUS OF DISCUSSION IN GERMANY

B. Baltes[1], K.J. Röhlig[1] and A. Nies[2]

[1] Gesellschaft für Anlagen- und Reaktorsicherheit (GRS) mbH, Germany
[2] Bundesministerium für Umwelt, Naturschutz und Reaktorsicherheit (BMU), Germany

1. Introduction

Long-term safety assessments for radioactive waste repositories in deep geological formations are part of the comprehensive demonstration of the safety of the loaded and sealed repository in the post-operational phase. This demonstration is conducted site-specifically on the basis of the geological, hydrogeological, geochemical and geotechnical state of the disposal system (engineered and natural barriers) as well as its long-term predictions.

The long-term safety analysis is carried out in three stages: Scenario analysis, consequence analysis with uncertainty and sensitivity analyses as well as demonstration of adherence to prescribed safety objectives. In the scenario analysis the potential evolution of the disposal system is studied. For the disposal system a variety of potential changes in system behaviour have to be considered especially because of the long time-spans involved. Scenarios, by regarding potential future developments, thus provide the context for carrying out safety analyses. They essentially determine the procedures in all phases of disposal evolution (planning, design, normal- and post-operation) during the data acquisition as well as during the development of models.

The discussion of scenarios provides an important basis for communication between the applicant and licensing authorities but also represents an essential element in the process of confidence-building measures.

2. Definitions and Classifications

2.1 *Scenario definition*

The following general definition has been established for the term "scenario":

"A scenario describes a possible system evolution that is specified by a combination of relevant factors."

It follows from this general definition that scenarios can be developed for each system (total system or partial system) upon identifying the relevant factors that characterise the system.

For a disposal system the definition is specified as follows:

"A scenario describes a potential (possible) evolution of a disposal system (repository, geosphere, biosphere) which is specified by a combination of relevant factors which characterise the disposal system."

The identification and selection of alternative evolutions of a disposal system for further treatment in safety analyses is carried out by means of scenario analyses.

2.2 *Disposal system evolution*

The possible evolutions of the total system in the sense of the definition given above on the one hand originate with natural i.e. endogenous and exogenous processes involving the entire system and on the other hand in the evolutions induced by human activities.

Natural processes are disposal system evolutions which are of natural origin. These comprise normal as well as disturbed evolutions in the disposal system; they include hypothetical initiating events and occurrences which involve bypassing or damaging of barriers. Basis for these considerations is the status of the subsystem, the components and barriers, as well as of the disposal system at the beginning of the post-operational phase. Thus, for example, the state of the engineered barriers at the beginning of the post-operational phase represents the starting situation and description of conditions for the scenario development. This includes consideration of uncertainties in the design and construction of engineered barriers and in the same way consideration of human failings in the manufacture, installation, and quality assurance of technical components.

By **human activities** is meant all those activities which intentionally or inadvertently alter the effectiveness of the barriers of the disposal system. These on the one hand are activities which have an influence on the effectiveness of the barriers or the site situation as, for example, the building of a dam that brings about a change in the groundwater flow regime, and on the other hand such activities that bypass the barriers and constitute a short-circuit between the repository and the biosphere. Examples of such **direct intrusions** are bore hole drillings or mining activities.

Looking further at safety analyses only those human activities are studied which inadvertently affect the isolating property of the disposal system. These activities are such that knowledge about the existence and whereabouts of the repository is lost to the memory of the living, or the potential danger from the activities presumably cannot be known. For the intentional intrusion into the repository or an intentional risk-taking in regard to influencing the whole disposal system, the intruders themselves should accept responsibility. These scenarios are therefore not considered further in the safety analyses.

2.3 *Scenario classification*

For yet further treatment in safety analyses, scenarios can be classified as to their probability of occurrence:

The class of **likely scenarios** includes those processes and evolutions that are associated with a high likelihood of occurrence based on the characterisation of the site. They comprise the normal geological evolution of the site for the period of time during which a stable geological site situation can be assumed. Moreover, other influences to be expected within this timeframe are taken into account – for example, the evolution of the system of engineered barriers or individual components. This means that in order to judge safety in this timeframe, comprehensive knowledge of the site and its evolution, its barriers and their behaviour, and the underlying climatic evolutions over the course of time must be on hand. Furthermore, in order to carry out the safety analysis, the description of the system and its evolution must be given.

To the class of **less likely scenarios** belong those events and processes the occurrences of which are held to be less probable or for which hypotheses must be made. This class contains scenarios of natural processes that describe disturbed evolutions of the disposal system, the consequences of which remain limited and hence also deviate little from expected evolutions. The possibility of describing the system and its evolution is equally as good as in the class of likely scenarios. However, the uncertainties in the assumptions, data and models are definitely larger than in the class of likely scenarios. Scenarios based on human activities (with the exception of direct human intrusions) similarly are assigned to the class of less likely scenarios.

To the class of **unlikely scenarios** belong those for which the likelihood of occurrence is either very low or cannot be given. Within this class of natural process scenarios site developments can also be found which lead to a drastic impact upon the barrier system. Such scenarios lead to situations going beyond the expected evolution of the disposal system. The consequences can far exceed the expected development. The site selection must be such that those scenarios insofar as they are site-related can be categorised as sufficiently improbable. Thus, through site characterisation confidence in the site and its qualities (e.g. a sufficiently low likelihood of occurrence for such scenarios) must be given.

Examples for the unlikely scenarios are those for which no precaution against damage can be pursued (so-called disruptive events), including external events such as a meteor strike on the repository.

Unintentional human intrusion into a repository (e.g. by exploratory drillings, driving a mining level) results in a short circuit between the repository and the biosphere because the functionality of the barriers is nullified due to total or partial disturbance of the barrier system. The consequences resulting from these scenarios may be different from those described earlier. They may lead e.g. to exposures to personnel due to the actions of unintentional intrusion. Long-term effects on the population according to such scenarios are likewise not to be excluded. The fundamental scientific basis is lacking for any prediction of human evolution, the way of human life, and human behaviour over the time-spans under consideration. Hence, in long-term safety analysis, selected stylised scenarios for direct human intrusion are regarded and the isolating quality of the disposal system is demonstrated.

Thus for the safety analysis the scenarios are classified in the following way:

The scenarios in the family of natural processes and human activities (except for direct intentional intrusion into the repository) are divided among the following classes according to likelihood of occurrence:

- Scenarios which are certain or highly likely
  → **likely scenarios**

- Scenarios whose likelihood of occurrence is regarded as low
  → **less likely scenarios**

Scenarios involving human activities which result in unintentional bypass to the system of barriers require special treatments.

- Scenarios which describe unintended intrusion upon a repository resulting from human activities
  → **unintentional human intrusion into a repository**

For scenarios, which need not be considered, decisive reasons for this have to be stated e.g. very low likelihood of occurrence.

3.   Scenario Development

The scenario development represents an identification and selection of relevant alternative developments of the disposal system for further treatment in safety analyses. The scenario development thus requires adequate knowledge of the disposal system which makes possible a description and characterisation of the entire system, its behaviour and evolution up to now and also in the future. Basis for this work is a comprehensive identification of the relevant site- and system specific factors influencing the system (features, events and processes, FEPs). The understanding of the system, for example of the geological and geotechnical situation, must be such that a prediction of the potential evolution of the system can be given with reasonable certainty. For this purpose exploration of the site and accompanying laboratory and in-situ studies are carried out. Appreciable attention in the investigations of the site is given to the interpretation of the history of the geological evolution of the site itself. This should provide a basis for predictions within a timeframe which is relatively short in terms of the geologically interpretable history of site-evolution. Further observations of nature e.g. natural analogues are essential to understand the system and its evolution.

Based on this, the following steps are distinguished for the scenario development:

Firstly, relevant factors essential to characterising the behaviour of the system under consideration (mostly: "FEPs") are gathered together. For this reason, generic data bases (e.g. the NEA databank) as well as site-specific information can be reverted to. The process of selecting phenomena regarded to be relevant for the analysis is partly based on subjective decisions. This holds as well when the decision process is stringently formalised or even automated because in such cases the (possibly subjective) decision is made by the definition of the selection criterion. Were the selection of e.g. the probabilities of occurrence of the phenomena drawn upon, then the question by which procedure this likelihood of occurrence was determined is brought up.

Secondly, the phenomena are then combined to potential evolutions (scenarios). There exist several possible methodologies for combining the phenomena (FEPS) to scenarios whereby none is distinguished through having advantages in comparison with the others. The development of scenarios depends on the purpose of the analysis to be carried out. So, for example, processes that describe natural site evolutions can be especially important for the site selection, while processes pertaining to the disposal system can be drawn upon for the safety analysis.

Finally, the hypothetical processes (scenarios) are grouped and differentiated with respect to further procedures regarding their place in an analysis and to the purpose of the analysis itself. The remarks concerning the subjectivity of such a decision-making process are valid here as well.

The process of scenario development must be transparent, i.e. it must be reproducibly documented for the licensing procedure. Hence, the individual steps must be well founded and the decision made by the experts tracebly presented.

4. Radiological Protection Objectives for the Post-operational Phase

The fundamental radiological safety objectives of the permanent disposal of radioactive wastes is to protect man and his environment from the ionising radiation. Following the ICRP philosophy and the developments of the ICRP Task Group on "Radiation Protection Recommendations as applied to the Disposal of Long-lived Solid Radioactive Waste" under the chair of A. Sugier the state of the development in Germany is as follows. The protection of future generations is attained via measures to isolate the radioactive wastes within deep geological formations and does not depend on active measures in the future. The basic precept is that the same protective goals should apply to future generations as to man living today.

In this context the individual dose applies essentially as the protective aim of long-term safety. For the post-operational phase it can be expected that the potential radiological contamination of the biosphere caused by a disposal is relatively constant over the time-span of interest and lasting longer than the lifetime of the people living then. From there an averaged individual lifetime dose can be used as evaluation standard for potential future radiation burdens. With this, it is to be considered that the annual individual dose determined for the far future may not be taken as a predicted dose burden. Moreover, long-term safety analyses are bound with the uncertainties resulting on the one hand from the description of the disposal system, and on the other hand from the long time-frames to consider. Hence, particularly with the increasing problem-time, the individual doses determined must be viewed as indicators of disposal safety.

For the above mentioned scenarios, except direct human intrusion, adequate protection of humans and the environment is attained through the process of "constraint optimisation" in connection with a dose constraint of 0.3 mSv/a. The process of optimisation means that all meaningful measures are laid hold of for the reduction of the individual dose estimated for the future during an iterative procedure for site selection, planning, development of the construction and operation of the repository. With increasing problem-time, however, but also with decreasing likelihood of the scenarios under consideration the dose-constraint is to be interpreted as a reference value.

The process of optimisation is fulfilled when the repository is completed with state-of-the-art science and technology, technical and managerial principles are realised, the 0.3 mSv/a constraint is adhered and actions on meaningful measures against inadvertent human intrusion are taken. This does not mean that if exceedence of the dose constraint is calculated in the consequence analysis, particularly in the far future of the disposal, the license must be denied. The evaluation of such a case should taken into account the prognostic nature of analysis, the design basis of the disposal, the conservativeness of the analysis, findings from observations of nature as well as the interpretation of the individual dose as a reference value.

Consequence analysis of unintentional human intrusion scenarios requires stylised assumptions. The process of optimising the multibarrier system cannot be applied, since by definition the system of barriers is no longer functional. The consequence of these scenarios can lead to direct exposure of humans on the one hand or to long-term burdens to men on the other. Thus, in siting and designing the disposal system greatest attention must be placed on preventing these scenarios. Unintentional human intrusions into a repository in the post-operational phase should not have deterministic radiation effects. Hence, to be considered in the evaluation is the level of the possible radiation exposure, the number of persons affected, the physical dimensions of a possible contamination, the possibility of limiting the consequences, and the countermeasures.

5. Outlook

The scenario development described above gives the current status of discussion in the professional circles in Germany. Further discussions in-depth are foreseen.

SCENARIO DEVELOPMENT AND ANALYSIS FOR A REPOSITORY IN SALT FOR HIGHLY RADIOACTIVE WASTE

Proposal for a screening process

Siegfried Keller

Federal Institute for Geosciences and Natural Resources, Germany

Abstract

Within the scope of a safety assessment of a site for a repository in a salt dome, a total of 32 scenarios containing 61 FEPs (features, events, and processes) have been analyzed. A possible method for sceening is presented. Three categories for evaluating the potential hazards were chosen to classify (1) the hazards resulting from the FEP, (2) the temporary aspects, and (3) the hierarchy of the barriers modified by the events and processes.

A fourth category takes the relevance of the FEP for this site into consideration. Additionally, all four categories are subdivided into evaluation classes.

A point system is used to evaluate the FEP in terms of the system of categories. This point system is subdivided into evaluating groups. High scores for an FEP means a high hazard potential.

Twelve of the FEPs in the geotechnical scenarios, 1 FEP in the climate scenarios, and 2 in the geological scenarios have the highest scores. The scenarios include processes and events that

- make water available for gas production leading to an increase in pressure,

- produce gas by microbial activity,

- lead to the development of migration paths and the resulting possibility of radionuclide transport,

- cause the surface of the salt dome to rise, and

- occur at the margins of continental ice.

The other FEPs have low scores, which means a low hazard potential. The FEPs with the highest scores should be included in a safety analysis. The processes with high scores are potential hazards for the near-field of the repository, but not for the biosphere, because no uninterrupted transport route from the repository to the biosphere is observed. These potential hazards exist for only a few thousand years after the repository has been closed if the mine shaft to the repository remains sealed during this period of time.

1. Introduction

Geological and geotechnical studies have to be carried out to determine the suitability of a salt dome for a permanent repository for radioactive waste. Within the scope of these studies, a scenario analysis has to be made of the long-term safety of a potential repository. The work can be conducted in two stages:

In the first phase, scenarios are being developed on the basis of possible geological, extraterrestrial, hydrogeological, and climatic processes and events or such resulting from the deposition of radioactive waste in the repository. The plans for the repository should also be taken into consideration, for example:

- All kinds of radioactive wastes are to be emplaced in the repository.

- The repository is to consist of two levels, one for exploration and one for the wastes.

- The wastes are to be emplaced in chambers and boreholes.

In the second phase, the following aspects will be taken into consideration in the scenario analysis:

- the geological situation determined during the site investigation,

- the final repository concept, based on the geological results, and

- the kind of wastes that will actually be emplaced in the repository.

These two stages are necessary because all of the information from the last three points may to be expected to be available only after the exploration phase.

2. The Scenario Development

2.1 Constraints on the choice of scenarios

The development of scenarios was limited to geological and geotechnical features events, processes (FEP). Of the multitude of possible FEP, there are some that lead to a special list of scenarios for a site when the plans for exploration drifts, borehole depths, types of wastes, etc. are taken into consideration. The scenario development, therefore, is based on the following assumptions and constraints:

- A new repository mine will be constructed, and no previous mining has been conducted in the salt dome.

- An upper level of drifts will be driven for exploration and a second one below that for emplacement of wastes.

- The radioactive wastes will be emplaced in the Main Salt of the salt dome at a depth of more than 850 m.

- The wastes will be emplaced in chambers and boreholes.

- Weakly, moderately, and highly radioactive, heat-producing wastes will be emplaced.

- Human activities were not taken into consideration in the scenarios.

- Processes in the biosphere will not be taken into consideration.

- Only FEP during the post-operations phase will be considered.

2.2 Features, events and processes (FEP)

Exogene and endogene geological events and processes will affect the present, initial features: the natural, geological barriers (the salt dome, the cap rock, the cover rock) and the artificial barriers (the waste containers, etc.). The site investigation work, the construction of the repository, and the emplacement of highly radioactive, heat-producing wastes also initiate processes that affect the host rock. Under certain conditions, numerous chemical reactions can occur that facilitate or hinder (chemical barriers) the migration of radionuclides. The interaction of these events and processes causes changes in the multi-barrier system (geological, engineered, and chemical barriers).

A scenario consists of the resulting changes over a period of time.

Taking into consideration the constraints mentioned in the preceding section, the "International List of Events and Processes" (IFEP, FEP database, version 1.0) prepared by the international Nuclear Energy Agency (NEA) was used to select scenarios relevant to the possible site. A total of 32 scenarios with 61 FEP have been identified so far (Table 1).

A numbering system is used for the FEP indicating time and spatial aspects and a classification of the scenarios. The abbreviations are given in Appendix 1. For example: A process with the number prefix NA_T_A is one that occurs in the near-field (NA_), belongs to the geotechnical scenarios (_T_), and occurs in the time period A (_A), i.e., at the beginning of the post-operations phase (see also Section 3.1.2).

2.3 Scenario groups

The scenarios and the FEP on which they are based can grouped in different ways. The classification is subjective and reflects the viewpoint being emphasized. Within the scope of this study, with its emphasis on geology, the following system has been used:

- geotechnical scenarios (T);
  15 scenarios with 29 FEP.
- hydrogeological scenarios (H);
  5 scenarios with 5 FEP.
- climatic scenarios (C);
  4 scenarios with 18 FEP.
- geological scenarios (G);
  7 scenarios with 8 FEP.
- extraterrestrial scenarios (EX);
  1 scenario with 1 FEP.

Since only one of the possible extraterrestrial scenarios (meteorite impact) is relevant in the long term, it has been grouped together with the geological scenarios.

3. Scenario Analysis

The objective of scenario analysis is to determine one or more key scenarios that contain the most important FEP that have the most probable hazard potential and are significant for a long-term geological prognosis and an assessment of the long-term safety of the repository. **Scenario analysis is understood as the selection of the scenarios (on the basis of the IFEP list of the NEA and the site specific constraints) and the evaluation of the scenarios with respect to the long-term safety of the repository.**

The methods used for our scenario analysis discussed below were chosen on the basis of the above-mentioned conditions and constraints related to geology and geotechnics. An evaluation of other events and processes related to future human activities would require a modified procedure.

3.1 *Methods*

Three categories were selected for the evaluation of the FEP for a qualitative classification of the hazards represented by the FEP for a permanent repository for radioactive wastes, for the biosphere, as well as time aspects of the FEP and the hierarchy of the barriers modified by the events and processes. A fourth category takes the relevance of the FEP to the specific site. All four categories are subdivided into subcategories (Figures. 2a & 2b). The categories and subcategories are described in the following sections. The evaluation of the FEP leads to an evaluation of the scenario classes and the individual scenarios. The evaluation yields a reduced set of FEP relevant to the long-term geological safety of the repository. These FEP will be the subject of an analysis of the consequences to be taken that will be carried out within the scope of a safety analysis.

A point system is used for assigning an FEP to the categories. A high point count indicates a high hazard potential (Table 1). A low point count indicates a low hazard potential. The total point count for an FEP is obtained by adding the points from categories 1-3 and multiplying by the points from category 4. Since indirectly categories 1-3 indicate the occurrence of damage and category 4 indicates the probability that an event or process will occur, the points are also indirectly a measure of the risk associated with that event or process.

The FEP are grouped in classes on the basis of their total points. The class limits were arbitrarily chosen: < 20, 21–35, 36–50, > 51. The highest total point count for an FEP was 54 (FEP: MAW-NA_T_A 1). The highest possible point count is 84. If an FEP has more than half of this point count, it is considered significant for the long-term safety of the repository and should be taken into consideration in an analysis of the consequences within the scope of the safety analysis. In this discussion, however, point counts of more than 36 will be included in order to take into consideration the two classes with the highest point counts.

The use of the point count method makes it possible to follow the screening process throughout the scenario development and analysis, providing greater transparency and building confidence in the results. The method also makes it possible to discuss the results in detail with other experts in order to reach consensus between institutions interested in performance assessment for a radioactive waste repository.

3.1.1   Description and basis of category 1

Category 1 has the three subcategories "transport path", "transport medium", and "transport mechanism", assigned small letters "a" to "c". The last-named subcategory is further subdivided: "favors migration" and "retards migration" (Figure 1a).

Subcategory "a" includes events and processes that lead to the development of transport paths in the salt rock or in the cover and country rock. The development of transport paths in the sense of a loss of integrity of the barriers is viewed as damage.

Subcategory "b" includes events and processes in which media (i.e., water and gases) for the transport of radionuclides are involved, for example, chemical reactions that produce or consume such transport media. This group of subcategories is not subdivided further because it is considered that the presence of water or gases in the near-field represents a hazard potential that speaks against the safe development of the repository.

Subcategory "c" includes events and processes in which the transport mechanisms are involved. This group of subcategories is subdivided into (c_1) mechanisms that favor the migration of radionuclides (e.g. convergence and diffusion) and (c_2) those that retard spreading (e.g. sorption and precipitation).

Category 1 is based on the significance of the three subcategories for the migration of radionuclides from the repository into the biosphere. Without the simultaneous presence of paths, media, and mechanisms for transport, migration would not be possible. The transport paths are of particular significance: If a path from the repository to the biosphere is not present, radionuclides cannot migrate to the biosphere even if transport media and mechanisms are available. This may be illustrated with a hypothetical example: If it is assumed that the engineered barriers have been carefully planned and constructed, then groundwater cannot penetrate to the wastes. If brine reaches the area between the bulkhead seals and the waste containers, releasing radionuclides, a transport mechanism in the form of convergence and transport media in the form of water and gases would be available, but a transport path exists only between the brine reservoir and the repository, not as far as the biosphere. The safety of the repository is not in danger, because none of the brine reservoirs observed in the central part of the salt dome have a connection with the permeable layers outside of the salt dome. The radionuclides would be spread only in the near-field of the repository; their concentrations would depend on their solubility in the brine and the physical and chemical situation.

Owing to the considerable significance of transport paths for the long-term safety of a permanent repository for radioactive wastes, all events and processes that facilitate the development of transport paths in combination with transport media and mechanisms receive the highest point count. The evaluation scheme for category 1 is shown in Figure 1a.

3.1.2   Description and basis of category 2

Category 2 is divided into six subcategories "A" to "F" according to the time of their occurrence of the events and processes and the extent to which they affect the barriers:

Subcategory A is given the highest point count, since the complete inventory of radionuclides is present in the period immediately after closure of the repository. The number of points is decreased stepwise from subcategories A to F (Figure 1a). If an event or process can occur during several of the time periods, it is assigned to the earliest one.

Subcategory A includes events and processes that are relevant immediately after the repository is closed, for example, mobilization of brine inclusions in the salt by the heat produced by the wastes, radiolysis of the rock salt, and convergence. Depending on the extent that they act on one or more of the barriers, they can cause a loss of integrity of those barriers.

Subcategory B includes the events and processes that can occur before the maximum temperature produced by the waste is reached within the repository. These are mainly chemical processes, heat production, and convergence and belong to the geotechnical scenarios. The first model calculations indicate the maximum temperature will be reached within the first 150 years. The strain field created in the salt rock by the increase in temperature can lead to further events and processes. The time at which the maximum temperature is reached is taken as the boundary to the next subcategory.

Subcategory C includes the events and processes that occur in the time between the reaching of the maximum temperature and the time the natural temperature field is established again. The model calculations show that this will occur after about 10 000 years. This time period includes events and processes that only slowly impair the stability of the barriers, leading to failure of the seals of shafts, boreholes, drifts or waste containers fail or to changes in the hydrogeological conditions.

For the time after about 10 000 years, a renewed ice age similar to the Weichsel glacial stage is predicted. The mean annual temperature will decrease, leading to permafrost conditions. Owing to the large influence of permafrost on groundwater flow rates and directions, this period of extremely different climate from that of today is taken into consideration in subcategory D.

Subcategory E covers the period of continental glaciation, which can change the morphology of the area and increase the hydraulic potential, further changing the hydrogeology. This time period is estimated to occur from about 60 000 to 100 000 years from now. This class includes events and processes associated with a maximum glaciation.

Subcategory F includes events and processes that occur over geologically long periods of time, more than 100 000 years, and can cause changes in the geological barriers. Subrosion is an example of such a process: With the average subrosion rate of 0.01-0.05 mm/year estimated for salt domes in NW Germany, the thickness of the salt barrier would be reduced by only 10-50 m in a million years. Thus, subcategory F is given the lowest point count, because after 100 000 years most short-lived radionuclides have already decayed and the remaining radionuclide abundance would be similar that of a rich, natural, uranium ore deposit.

3.1.3   Description and basis of category 3

Category 3 classifies the individual barriers in terms of the significance of a loss of integrity or retention capability. In order to be able to take the simultaneous or successive loss of integrity of several barriers into consideration, the individual subcategories of this category can be combined, resulting in a higher point count. Higher point counts indicate a higher probability of the migration of radionuclides (Figure 1b).

Since the repository is in salt rock, the salt dome is given the highest significance (subcategory I). The repository may be considered essentially safe if the integrity of this barrier is not impaired. Subcategories I is divided into subcategories I_1 to I_3 depending on whether complete or limited loss of integrity occurs and whether the emplacement areas are affected.

Subcategory II includes events and processes that affect the cover rock. The cover rock consists mainly of permeable, unconsolidated rock. Hence it is given a few points than for the salt dome. Although in the long-term, the cover rock cannot hinder radionuclide transport, its function as a barrier receives greater weight than that of the engineered barriers. This is due to the long transport times in the groundwater in the deep aquifer (low flow rate) and the possibility of sorption of the radionuclides, precipitation at a redox front, or dilution.

Subcategory III includes events and processes that affect the ability of the engineered barriers to retain radionuclides. Subcategory III is divided into subclasses III_1 (containers) and III_2 (backfill and bulkhead seals) because the various events and processes can affect the integrity of one of the two types of barriers or both. The containers are the more important of the two, because failure of a container before consolidation of the backfill would lead to immediate spreading of radionuclides within the repository. The failure of both types of engineered barriers at an early stage is possible in several scenarios and therefore the significance of these barriers is considered to be low.

The significance of subcategory IV (chemical composition of the near-field) is considered to be low for a repository in salt rock. Besides optimum backfilling with crushed salt, the isolation of the waste is guaranteed by the properties of rock salt (e.g. low permeability and self-annealing by convergence). The chemical composition of the salt in the near-field of the repository can favor or retard the migration of radionuclides. Since suitable substances that can retard migration (e.g. by sorption or precipitation) can be added to the backfill, such measures are that add to the safety of the repository are taken into consideration in subcategory IV.

3.1.4   *Description and basis of category 4*

Category 4 takes the relevance of an FEP to the repository site into consideration. This category indirectly indicates the probability of the occurrence of events and processes. Hence, the highest point count is assigned to FEP that have been demonstrated to be present at the site (subcategory i). It is assumed that such events and processes will occur again, favoring or retarding migration of radionuclides (Figure 1b).

The next highest point count is assigned FEP in subcategory ii. Such FEP are assumed to be possible at this site in analogy to comparable sites in salt rock or on the basis of theoretical considerations derived from data obtained at the site. A good example is the simulation of experiments conducted in the Asse mine to simulate heat production by highly radioactive waste. The results of these experiments indicate the possibility of brine migration to the wastes and radiolysis of the water.

Subcategory iii includes FEP that are plausible for the site on the basis of theoretical considerations. For example, if brine fills part of the repository mine, convergence can press the brine out again. The process is theoretically plausible, but cannot be demonstrated or assumed on the basis of observations at this site or comparable sites. The brine would not necessarily be pressed out because there are processes that could quickly close migration paths. This is supported by the observation of old brine enclosures at the site. If migration paths were available for these brines, convergence would have closed the cavities and large volumes of brine would not be observed.

3.2   **Results of scenario evaluation**

Classification of FEP with respect to their possible hazard potential for the biosphere was facilitated by listing them in a table (Table 1). Of the 61 FEP that have been determined so far, the largest group (29) belong to the geotechnical scenarios. Of these, twelve belong to the two classes of FEP with the highest point counts (36 – 50 and > 51). Of the FEP in the other types of scenarios, only three have point counts in the two highest point count classes (one FEP in the climatic scenarios [C] and two in the geological/extraterrestrial scenarios [G & Ex]). If half of the possible point count (i.e. 42) is considered as the boundary between significant and less important FEP, then the number of FEP in the two highest point count classes is reduced to 8, of which one belongs to the climatic scenarios and seven belong to the geotechnical scenarios (light brown and light yellow lines in Table 1).

FEP with point counts less than 36 will not be included in the scenario analysis in the next section.

With the evaluation scheme presented here, it is possible to reduce the number of FEP for the selection of scenarios to be given priority in the safety analysis.

3.3   *Analysis of the scenario evaluation*

The FEP of the two point count classes 36 – 50 and >51 are considered significant, since it is assume that they represent the highest hazard potential for the biosphere. These FEP are listed in Table 2. They have in common that they are associated with the conditions resulting from the emplacement of radioactive, heat-producing wastes together with irradiated organic material). These FEP involve the availability of water from different sources and gas production by radiolysis, microbial decomposition, and corrosion, with an increase in pressure and the formation of migration paths from a previously stable, sealed repository.

The water can come from sources in the near-field, e.g. the moist crushed salt used as backfill, migration of brine in the temperature gradient towards heat-producing waste, or from brine enclosures migrating through fractures resulting from convergence of the repository cavities (FE_T_A1). Besides being a source of gases produced by radiolysis or possibly corrosion, the water causes rapid compaction of the backfill (i.e., rapid decrease in permeability), which must occur for gas production to lead to an increase in pressure. Heat production can lead to addition migration paths by changing the strain conditions in the host rock.

Only a combination of FEP lead to migration paths and a hazard potential for the biosphere.

The possibility of microbial decomposition of low- to intermediate-level radioactive waste receives a particularly high point count. This is because this process occurs early and because the containers may possibly be destroyed. The water for this process is provided by the waste and containers themselves. The amount of decomposable material can be quite large. If the amount of gas produced is sufficiently large, the scenario indicates that the gas pressure can increase to the point that the salt rock is fractured, forming migration paths. A safety analysis, therefore, requires an estimate of the amount of water that will actually be available, the amount and kinds of gas that would be produced, and the extent to which migration paths would be opened in the host rock.

The processes "epirogenetic uplift" and "ascent of the diapir" receive high point counts (40). This is because, on the one hand, these processes fracture the cover rock (forming migration paths) and increase subrosion of the surface of the salt dome and, on the other hand, these processes have high probability of occurrence (based on results of the site investigation). This is also the case for the process formation of ice marginal valleys (FE_C_E 2.2) by meltwater under high hydrostatic pressure.

This process would also provide a transport mechanism for contaminants and, hence, receives a high point count of 48.

The events and processes (12 with point counts > 36) in the geotechnical scenarios represent potential hazards that would lead to the release and transport of radionuclides in the immediate area of the repository. They would be significant only within the first thousand years after the closing of the repository, because the short-lived radionuclides responsible for the radiolysis of water will have decayed by this time, the materials that can corrode or decompose will have been used up, and heat production and its effects will be declining. The radionuclides in the immediate repository would, therefore, be distributed (and "diluted") in the near-field of the repository. These processes do not necessarily lead to transport into the biosphere. For this, continuous, stable migration pathways are necessary, and these are not possible with a carefully planned repository concept (repository location, backfill, amounts and types of waste). To avoid processes that could possibly lead to continuous migration pathways, measures should be taken that would maintain dry conditions in the immediate neighborhood of the wastes for the first thousand years.

The scenarios discussed here are generally valid for the repository concepts discussed up to now (one or two levels, emplacement in drifts or boreholes). They are valid not only for the different parts of the repository, but also for the repository as a whole. Further, more detailed scenarios should be discussed when the results of the geological investigations are available and the compositions of the wastes that will be emplaced in the different parts of a repository are known.

In summary, a model is proposed with the following steps for a safety analysis:

- quantification of the available water,

- quantification of the possible amounts of gas,

- estimation of the possible increase in pressure resulting from gas formation and the possible migration paths formed if the frac pressure is exceeded,

- determination of a continuous migration path from the repository to the surface of the salt dome, and

- quantification of radionuclide transport from the repository to the biosphere in the case of the formation of an ice marginal valley.

This model assumes the seal of both shafts will be remain intact for the first thousand years.

Enclosure 1.   List of abbreviations

BGR	Federal Institute for Geosciences and Natural Resources, Hannover, Germany
DE	Cover rock
E	Event
EB	Emplacement area
EX	Extraterrestrical Scenario
FE	Far-field
G	Geological Scenario
HAW	Highly radioactive, heat-producing wastel
HAWC	Vitrified, higly radioactive waste, Type COGEMA
H	Hydrogeological Scenario
IFEP	International list of "features", "events" and "processes" of Nuclear Energy Agency (NEA)
C	Climatic Scenario
LAW	Weakly radioactive wastel
MAW	Moderately radioactive wastel
NA	Near-field
NEA	Nuclear Energy Agency (Paris, France)
P	Process
SA	Salt dome
T	Geotechnical Scenario
E	Event
FEP	Feature, Event, Process

Table 1. Evaluation of FEPs for scenario analysis

Scenario	Number	FEP	Category (explanations in text and figs. 1a,b)				Total (1+2+3) x 4
			1	2	3	4	
Heat production by radioactive waste	NA_T_A 1.1	**Migration of brine in temperature gradient:** Corrosion, radiolysis of water	$c_1+b=3$	A=6	$I_2=3$ $III_1=1$	ii=3	39
	NA_T_A 1.2	**Thermally induced release of gases from pores and fluid inclusions:** Production of CO_2, HCl, decrease in pH of the brines and pitting of waste containers	b=2	A=6	$III_1=1$ $IV=1$	ii=3	30
	NA_T_B 1	**Maximum temperature and compression in repository area:** Change in properties of bulkhead seals and host rock	a=3	B=5	$I_1=2$ $III_2=1$	iv=1	11
	FE_T_B 2	**Change in temperature field at top of salt dome:** Tension and fracture formation, entry of groundwater	a+b=5	B=5	$I_1=2$	ii=3	36
Corrosion	NA_T_A 2	**Corrosion of steel containers and mining equipment:** Generation of gas under anaerobic conditions, reducing environment, redox front	$a+b+c_2=4$	A=6	$I_1=4$ $III_1=1$ $IV=1$	ii=3	48
Radiation	NA_T_A 3.1	**Radiolysis of water:** Gas production	a+b=5	A=6	$I_3=4$ $III_1=1$ $IV=1$	ii=3	51
	NA_T_A 3.2	**Radiolysis NaCl:** Fluid-assisted recrystallization, possible gas production	0	A=6	$IV=1$	ii=3	21
Ignition of gases	NA_T_A 4	**Ignition of gases with rapid release of energy:** Assumes presence of oxygen and sufficiently high temperatures, limited fracturing of the salt rock	a=3	A=6	$I_2=3$	iii=2	24
Formation of fissures	NA_T_B 2	**Fracturing due to elevated temperature and gas pressure:** Formation of migration paths in the salt rock, mobilisation of brine, entry of groundwater	a+b=5	B=5	$I_2=3$ $III_2=1$	iii=2	28
Convergence	NA_T_A 5.1	**Cavities and repository drifts converge:** Connections between cavities closed, reduced permeability	a=3	A=6	$III_2=1$	i=4	40
	NA_T_A 5.2	**Partial closure of fractures in excavation damage zones:** Reduced permeability	a=3	A=6	$I_1=2$	i=4	44
	NA_T_A 5.3.1	**Rapid reduction of backfill porosity because backfill additives and/or moisture are present:** Facilitates increase in gas pressure	0	A=6	0	ii=3	18

Table 1 (cont'd). **Evaluation of FEPs for scenario analysis**

Convergence	NA_T_A	5.3.2	**Slow reduction of backfill porosity because the backfill is dry:** Permeability and storage volume for gases is thus present.	$a=3$	$A=6$	$III_2=1$	ii=3	**30**
	FE_T_A	1	**Stress in adjoining Main Anhydrite:** Development of fractures, mobilisation of brines	$a+b=5$	$A=6$	$I_1=2$	ii=3	**39**
	NA_T_A	5.5	**Deformation of pillars and bulkhead seals:** Migration paths between emplacement areas	$a=3$	$A=6$	$I_2=3$	ii=3	**36**
	NA_T_A	5.6	**Contaminated brines pressed out of repository area:** Migration of contaminants into far-field	$a+b+c_i=6$	$A=6$	$I_2=3$	iii=2	**30**
	NA_T_B	3.1	**Closure of remaining cavities:** No storage volume for gases, increasing gas pressure	0	$B=5$	0	ii=3	**15**
	NA_T_B	3.2	**Closing of fractures in excavation damage zones:** No storage volume for gases, increasing gas pressure	0	$B=5$	0	ii=3	**15**
	NA_T_B	3.3	**Backfill totally compacted:** No storage volume for gases, increasing gas pressure	0	$B=5$	0	ii=3	**15**
Radioactive gases	NA_T_B	4	**Generation of radioactive gases:** Existing permeability allows contamination of emplacement area and migration of radioactive gases into far-field	$a+b=5$	$A=6$	$I_1=2$	iii=2	**26**
Movement of containers	NA_T_A	6	**Reduced distance between containers:** Elevated concentration of fissionable material	0	$A=6$	$III_1=1$	iv=1	**7**
Moisture in backfill	NA_T_A	8.1	**Backfill becomes moist during temporary storage at surface:** Corrosion, radiolysis of water, increasing gas pressure	$a+b=5$	$A=6$	$I_3=4$ $III_1=1$ $IV=1$	ii=3	**51**
	NA_T_A	8.2	**Moisture derived from water of crystallization:** Corrosion, radiolysis of water, increasing pressure	$a+b=5$	$A=6$	$I_3=4$ $III_1=1$ $IV=1$	ii=3	**51**
Microbial degradation	MAW_NA_T_A	1	**Microbial degradation of organic materials:** Gas production, corrosion of containers and decomposition of waste	$a+b+c_i=6$	$A=6$	$I_3=4$ $III_1=1$ $IV=1$	ii=3	**54**
Exploration boreholes poorly sealed	FE_T_B	1	**Poorly sealed exploration boreholes in vicinity of emplacement areas:** Migration paths	$a=3$	$B=5$	$III_2=1$	ii=3	**27**

Table 1 (cont'd). **Evaluation of FEPs for scenario analysis**

Safety margin to Main Anhydrite	FE_T_B	3	**Incorrect interpretation of exploration results:** Safe distance of emplacement areas to brine pockets larger than assumed, mobilisation of brines	a+b=5	B=5	$I_2=3$	iv=1	13
Fractures in the salt rock	FE_T_B	4	**Fractures generated by increasing gas pressure and/or heat production become connected with the natural fracture network:** Migration paths from repository to cover rock	$a+b+c_1=6$	B=5	$I_3=4$	ii=3	45
Loss of integrity of the bulkhead seals	FE_T_C	1	**Alteration of bulkhead seals:** Migration through bulkhead seals as a result of increased permeability	$a+b+c_2=4$	C=4	$III_2=1$	iii=2	18
Loss of integrity of the shaft seals	FE_T_C	2	**Alteration of shaft seals:** Migration of groundwater; crystallization of salt as a result of reactions between NaCl and $MgCl_2$-saturated brines blocking migration paths	$a+b+c_2=4$	C=4	$III_2=1$	iii=2	18
Periglacal effects	FE_C_D	1.1	**Permafrost in uppermost cover rocks:** Sealing of upper aquifers	0	D=3	II=2	ii=3	15
	FE_C_D	1.2	**Change in chemical content of the groundwater:** Increase in salinity of the groundwater	b=2	D=3	0	iii=2	10
	FE_C_D	1.3	**Change in morphology due to permafrost:** Modification of hydraulic conditions (e.g. aquifer permeability, discharge/recharge areas)	0	D=3	0	i=4	12
	FE_C_D	1.4	**Cryofracturing in top of salt dome:** Entry of groundwater into the salt rock, locally increased subrosion	a=3	D=3	$I_1=2$ $II=2$	iv=1	10
Permafrost above salt dome at margin of ice sheet	FE_C_E	1.1	**Ice movement modifies morphology:** Modification of hydraulic conditions	$c_1+b=3$	E=2	II=2	i=4	28
	FE_C_E	1.2	**Development of taliki:** Reduced permafrost thickness, groundwater flow paths and discharge areas modified	$c_1+b=3$	E=2	II=2	ii=3	21
	FE_C_E	1.3	**Meltwater on/in ice sheet modifies hydraulic gradients:** Increased groundwater flow rate, exchange of saline groundwater with fresh water	$c_1+b=3$	E=2	II=2	ii=3	21
	FE_C_E	1.4	**Groundwater recharge from meltwater:** Modification of area of recharge	b=2	E=2	II=2	iii=2	12

95

Table 1 (cont'd). **Evaluation of FEPs for scenario analysis**

Category	FE code	No.	Description					Product
Ice sheet above salt dome	FE_C_E	2.1	**Sediments disturbed by exaration:** Increase in hydraulic conductivity of cover rock	$a+c_i=4$	E=2	II=2	i=4	**32**
	FE_C_E	2.2	**Development of subice channels by meltwater under high pressure or by exaration down to the top of salt dome:** Deposition of unconsolidated sediments with high hydraulic conductivity	$a+b+c_i=6$	E=2	$I_1=2$ II=2	i=4	**48**
	FE_C_E	2.3	**Modification of morphology due to movement of ice sheet:** Deposition of moraines, discharge and recharge areas changed	$c_i=1$	E=2	II=2	i=4	**20**
	FE_C_E	2.4	**Reduction of permafrost thickness below thick ice sheet:** Change in hydraulic conductivity	$b=2$	E=2	II=2	ii=3	**18**
	FE_C_E	2.5	**Development of lakes behind ice dams:** Reduced permafrost thickness, groundwater recharge, increase in hydraulic potential	$c_i+b=3$	E=2	II=2	iii=2	**14**
	FE_C_E	2.6	**Fractures develop after retreat of ice sheet from above salt dome (fracturing perpendicular to a former compression direction due to expansion of salt rock on release of load, dependent on ice thickness):** Entry of groundwater into salt rocks	$a=3$	E=2	II=2	iii=2	**14**
	FE_C_E	2.7	**Falling sea-level:** Increasing down-cutting of rivers, migration paths become shorter owing to reduction of cover rock thickness	$a+b=5$	E=2	II=2	iv=1	**9**
Greenhouse effect	FE_C_A	1.1	**Development of a humid, warm climate:** Groundwater table rises	$b=2$	A=6	II=2	iv=1	**10**
	FE_C_A	1.2	**Development of a dry, warm climate:** Lowering of groundwater table, increasing groundwater salinity due to high evaporation	0	A=6	II=2	iv=1	**8**
	FE_C_A	1.3	**Melting of Arctic and Antarctic ice caps:** Sea level rises, flooding of area above repository	$b=2$	A=6	II=2	iv=1	**10**
Epeirogenesis	FE_G_F	1.1	**Uplift:** Erosion of cover rock, decrease in depth to top of salt dome, increasing subrosion, development of stress-release fractures	$a+b=5$	F=1	$I_1=2$ II=2	i=4	**40**
	FE_G_F	1.2	**Subsidence:** Cover rocks flooded by sea, new sediment deposited, depth to top of salt dome increases	$c_2+b=1$	F=1	0	i=4	**8**

Table 1 (cont'd). **Evaluation of FEPs for scenario analysis**

Earthquakes	FE_G_F	2	**Rapid release of stress in lithosphere:** Development of fractures in cover rock and country rock	$a=3$	$F=1$	$I_1=2$ $II=2$	$ii=3$	24
Tectonic deformation	FE_G_F	3	**Long-term movement of crustal units:** Development of faults in cover rock and country rock	$a=3$	$F=1$	$I_1=2$ $II=2$	$ii=3$	24
Igneous activity	FE_G_F	4	**Intrusion of basalt into salt rock:** Alteration of salt rock, development of migration paths	$a=3$	$F=1$	$I_3=4$ $II=2$	$ii=3$	30
Subrosion	FE_G_F	5	**Dissolution of salt rock by groundwater:** Subrosion of top of salt dome, mean rate ~0.01 mm/yr	$b=2$	$F=1$	$I_1=2$	$i=4$	20
Salt diapirism	FE_G_F	7	**Uplift of salt dome:** Development of faults and fractures in cover rock, increasing subrosion rate	$a+b=5$	$F=1$	$I_1=2$ $II=2$	$i=4$	40
Main Anhydrite	FE_G_F	6	**Change in local stress fields:** Fractures develop in brittle rocks (anhydrite), and brine in the Main Anhydrite is mobilized	$a+b=5$	$F=1$	$I_1=2$	$i=4$	32
Meteorite impact	FE_EX_F	1	**Meteorite impact:** No significant damage caused by small meteorites, complete destruction of repository by bolide impact	$a+b+c_i=6$	$F=1$	$I_3=4$ $II=2$	$iv=1$	13
Migration of radionuclides through fractures	FE_H_B	1	**Convergence, diffusion, hydraulic gradient:** Migration of radionuclides if transport paths are available	$a+b+c_i=6$	$B=5$	$I_1=3$	$iii=2$	28
Migration of radionuclides through shafts	FE_H_C	1	**Lost of integrity of shaft seal:** Migration of radionuclides through shaft into cover rock, migration paths from emplacement areas towards the shafts, physicochemical environment favors migration	$a+b+c_i=6$	$C=4$	$I_3=4$	$iv=1$	14
Migration of radionuclides through exploration boreholes	FE_H_C	2	**Lost of integrity of borehole seals:** Migration of radionuclides through exploration boreholes into salt rock containing a natural fracture system, limited spreading of radionuclides in surrounding salt rock	$a+b+c_i=6$	$C=4$	$I_2=3$	$iv=1$	13
Groundwater velocity	FE_H_C	3	**Increase/decrease of groundwater velocity:** Faster/slower transport of radionuclides, migration times of radionuclides towards biosphere decreases/increases	$c_i+b=3$	$C=4$	$II=2$	$iv=1$	9
Groundwater flow direction	FE_H_C	4	**Shortening/lengthening of migration paths:** Reduction/extension of radionuclide migration time	$a+b=5$	$C=4$	$II=2$	$iv=1$	11

Table 2. **List of FEPs with high point counts > 36**

Scenario Groups	FEP-No.	*FEP*	point counts
Geotechnical Scenarios (T) (• 12 FEPs)	*MAW_NA_T_A 1	Microbial degradation of organic materials: Gas production, corrosion of containers and decomposition of waste.	54
	NA_T_A 3.1	Radiolysis of water: Gas production.	51
	NA_T_A 8.1	Backfill becomes moist during temporary storage at surface: Corrosion, radiolysis of water, increasing gas pressure.	51
	NA_T_A 8.2	Moisture derived from water of crystallization: Corrosion, radiolysis of water, increasing pressure.	51
	NA_T_A 2	Corrosion of steel containers and mining equipment: Generation of gas under anaerobic conditions, reducing environment, redox front.	48
	FE_T_B 4	Fractures generated by increasing gas pressure and/or heat production become connected with the natural fracture network: Migration paths from repository to cover rock.	45
	NA_T_A 5.2	Partial closure of fractures in excavation damage zones: Reduced permeability.	44
	NA_T_A 5.1	Cavities and repository drifts converge: Connections between cavities closed, reduced permeability.	40
	Na_T_A 1.1	Migration of brine in temperature gradient: Corrosion, radiolysis of water.	39
	FE_T_A 1	Stress in adjoining Main Anhydrite: Development of fractures, mobilisation of brines.	39
	FE_T_B 2	Change in temperature field at top of salt dome: Tension and fracture formation, entry of groundwater.	36
	NA_T_A 5.5	Deformation of pillars and bulkhead seals: Migration paths between emplacement areas.	36
Climatic Scenario (C) (• 1 FEP)	FE_C_E 2.2	Development of subice channels by meltwater under high pressure or by exaration down to the top of salt dome: Deposition of unconsolidated sediments with high hydraulic conductivity.	48
Geological Scenarios (G+EX) (• 2 FEPs)	FE_G_F 1.1	Uplift: Erosion of cover rock, decrease in depth to top of salt dome, increasing subrosion, development of stress-release fractures.	40
	FE_G_F 7	UPLIFT OF SALT DOME: DEVELOPMENT OF FAULTS AND FRACTURES IN COVER ROCK, INCREASING SUBROSION RATE.	40

* Abbreviations see **enclosure 1**

Figure 1a. **The subcategories of categories 1 & 2 and the evaluation points (x) for the scenario analysis**

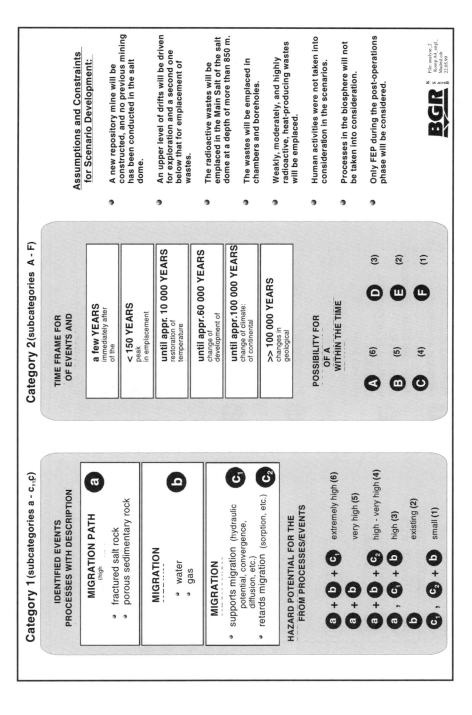

Figure 1b. The subcategories of categories 3 & 4 and evaluation points (x) for the scenario analysis

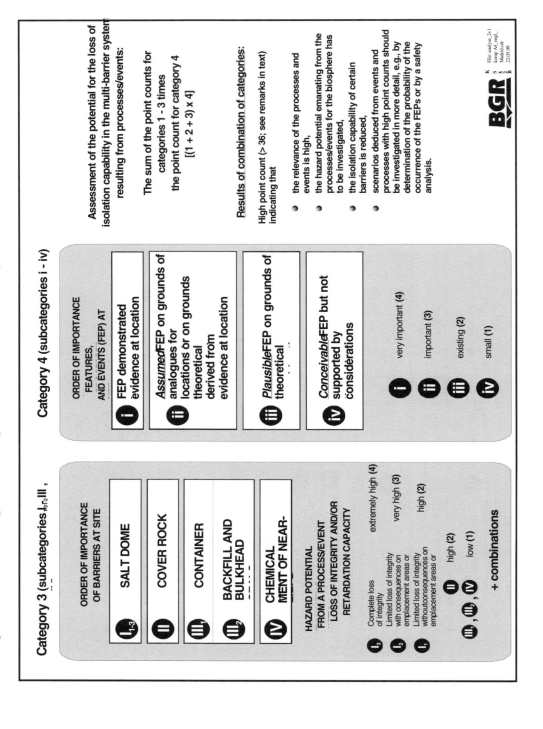

Paper 3

THE PROSA METHODOLOGY FOR SCENARIO DEVELOPMENT

J.B. Grupa
NRG – The Netherlands

Abstract

In this paper a methodology for scenario development is proposed. The method is developed in an effort to convince ourselves (and others) that all conceivable future developments of a waste repository have been covered. To be able to assess all conceivable future developments, the method needs to be comprehensive. To convince us and others the method should be structurised in such a way that the treatment of each conceivable future development is traceable. The methodology is currently being applied to two Dutch disposal designs. Preliminary results show that the elaborated method functions better than the original method. However, some elements in the method will need further refinement.

1. Introduction

NRG's existing strategy for scenario development, the "PROSA-methodology", has been further developed. The reason for this was that application of the original method to a new disposal concept revealed a number of flaws. This paper describes this further developed PROSA-methodology.

In section 0 a working definition of "scenarios" is given. This definition is based on methods that have been used in e.g. probabilistic assessments for nuclear reactors. The implications of adopting this working definition are discussed.

Section 0 describes the proposed approach for scenario development in detail. In Section 0 the accomplishments of the proposed method are evaluated.

2. Scenarios in a Performance Assessment

In general a scenario describes one out of many conceivable evolutions of a disposal facility. However, this general definition has to be elaborated if we want to assess the comprehensives of scenarios in a probabilistic analysis.

In a risk study non-catastrophic as well as catastrophic scenarios will be assessed. To illustrate shortcomings in the above-mentioned general description of scenarios, focus on a

101

catastrophic scenario. Assuming a pessimistic point of view, it will always be possible to develop a catastrophic scenario. A very rational response is to consider at the same time the probability of such a catastrophic scenario, in order to investigate whether this scenario can be a significant threat to individuals or to society.

However, estimating the probability of a scenario is not straightforward. The probability that reality will develop exactly as described in a scenario (i.e. *one* conceived evolution of the facility) is zero or almost zero. In technical terms: the probability of a realisation of the scenario is (almost) zero. A common technique to solve this problem is to expand the definition of "scenario" to make it cover much more than one realisation. In the concept presented in this paper all look-alike realisations are gathered in one scenario, the range of consequences of these realisations are evaluated, and the probability is estimated.

A working definition of "scenario"

- A scenario consists of a large number of "look-alike" realisations.

- The probability of occurrence of a scenario is the sum of the probabilities of each "look alike" realisation contained in the scenario.

- The consequences of a scenario can be presented as a range of consequences. This range is composed of the consequence of each look-alike realisation contained in the scenario.

In a probabilistic assessment, an ideal working procedure would be as follows:

Assume a hypothetical computer programme that can generate at random a large number of descriptions of equally probable realisations, i.e. the programme generates "simulated realisations". A team of experts evaluates each simulated realisation by (1) determining which scenario represents this simulated realisation, and (2) determining what the consequences of the realisation are. After paying the experts for their work, we can use common statistic techniques to estimate the probability of each scenario and determine the range of consequences of each scenario.

Implications of adopting this working definition

Even the ideal working procedure can cause problems, particularly the association of a realisation with a scenario: a second group of experts could use a different set of scenarios, and consequently associate realisations with other scenarios. In most performance assessments a "normal evolution scenario" is defined. One research group associates a given realisation with the normal evolution scenario, whereas others would associate the same realisation with a dedicated "altered evolution scenario". It is important to recognise this problem, especially if results of performance assessments are published and compared with other publications.

For a given performance assessment this will not cause inconsistencies. Actually, an extreme option is to incorporate all realisations in one "overall" scenario. Regarding possible consequences and probabilities, in an adequate statistic treatment no information is lost by gathering all simulated realisations in one scenario. The problem relates to the presentation of results, and not to the internal consistence of a performance assessment.

Some remarks

Earlier in this section a working definition of scenarios has been given. Now the role of scenarios can be added: scenarios are used to communicate about the results of an assessment.

Further, the conceptual separation of "scenario" and "realisation" will turn out to be a key element in the methodology for scenario development. In fact, this concept allows us to decide whether or not given events and processes are incorporated in one or more realisations in a scenario.

3.   A Proposed Method for Scenario Development

The computer programme, mentioned in Section 0, that generates realisations does not exist. However, the basic ingredients for realisations are found in FEP-catalogues.

FEPs

In the eighties numerous research organisations started creating catalogues of processes and events that can affect future "realisations" that may result in exposure of individuals. Each item in such a catalogue is called a FEP (Feature, Events and Processes). ECN/NRG has developed such a FEP-catalogue, published in the *PROSA final report.*[1]

FEPs and realisations

Today we use FEPs as building blocks for realisations. Hypothetically we could evaluate systematically all possible FEP combinations. One of the FEP combinations for a given repository in salt is:

FEP 3.3.4:   *Embrittlement, cracking*
The waste container in the disposal concept is not able to endure the lithostatic pressure of the host rock. After at maximum 100 years the container wall will crack.

FEP 1.4.10:   Subrosion
The salt formation may slowly dissolve in the ground water. This process is called subrosion. After about one million years the waste disposed in the salt formation could be exposed to groundwater.

FEP 3.2.7:   Leaching of nuclides
If the waste matrix is exposed to the groundwater, the radionuclides will slowly dissolve in the groundwater.

FEP 1.5.5:   Groundwater flow
The groundwater eventually reaches the biosphere (river, lake, sea).

FEP 1.6.1:   Advection, convection and dispersion
Radionuclides dissolved in the groundwater are transported with the groundwater.

FEP 1.8.7:   Uptake of nuclides by animals and plants
Some radionuclides that are dissolved in the groundwater enter the food chain.

FEP 1.8.4:   Evolution

---

1.   J.Prij e.a. *PROSA. Probabilistic Safety Assessment.* Final Report. Petten, November 1993.

The food chain and exposure pathways will be affected by evolution.

NRG's experts would categorise this combination as part of the so-called "normal evolution scenario" or "subrosion scenario" for a repository in salt. Two observations regarding this FEP combination are:

1. The FEP combination represents a large number of possible realisations, mainly because the process parameters have not been quantified (i.e. FEP 1.4.10 represents all average subrosion rates larger than zero, but smaller than about 0.5 mm/year).

2. The "subrosion scenario" accounts for more processes than given in this FEP combination: e.g. fault activation in the overburden, diapirism, climate changes, etc.

Scenario development

A major practical problem is that the number of FEP combinations that can be obtained with the PROSA catalogue is about 10^{260}. Fortunately, the vast majority of these FEP combinations does not result in release of waste from the repository, and does not lead to exposure.

For scenario development a methodology is needed that automatically discards those combinations that will not result in exposures. However, even this will not be sufficient, because there are still much too many FEP combinations that result in exposure. The combination above can be expanded with any out of a large number of FEP combination, and still lead to exposure (most of the FEPs that can be added will not actually change the evolution of the repository). So, the methodology should also discard those combinations that already have been accounted for in known scenarios.

Therefore the proposed method for scenario development is an iterative method. Given an incomplete set of scenarios, the method aims at identifying those FEPs that are not accounted for in the incomplete set of scenarios. Once such a FEP is identified, it is possible to add a new scenario to account for this FEP.

To be able to identify the FEPs that could lead to new scenarios, a visualisation of scenario descriptions is developed. This visualisation is based on the "multi barrier state" approach, which has been used e.g. in the SKI/SKB scenario development study[2] and in PROSA.

The performance of a repository in a given scenario is determined by the effectiveness of barriers between the waste and individuals. These barriers can be visualised in a Multi Barrier System (note the shift from Multi Barrier *State* to Multi Barrier *System*). The anticipated initial situation of a repository can be visualised by the Multi Barrier System presented in Figure A. This particular choice is used by ECN/NRG. For other disposal concepts another arrangement may be more suitable.

---

2. A Systematic Approach to the Overall Evaluation of a Natural Analogue: Objectives and Planning. In: Alligator Rivers Analogue Project, Progress Report 1 June 1989-31 Augusts 1989. SKI/SKB, ANSTO 1989.

Figure A. **Initial barriers between radioactive material and man**

Radioactive Material (RM)	
Waste Matrix (WM)	
Technical Barrier (TB)	
Host Rock (HR)	
Overburden (O)	
Biosphere (B)	
Man (M)	

In the original approach those FEPs would be identified that short circuit one or more of these barriers. However, this approach ignores the difference between a short circuit and a process that describes transport through a barrier (or subsystem). The evaluation options of the FEPs in terms of "short circuit" or "no short circuit" lacks the level of detail that is needed for a proper evaluation.

Our experience is that those FEPs that were associated with short circuits actually would allow new transport processes, which would only sometimes really behave as a short circuit. In the improved method this is recognised. The improved method first identifies "old" transport processes, and subsequently identifies those FEPs that allow "new" transport processes.

The improved method consists of the following steps:

1. Definition of Multi Barrier Systems (MBSs) for each known scenario.

2. Classification of all FEPs for each subsystem (or barrier) in each MBS.

3. One or more new scenarios are added as a result of the FEP classification.

4. Goto step 1 (iterative process).

Scenario development - step 1

The first step to improve the methodology was to focus on those FEPs that cause transport through the subsystems or barriers. This is meant to discard all FEP combinations that will not result in exposure, as mentioned earlier. However, to be able to do so, knowledge of the scenario is needed: one should know which barriers or subsystems are relevant for the given scenario, and one should know what the effectiveness is of the processes accounted for in the scenario.

So, for each known scenario an MBS must be developed, based on the experience from performance analyses for these known scenarios.

Further, as a part of defining the MBS, the FEP catalogue is screened for those FEPs that describe the transport through the subsystems (or barriers) for the given scenario. Again, to be able to do so knowledge about the performance of the system for the given scenario is needed. Those "transport FEPs" are defined as "secondary FEPs". An example of the result of step 1 is presented in Figure B.

Figure B. **Multi Barrier System for the subrosion scenario**

	Radioactive Material (RM)	*Secondary FEPS:*	
	Waste Matrix (WM)	3.2.7	*Leaching*
	Host Rock (HR)	1.4.10	*Subrosion*
	Overburden (O)	1.6.1	*Advection,dispersion*
	Biosphere (B)	1.8.7	*Uptake of nuclides*
Man (M)			

In Fufire B only one secondary FEP per subsystem is given. However, if the scenario accounts for more than one transport process through a subsystem, more than one secondary FEP should be given in the MBS of the scenario. Further, the subsystem "technical barriers" has been removed from the MBS of the subrosion scenario, because in this scenario this barrier will be short circuited completely.

At the end of step 1 each known scenario should be described as an MBS including the secondary FEPs. Note that the number of the subsystems and the description of the subsystems may be different for each scenario.

Scenario development – step 2

In this step in the proposed method so-called **primary** FEPs are identified. A primary FEP changes a subsystem (or more subsystems) to such an extend, that the secondary FEPs identified earlier are not adequate to describe the transport through the altered subsystem. A primary FEP is FEP 1.2.14: undetected geological features – an undetected anhydrite vein allows water intrusion from the overburden to the disposal facility and therefore allows other transport processes than subrosion.

Other FEP classifications are:

- **Variant** FEPs do not cause transport through the subsystem, but influence the magnitude of the transport (e.g. evolution influences the transport through the biosphere).

- **Other** FEPs are FEPs that have no effect at all in the given scenario.

Scenario development – step 3

Given the primary FEPs identified in step 2, new scenarios must be developed. For example, in the PROSA FEP – catalogue 34 primary FEPs have been identified that affect "subrosion-transport" through the rock salt. From these 34 primary FEPs six cause a (water-) permeable connection between the subsystem "technical barriers" and the subsystem "overburden". Due to a water-permeable connection the facility will be flooded. This "new" situation should be analysed in a "new" scenario. Actually, the scenario following from this example has already been analysed as the "brine intrusion scenario".

Scenario development – step 4

For the new scenarios the FEP-catalogue has to be evaluated to identify possible (new) primary FEPs. The first step is to develop the MBS for the new scenario's as in step 1.

For the example scenario in step 3 the new Multi Barrier System is presented in Figure C.

Figure C. **Altered Multi Barrier System**

Radioactive Material (RM)		
Waste Matrix (WM)	3.2.7	*Leaching*
Technical Barrier (TB)	3.3.4	*Cracking*
	1.6.1	*Advection, disperison*
(water-)Permeable Connection (PC)	1.6.1	*Advection, dispersion*
Overburden (O)	1.6.1	*Advection, dispersion*
Biosphere (B)	1.8.7	*Uptake of nuclides*
Man (M)		

Given the existing MBS and the primary FEPs, it is often not straightforward to develop a new MBS. Our experience is that the optimal description of the MBS is developed in close interaction with the actual analyses (e.g. dose calculations) of the scenario related to the new MBS. This analysis shows which barriers are most relevant for the scenario. Knowledge of the relevant barriers is essential for defining the new Multi Barrier System for the scenario.

Is the proposed method consistent with the working definition of scenarios?

A scenario consists of a large number of "look-alike" realisations.

The scenario and the associated MBS description covers indeed a large number of look-alike realisations. The full range of realisations covered by the scenario depends on (1) the "variant FEPs" identified for the scenario, and (2) the range of values for process parameters allowed within a FEP.

- The probability of occurrence of a scenario is the sum of the probabilities of each "look alike" realisation contained in the scenario.

The probability of the scenario depends on the probability of the "event FEPs" in the scenario description, and the probability that the value of a process parameter will be within the range accounted for in the FEPs.

- The consequences of a scenario can be presented as a range of consequences. This range is composed of the consequence of each look-alike realisation contained in the scenario.

Given sufficient statistical information about the values for the process parameters, it is possible to calculate the range of consequences for a scenario.

4.   Evaluation of the Proposed Method

Compared to the original PROSA method, new elements in the proposed method are:

1. The definition of a scenario is strictly coupled with probabilistic analysis.
2. A conceptual difference between "scenario" and "realisation" has been introduced.
3. The Multi Barrier System is now used as a tool to obtain a more precise description of each single scenario, especially in terms of the range of realisations covered by a scenario.
4. The definition of the FEP categories has been improved.
5. The methodology allows ongoing scenario development.

Pro's:

We think that the proposed working definition of "scenario" is in agreement with an internal consistent performance assessment. Further we think that the MBS visualisation of scenarios eases the iterative process of scenario development. Additionally the graphical presentation eases tracebility, and could contribute to the persuasiveness of the method.

Con's:

The major problem encountered is that some transport processes are not related to a single FEP. Regard for example the transport of radionuclides in case of the water intrusion scenario in a repository in salt rock. After the intrusion, due to the *creep of rock*, the cavities that are filled with water are *squeezed*. This may result in *advective transport* of radionuclides through the permeable connection. Here three FEPs (1: creep of rock; 2: squeeze; 3: advective transport) determine the transport through the subsystem. The problem has been solved only provisionally by the afore mentioned interaction between the performance assessment and the development of the MBS. This solution, however, is not sufficiently transparent and decreases the persuasiveness of the method.

Consideration:

The proposed method probably will never "end", because (1) it is an iterative process were each iteration can result in new scenarios, and (2) the FEP catalogues are growing with time. Although this is unsatisfying from an technical point of view, we think that this continuing refinement, that is built-in in the proposed method, represents the actual progress of the work.

The proposed method is currently being applied for two Dutch repository designs. Given the goals of the Dutch research programme – investigation of the consequences of design modifications to enable retrievability of the waste – the proposed method is adequate for the time being. However, as research is continuing the method should be enhanced further.

Further developments

The definition of secondary FEPs has to be elaborated. A transport process consists of two types of FEPs: "driving FEPs" (creep of rock, squeezing) and a "transport FEP" (advective transport in brine). We found difficulties in the classification of some FEPs in the PROSA FEP catalogue. Clearly, better wording of the FEP descriptions is needed. The proposed visualisation of an MBS suggests that an MBS is statical, i.e. the sequence of events in a scenario is not visualised. The problem, however, relates to a possibly wrong interpretation of the visualisation, not to a flaw in the proposed methodology.

Paper 4

ENRESA'S METHODOLOGY FOR SCENARIO DEVELOPMENT AND EXPERIENCE OF APPLICATION IN PERFORMANCE ASSESSMENT

Jesús Alonso (ENRESA), **Emiliano González** (INITEC), **Celsa Ruiz** (CIEMAT)

1.   Introduction

The performance assessment strategy established by ENRESA for its Deep Geological Disposal Project is based on a systematic process that will permit through iterative steps to predict the capability of the disposal system to comply with the established safety criteria.

Within this context, a first level of performance assessment was completed for a repository in a granite formation in 1997, and in 1998 a performance assessment of similar scope was carried out for a repository in clay rock. For these two assessments an interim methodology for scenario development was established and then applied with a limited scope. In 1998 ENRESA started a new iterative performance assessment of a repository in a generic granite formation named ENRESA-2000, with the development of a more formalised and systematic methodology for scenario development, which is scheduled for completion by summer 1999.

The object of this paper is to describe the objectives and the scope of the scenario development in ENRESA-2000, to present the methodology which is being followed, and to stick out the practical experience of application obtained to date.

2.   ENRESA's Methodology for Scenario Development

The ENRESA-2000 methodology for scenario development was preceded by a comprehensive examination of most work published in this field. The reference methodology finally chosen was similar to the one described in the exercise SITE-94 performed by SKI.

Regulations and objectives of Scenario Development

The Spanish Nuclear Safety Council has made an official statement with regard to the acceptance criteria to apply to the installations for the final disposal of radioactive wastes, establishing that in order to guarantee safety, the criterion shall be an individual risk lower than 10^{-6}/year. No reference has been done to any aspect regarding scenarios.

In ENRESA-2000, the already started activity of Scenario Development tries to identify a group of scenarios that as a whole are appropriate to analyse the capacity of the system to perform its function under any conceivable future evolution.

Position of Scenario Development in the Assessment – Interfaces

Scenario Development should start necessarily from the objectives and scope aimed for in the assessment, the regulations to consider and the description of the disposal system.

The level of detail to which the definition of scenarios should arrive will have to be accomplished in a progressive way, being completed in the successive stages of the evaluation. In principle, the analysis consists in the systematic management of the existing information, as well as the one supplied by the experts. It must be decided in a pragmatic way an adequate level of detail, sufficient to define, without ambiguities, the scenarios to consider, which will be deepened and amplified in the following stages of the evaluation. Throughout all the evaluation, it will have to be guaranteed in a systematic way that these subsequent developments will be consistent with the conclusions of the scenario analysis and in other case, to perform the appropriate iterations within the evaluation.

Methodology

Starting with the objectives and the scope of the evaluation and with the defined system, the methodology establishes as a firs step the **"identification of a Reference System"** of the repository, given the impossibility of studying the repository as a closed system without external influences. That is to say, it compels to the establishment of some spatial limits that will encompass the set of subsystems that are going to be modelled and of some temporary limits (initial conditions and time span of the assessment) that fix the extent of the type of phenomena that can occur.

The Reference System is defined as the organised set of all the FEPs and their interrelationships, included within some spatial and temporary limits of the disposal system, that affect directly or indirectly, for a given set of external conditions, to the release and transportation of radionuclides and to their potential consequences.

This Reference System is going to serve as starting point in all the Scenario Development and the methodology that it is being applied continues a series of stages for its achievement.

The complete definition of the Reference System and the external conditions that can influence it, begin with the step **"FEP identification"**. Though it is impossible to demonstrate that the identified list of FEPs is complete for a specific detail level, the application of a systematic procedure sufficiently flexible to permit future iterations, and the possibility of registering all the judgements and reasoning behind the list, permits at least, to guarantee sufficiency. In this sense, the methodology establishes the use of a combination of different methods of identification in such a way that remains compensated the weak points of each one of them. In ENRESA-2000 two complementary methods have been used:

- identification of FEPs by expert judgement, supported by interaction matrices; and

- compilation of a FEP list from other already existing lists.

Each identified FEP is accompanied with its description, causes, effects, possible importance in the disposal system, degree of knowledge, etc., incorporating all this information in a data base.

With the FEP list obtained in this way, it begins the stage **"classification of factors"**, according to a plan that incorporates the differences between factors of the Reference System and external factors, in order to facilitate the subsequent steps of the methodology.

The following stage is **"screening of factors"**. This stage helps to adjust the list to the specific circumstances of the evaluation. The elimination of a given FEP must be justified with the criterion that is supposed will eliminate it from a definitive evaluation, though in a given moment could not be argued thoroughly such determination by lack of data, models or of the understanding of the phenomenon. This is an important stage in the methodology, where the criteria should be defined very clearly and all the information associated with each FEP registered for successive evaluations. The screening must be consistent with the objectives, scope and technical criteria of the evaluation.

Last step in the procedure is **"scenario construction"**. External FEPs are combined successively with the FEPs of the Reference System to form scenarios. Since the consequences of a given FEP can be altered by its interaction with other ones, each FEP is analysed according to its possible interactions. Each determined scenario, composed of a group of FEPs, will give origin to the development of an influence diagram, which will provide the framework upon which the quantitative description of the repository performance can be constructed.

The review of the diagram will be carried out by a number of people with expertise in different disciplines in order to cover all the aspects of the long term performance.

The evaluation of a complex influence diagram for a defined scenario has proven to be time consuming, since there are large number of FEPs and influences that should be analysed in detail. Therefore, once the influence diagram was reviewed, it will have to be simplified having into account the limited scope of the assessment. This now reduced influence diagram will be used to formulate the Reference Scenario and identify calculations and modelling needs for quantitative estimates.

Final step in the methodology is **"selection of scenarios to be quantitatively analysed"**. In ENRESA-2000, apart of the human intrusion scenarios, which are not considered due to the scope of the project, the quantitative analysis includes the following scenarios:

The Reference Scenario, which will consider the evolution of the Reference System, assuming that external FEPs will not be involved. Basic premises for this scenario are: 1) the repository construction and operation will follow the planned design and 2) the actual geosphere and biosphere conditions will be maintained during all the analysis.

This scenario is conceived as a practical tool to understand the functioning of the Reference System, also as a starting point for the construction of other scenarios.

Other scenarios appear as a consequence of applying the external FEPs to the Reference System. First of all, a "*Climatic scenario*", which contemplates the climatic evolution in Spain and its consequences, will be constructed. From this point, named "*Alternative scenarios*" will be constructed as a consequence of the occurrence of other external FEPs. Later, these scenarios will be screened out and grouped in families that can be analysed as a whole.

Additionally, *"What if scenarios"* will be considered in order to analyse the uncertainty in the initial description of the system, specific aspects in the regulations or only to increment the knowledge about the role of the barrier or determined features of the repository.

3. Experience of Application

By the time of writing this paper, just the task "FEPs Identification", which includes the descriptions and the final list of FEPs for the assessment, have been finished. Due to this fact, the practical aspects analysed and the conclusions presented are of preliminary nature and may change in the future.

Work Context

The participants involved directly in the activity Scenario Development of ENRESA-2000 are two independent teams: CIEMAT (Department of Energy Environmental Impact), as the R&D group for scenario development, and IP (ENRESA´s Project Engineering). These groups co-ordinate the whole activity and accomplish directly several of its tasks.

The necessary integration between performance assessment and scientists is achieved making large use of expert judgement, by the so-called GTIs groups. In this exercise, the method for scenario development has been structured around these groups. The basic function of GTIs is to provide expert judgement in informally and formally elicited ways, in order to establish a well structured decision making process, that can be very useful to support essential parts of the information used. R&D people working for ENRESA in Performance Assessment were organised among seven GTI groups according with their fields of specialisation.

In practice, due to the large amount of different specialists participating in the Scenario Development activity, the application of the methodology and the systematic of work had to be organised around a Technical Procedure to be followed by all the involved organisations in the activity. The Procedure defines in concrete terms, step by step, the different tasks that constitute the activity and identifies the responsibilities of each one of the involved parts.

The objectives, the organising and regulatory aspects and the scope of the assessment were specified in a document named "Document of Context". Also, a preliminary description of the disposal system, including the radioactive waste, the site and the repository design, was prepared in advance to the specific scenario development tasks in another document. Both were handed out between the people involved in the activity.

Identifying FEPs

Regarding the identification of FEPs, as mentioned previously under the epigraph of methodology, two methods have been combined in ENRESA-2000 in order to assure completeness (Figure 1):

1. Identification and description of FEPs by GTI experts by means of three RES interaction matrices (source term, near field and far field).

2. Elaboration of a list of FEPs by two independent groups starting on existing lists obtained from similar repository systems. These lists correspond to SITE-94 (SKI), KRISTALLIN-1 (Nagra) and ENRESA-97 (ENRESA). This task was concluded with the unification of the lists from both groups.

Figure 1. **Process of identifying FEPs**

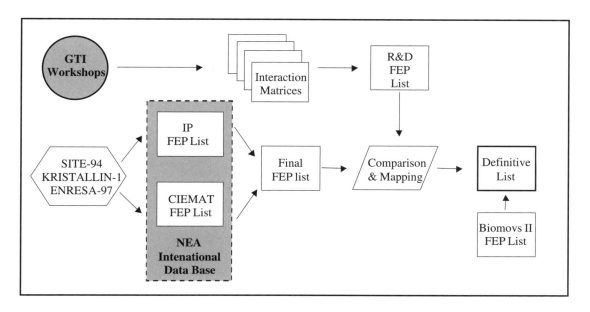

These two methods gave the necessary output in order to carry out a definitive list of FEPs with the exception of the biosphere FEPs, where BIOMOVS II international list of FEPs was considered.

In advance to the planned workshops to be held with the participation of the GTI specialists, a questionnaire was handed out to the members of these groups. The idea was that the experts could fill it out with a preliminary description of the FEPs under their area of expertise, with the aim of making possible that they could work out the topic in advance for each of the workshops, just in order to make easier the subsequent workshop activities. The questionnaire included items such as: name and type of the FEP, general description, causes and effects, current knowledge and bibliographic references.

As a starting point three workshops were held by ENRESA, where the experts, from more than ten different organisations working for ENRESA, filled out three RES matrices regarding the following subsystems: source term, near field and far field. The purpose of this interaction matrices was to be able to structure and visualise the reference system in order to facilitate the subsequent identification of FEPs and also to be a kind of check-list for the definitive list of FEPs (Figure 2). After the workshops each expert was requested to prepare a list with the FEPs under their speciality. Finally, all these lists were put together and merged in a single list.

Subsequent to the mentioned workshops, both CIEMAT and IP prepared in parallel two independent lists of FEPs. These two lists, with basically the same structure of the NEA International Database, were obtained from other lists performed by some national radioactive waste management agencies. Once this work was completed, the two obtained lists (one from CIEMAT and one from IP) were confronted in a workshop in order to obtain a single list.

Figure 2. **Field of specialisation of the GTI groups**

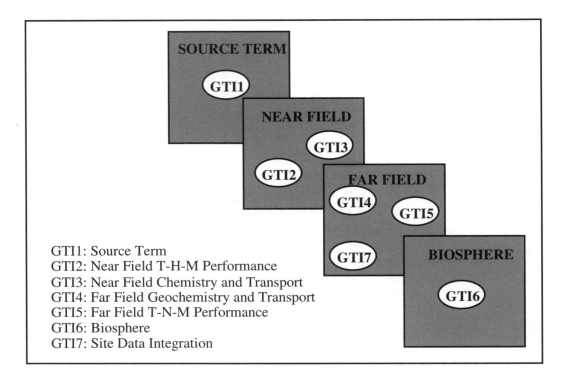

Finally, the list obtained from the experts of the GTIs and the List obtained between CIEMAT and IP, were compared in order to derive a complete and consistent list of FEPs. With this list, a preliminary description of the FEPs was undertaken by CIEMAT and then distributed to the GTI experts for revision. The ended product was the definitive ENRESA-2000 list of FEPs.

The software FileMaker Pro 4.0 was used by both, CIEMAT and IP, in order to collect all the information referred to the list of FEPs in the framework of the NEA International Database. For the biospheric FEPs ENRESA used a specific software developed for FEP database and RES matrices.

Classifying and screening FEPs

The next step was to classify the different FEPs in order to provide the organisation needed to begin to develop scenarios. Regarding the Reference System the classification scheme distinguished basically two types of FEPs: belonging and external to the Reference System

Afterwards, screening procedure assured the selection of the most significant FEPs. Disruptive geological FEPs have been screening on very general criteria due to the fact that the site of the assessment is generic. The following screening criteria has been used for FEPs:

1.   Negligible consequences on repository system.

2. Very low probability of occurrence.

3. Related to future human acts.

Therefore, using these determined screening criteria, some FEPs were eliminated of the final FEP list. Some examples of screened out FEPs are:

- Large meteorite impact (very low probability).

- Accumulation of He in the canister (low consequences for a short lived canister).

- Glaciation (very low probability in Spain).

- Magmatic activity (very low probability by the site selection plan).

- Retrieval of the repository materials (responsibility of the future generations).

Conclusions

As the Scenario Development activity of ENRESA-2000 is still under its way, these conclusions are only referred to its first already finished task" FEPs Identification".

1. FileMakerPro has proved to be an acceptable database for ENRESA´s FEPs, with the important advantage to hold the NEA FEP database files on it.

2. Workshops between specialists and people working in PA has shown to be a very efficient way for constructing interaction matrices when the diagonal elements are defined in advance by the PA working group.

3. In ENRESA-2000, the long time required to carry out all "Scenario Development" tasks (more than one year) is showing to be an important practical constraint, since the outputs from this activity are inputs to the rest of the assessment. This exercise now foreseen practical overlaps between these activities and the rest.

4. The experience acquired by ENRESA in FEPs identification, to assure a high degree of and comprehensiveness, has shown that this is a very important resource consuming task (independent groups of people working on different FEP lists, elaboration of interaction matrices, etc). It would seem to be more profitable to adapt a generic and complete list from the bibliography to the specific conditions. To this effect, the NEA, with the launching of its FEP Database, has started a very promising way of optimising this kind of activities.

SCENARIO SELECTION AND DEMONSTRATING COMPLIANCE BASED ON RISK, DOSE AND COMPLEMENTARY CRITERIA

Stig Wingefors, Björn Dverstorp, Christina Lilja and Magnus Westerlind
Swedish Nuclear Power Inspectorate, Sweden

1.   Introduction

The Swedish Radiation Protection Institute, SSI, has recently finalised regulations concerning the final management of spent nuclear fuel and nuclear waste [1]. These regulations set the basic radiological standards for the protection of human health and the environment. The regulations of course have implications on e.g. the scenario selection for safety assessments of geological disposal.

The Swedish Nuclear Power Inspectorate, SKI, is currently developing corresponding regulations concerning the long-term safety of disposal. SKI's regulations will contain requirements on the construction and operation of a repository and on how to demonstrate compliance with the radiation protection criteria prescribed by SSI. Thus, the regulations will address construction and the issues to be covered in the safety assessment of long-term performance.

SKI and SSI have initiated collaboration on the development of safety indicators complementary to dose and/or risk, with the aim to investigate the possible usefulness as regulatory guidance.

The purpose of this paper is to give an overview of the recent regulatory development in Sweden, since it has strong influence on the industry's scenario selection, demonstration of compliance etc.

2.   Regulatory Framework

2.1   SSI's regulations

SSI's regulations concerning the final management of spent fuel and nuclear waste entered into force 1 February 1999, and the main issues are presented below. It should be pointed out that the general requirements in SSI's regulations apply to handling, treatment, transportation, interim storage prior to, and in connection with, final disposal as well the final disposal of spent fuel and nuclear waste. Thus, the regulations are not limited to the disposal, although they may have the largest impact in this field.

2.1.1   Optimisation and BAT

The regulations require that the entire disposal system (i.e. encapsulation, transportation and disposal) for final management should be optimised. However, SSI also states that there are several limitations with respect to the possibility of the full optimisation of the system. These include for example the balancing of doses from operation and hypothetical doses in a distant future.

In the regulations, it is specified that the outflow of radioactive substances for a period of one thousand years after repository closure must be included in the collective dose calculation. To account for the fact that an outflow can result in doses in the future, the dose calculation should be carried out for a longer period of time than 1 000 years, therefore 10 000 years is specified as the upper boundary for the calculation. Thus, the annual global collective dose (as a result of an outflow over a period of 1 000 years) should be calculated and totalled for a period of 10 000 years. It should be stressed that SSI does not consider the collective dose calculated in this way as a prediction of a "real" detriment. The collective dose is primarily intended for comparison of different management and disposal options.

SSI requires consideration of best available technique (BAT) in the final management and disposal of spent fuel and nuclear waste. It should be noted that SSI's definition of BAT includes consideration of costs. Thus, BAT in this context is defined as "the most effective measure available to limit the release of radioactive substances and the harmful effects of the releases on human health and the environment, which does not entail unreasonable costs."

2.1.2   Protection of the individual

The regulations stipulate that "a repository for spent nuclear fuel or nuclear waste shall be designed so that the annual risk[1] of harmful effects[2] after closure does not exceed 10^{-6} for a representative individual in the group exposed to the greatest risk."

This requirement has several implications on the selection of scenarios for the safety assessment of geological disposal. The most obvious implication is the use of risk as a criterion, which emphasises the probability of scenarios to occur. SSI comments that the criterion applies to a repository undisturbed by man. Thus, intrusion scenarios are excluded (but should be addressed separately).

SSI comments the "low-probability/high-consequence" problem in the way that scenarios that give doses above 1 mSv/year must be assessed separately. Furthermore, the use of risk does not mean that the dose calculation can be skipped over. All of the stages in the calculation must be reported.

An important point is that SSI does not expect compliance to be demonstrated by a single "exact" risk figure. Instead, the risk must be assessed from a risk profile, which is obtained by weighing together consequences and probabilities for different scenarios. The concept risk profile is to be understood as calculated, or otherwise assessed, consequences and probabilities for a relevant

---

1. Risk is defined as the product of the probability of receiving a radiation dose and the harmful effects of the dose.

2. Harmful effects are defined as cancer (fatal and non-fatal) as well as hereditary effects.

choice of possible scenarios. Closely linked to this is the grouping of scenarios into different classes, depending on their likelihood, which is elaborated further in SKI's regulations.

An important, but perhaps easily overlooked, feature is that the risk criterion does not apply to a critical group (as defined by the ICRP) but to the group at greatest risk. One criterion for the ICRP critical group is that the range of doses to the individuals in the group should be within a factor of ten. The group at greatest risk used in SSI's regulations may instead have a range in risk, which is ten times higher, i.e. a factor of 100. Thus, this group may be larger and geographically more spread than the traditional critical group. This means that efforts have to be made to identify and assess exposure pathways on a regional scale.

2.1.3   Environmental protection

The regulations include qualitative requirements for the protection of biodiversity and sustainable use of biological resources. The requested description of biological effects of radiation shall be based on available knowledge. Thus, a detailed analysis is only expected for the short-term. SSI does not, at present, consider it justifiable to formulate quantitative criteria for environmental protection. Above all, this is due to gaps in scientific knowledge, with respect to radiosensitivity of various organisms, synergetic effects etc. SSI continues to investigate whether criteria can be derived from existing documentation, based on an ecotoxicological approach.

2.1.4   Intrusion and access

As mentioned above the risk criterion of 10^{-6} does not apply to intrusion into a repository. The reason, of course being the inherently speculative nature of intrusion scenarios. However, intrusion (defined as unintentional human action) scenarios shall be defined and assessed.

If measures are planned to facilitate future access, e.g. for inspection, repair or retrieval, these must be analysed with respect to their impact on the performance of the repository.

2.1.5   Time periods

SSI requires the assessment for a repository's performance to be reported for two time periods; the first thousand years after closure and the time after thousand years.

For the first thousand years SSI's opinion is that reliable quantitative analyses can be made of the radiological impact, i.e. it is an upper bound for the estimation of radiological detriment (i.e. risk or dose).

SSI requires that assessments, in different time periods, shall always include a case based on the current (at the time of the application) biosphere conditions. Current conditions refer to the existing circumstances and the conditions for the biota and the society. However, the concept also includes the fact that known trends are taken into consideration, such as land elevation.

For longer times (more than one thousand years) the biosphere, and in particular the society, may change substantially. Thus, different scenarios must be assessed, and estimated risks (or doses) can only be regarded as indicators of performance of a repository. The capability of the repository to isolate and retain the waste can instead be evaluated using safety indicators complementary to dose and risk.

2.2 SKI's regulations

SKI's premises for regulations concerning the long-term safety of geological disposal were presented in 1997 [2], and circulated widely for comments. The main principles built on earlier recommendations issued jointly by the Nordic safety authorities, the so-called Nordic Flagbook [3], as well as other principles discussed and issued by the ICRP and the IAEA.

The ideas in the discussion paper from 1997 have now been further developed and presently draft regulations are being prepared for submission.

2.2.1 Basic safety requirements

With the aim to ensure that spent fuel and nuclear waste is disposed of in accordance with SSI's radiation protection criteria the following basic safety requirements are proposed by SKI:

- The level of risk associated with geologic disposal must comply with SSI's criteria and be consistent with levels that are considered acceptable for other nuclear activities.

- The assessment of safety shall be based on the risk profile derived from a performance assessment of relevant scenarios.

- Repository safety (performance) shall be based on several functions of technical and natural barriers, in which the failure of a single barrier function may not impair the overall performance of the repository.

- A geologic repository shall be designed in a way that obviates the need for post-closure monitoring.

- QA should be implemented for the operational phase to ensure that the various barriers of the repository will perform as intended and that the safety analysis report is properly updated. A renewal of the report will be required with an interval of ten years until closure of the repository.

- A research programme on the long-term safety shall be reported regularly to SKI until closure of the repository.

2.2.2 Design and construction

The repository shall be designed and constructed as to meet design basis requirements specified in the safety analysis report.

SKI requires, as do SSI, that best available technique (BAT) is considered in the design and construction of a repository.

The performance of the repository should be assessed for as long as safety functions are required, for ten thousand years as a minimum, but not longer than one million years.

According to the regulations, a scenario shall include a description of how a given combination of external and internal FEPs influences the repository performance. This includes:

- External events like climate changes and their importance for the performance (permafrost, land elevation) as well as effects of human actions.

- Internal conditions like performance of engineered barriers and the surrounding rock.

As discussed above SSI's risk-based criterion for individual protection puts assignment of scenario probabilities into focus. However, SKI does not believe that a fully probabilistic safety assessment, with probability estimates assigned to individual scenarios, will provide a good basis for demonstrating compliance. Instead SKI favours the use of a so-called risk profile, as presented in section 2.1.2 above.

Thus, SKI suggests that scenarios be divided into three classes:

- The main scenario
- Less likely scenarios
- Residual scenarios.

Main scenario

The main scenario should be defined based on a description of a likely climate evolution and reasonable assumptions about the initial state/properties of the Process System[3], including the engineered barrier system (EBS). Thus, the basis for identifying/defining the main scenario are external events with high probability to occur (or events which cannot be shown to have low probability of occurrence) and assumptions about the likely internal conditions. The main scenario will constitute the basis for judging compliance with the radiation protection criteria. Also, the main scenario will be the starting point for analyses of the importance of uncertainties.

The main scenario should typically cover the next glacial cycle of about one hundred thousand years (for long-lived nuclear waste and spent fuel).

Less likely scenarios

Less likely scenarios include variations of the climate evolution, e.g. alternative time sequences for glaciations, sea level changes, land elevation etc. A special case of scenarios belonging to this class is human action scenarios, including effects of human intrusion on barrier performance. It should be noted that the emphasis is on the effects on barrier performance and not on consequences for the intruder. These consequences are instead treated as residual scenarios.

---

3.   FEPs, and their interactions, which directly or indirectly affects the performance are assigned to a Process System with well-defined boundaries [4].

When assessing the less likely scenarios it is necessary to account for both consequences and likelihood of occurrence. For each scenario it will be required to estimate the probability distribution in time of consequences. It can be foreseen that expert judgement will play an important role, but so far no regulatory guidance has been developed in this respect.

Residual scenarios

Residual scenarios include extreme natural events, consequences to intruders and other events of a "what-if" character. Thus, these scenarios are meant to illustrate performance of individual barriers rather than providing a basis for judging compliance.

Scenarios, models, uncertainties

A systematic approach should be adopted with regard to the identification of scenarios, processes and uncertainties that could affect repository performance. In addition, a comprehensive documentation must be provided of how validation of models, assumptions and data for the intended use has been achieved.

SKI considers both deterministic and probabilistic analyses and sensitivity analyses important elements of performance assessment calculations. Model uncertainties should be analysed by applying several alternative models.

SKI also emphasises that the evaluation of safety assessments is not restricted to checking whether or not estimated consequences of releases radioactive substances comply with specified criteria. Most of the evaluation focuses on investigating whether all essential processes and their inherent interactions have been included, or addressed, in the assessment and whether they have been correctly described from a technical/scientific perspective.

3.   Complementary Safety Indicators

Safety indicators for the assessment of radioactive waste have been discussed and proposed for many years, e.g. within the Nordic countries and the IAEA [5 and references therein]. With the development of regulations concerning the long-term safety of repositories, SKI and SSI have also begun collaboration on the possible regulatory use of safety indicators complementary to dose and risk. The difficulties with the use of dose and risk are to large extent due to the long time-scales needed to be considered in waste disposal. The future cannot be predicted in detail but instead different scenarios, with different probabilities of occurrence, must be assessed. Some parts of a disposal system can be predicted or analysed with high confidence for very long periods of time, e.g. geological formations, while for example the evolution of the biosphere, and in particular the society, become quite uncertain within less than one thousand years. Thus, there may be considerable uncertainty in doses (or risks) derived from the safety assessment of a repository. For this reason the focus for SSI's and SKI's collaboration is on the use of safety indicators for assessing the long-term performance ($\geq 10^3$ years).

3.1 A system of safety indicators

It has to be recognised that different safety indicators fulfil different purposes in the successive stages of, e.g. a disposal project and in its licensing. It would, therefore, be appropriate to develop a hierarchical system of safety indicators applicable to disposal.

Intimately linked to safety indicators are the corresponding criteria or reference values. Preferably it should be possible to compare each indicator with a criterion. For example, a calculated flux of radionuclides from a repository could be compared with a flux of natural radionuclides. However, safety indicators may be useful also in the absence of an established criterion or reference value. In this case the indicators can be used for comparative purposes. For example, different options in the design of a repository may be assessed by comparison of calculated fluxes. An alternative is to use the indicators for indirectly showing compliance with other criteria. For example, a calculated environmental concentration of radionuclides may indirectly indicate compliance with a dose criterion.

One starting point for SKI's and SSI's work is the hierarchy of proposed indicators as developed in the present IAEA work, which is illustrated in Table 1.

Table 1. **Overview of safety indicators**

	Primary safety indicators		Secondary safety indicators	
	Location	**Reference**	**Location**	**Reference**
Fluxes	Geosphere/ Biosphere Interface; EBS (steady state conditions)	Natural fluxes from geosphere; Through surface environment; into river basins	EBS (in general)	Flux criteria derived from safety assessments
Concentrations	Surface environment; Shallow groundwater; Near surface rock	Corresponding natural concentrations; Maximum permissible concentration	EBS; deep geosphere	Derived concentration criteria (less applicable)
Times	Waste package containment time; transfer time through EBS; transfer time to biosphere	Crossover time based on hazard indices	EBS (range of containment times)	Derived Ranges

Primary safety indicators

Primary safety indicators should provide some measure or indication of radiological impact on human health and the environment. The indicators should be possible to assess against, or compare with, criteria or references independent of the safety assessment itself. These criteria or reference values should have a similar general validity as dose or risk. Examples of two potential safety indicators, which fulfil these requirements, are the fluxes of radionuclides leaving the geosphere and the concentrations of radionuclides in the surface or near-surface environment. Both of these quantities can be compared with reference values based on existing natural conditions.

Secondary safety indicators

Secondary safety indicators are those which can be assessed against sub-system criteria, or references, derived from safety assessments based on dose or another primary safety indicator. Examples from this category are fluxes through engineered barriers and release rates from waste forms. Like the primary ones, the secondary safety indicators provide measures of safety for a disposal facility, but these measures are not possible to compare with corresponding data independent of the safety assessment.

Performance indicators

Performance indicators are safety indicators on a third hierarchical level and do not, by themselves, describe the function of a barrier in terms of its ability to restrict radionuclide release. Rather, they describe intrinsic properties that a repository component should have, in order to be effective as a barrier or to preserve the safety functions of larger parts of the system. References for performance indicators, also called technical criteria, may, for example, be derived from subsystem criteria established by the regulatory authority or by the proponent of a disposal system. Technical criteria should be established, at the latest, before building of facilities, and it must then be ensured that these criteria can be met in practice. Examples of such performance indicators are waste load per package, metallurgical properties of waste canisters, composition and density of clay buffers and backfills, and fracture frequency and other properties of the host rock.

In summary, SKI's and SSI's collaboration consists of two major tasks, which will be carried out in parallel. The first task is to develop the hierarchical system of complementary safety indicators, and to evaluate whether it can be a useful regulatory tool. The second task, aims to assemble, analyse and publish data on concentrations and fluxes of natural radionuclides to serve as possible reference data in the use of safety indicators.

4.   Summary and Future Work

In summary, the Swedish regulatory framework for the management and disposal of spent fuel and nuclear waste has evolved during the last few years. The SSI has issued the basic radiation protection criteria, and shortly SKI expects to submit draft regulations for the long-term safety of geological disposal. So far, the main efforts have concerned the formulation of general requirements. Consequently, the future work will be more directed towards regulatory guidance on compliance issues.

Starting from the experiences from the SITE-94 project [4] SKI has continued to develop tools and procedures for safety assessments, some of the efforts are presented elsewhere in this workshop [6]. Some topics, which SKI are currently working with or planning, relevant to this workshop are:

- Development of software for managing and presenting FEPs etc. [6].
- Development of an encyclopaedia with descriptions of FEPs relevant to a disposal [6].

- Definition of process influence diagrams for the SFR facility. It should be mentioned that SKB will present a new safety analysis report for SFR ca. 2000/2001. Thus, SKI and SSI have both begun preparations for the review.

- Improvement of the climatic evolution scenario used in SITE-94.

- SKI will together with SSI develop a regulatory strategy on the treatment of future human actions.

- As mentioned above work has begun on the regulatory use of complementary safety indicators.

The general aim is to support the development of regulatory criteria and to maintain and develop the necessary regulatory competence for the future review of licence applications for disposal of spent fuel and nuclear waste.

References

1. The Swedish Radiation Protection Institute's regulations concerning the final management of spent nuclear fuel and nuclear waste, SSI FS 1998:1 (1998). (Presently only in Swedish)

2. SKI Memorandum 97017, Premises for regulations concerning safety in connection with the final disposal of spent nuclear fuel etc. (1997).

3. The radiation protection and nuclear safety authorities in Denmark, Finland, Iceland, Norway and Sweden, Disposal of High Level Radioactive Waste: Consideration of Some Basic Criteria, (The Nordic Flagbook) (1993).

4. SKI SITE-94, Deep repository performance assessment project, SKI Report 96:36 (1996).

5. Wingefors S., Westerlind M., Gera F., The use of safety indicators in the assessment of radioactive waste disposal, in proceedings from an International Symposium on Radioactive Waste Disposal: Health and Environmental Criteria and Standards, Stockholm, 31 August – 4 September 1998 (in press).

6. Chapman N.A., Robinson P., Jack J., Stenhouse M., Miller B., Dverstorp B., Lilja C., Sundström B., Development of a comprehensive performance assessment systems analysis methodology and supporting tools, and their application in scenario evaluation, paper presented at OECD/NEA workshop on scenario development, Madrid 10-12 May 1999.

DEVELOPMENT OF A COMPREHENSIVE PERFORMANCE ASSESSMENT SYSTEMS ANALYSIS METHODOLOGY AND SUPPORTING TOOLS, AND THEIR APPLICATION IN SCENARIO EVALUATION

Neil A. Chapman[1], Peter Robinson[1], Jonathan Jack[1], Mike Stenhouse[1], Bill Miller[1], Björn Dverstorp[2], Christina Lilja[2] and Benny Sundström[2]
[1]QuantiSci; Melton Mowbray, UK & Denver, USA
[2] SKI; Swedish Nuclear Power Inspectorate, S-106 58 Stockholm, Sweden

1.   Introduction

As part of its regulatory function, SKI is developing an independent performance assessment (PA) capability to allow it to evaluate SKB's RD&D programme and upcoming licensing submissions. This capability is built upon the Systems Approach (Chapman *et al.*, 1995), originally developed as part of the SITE-94 project (SKI, 1996), and is intended to allow SKI to test concepts, develop safety criteria, evaluate and report on SKB safety assessments, and demonstrate whether compliance is being achieved.

SKI view systems and scenario analysis as the fundamental basis for safety assessment. The approach which SKB would be expected to adopt, and which SKI would apply in its evaluations, is based on the identification of FEPs (features, events and processes) and their influences on each other, the construction of scenarios which incorporate these FEPs and QA audit techniques for demonstrating that the system has been evaluated comprehensively. Both the SKB and SKI methodologies approach this in a similar fashion, although the concepts and tools used by each organisation are rather different.

This paper describes developments in the production of supporting software tools, which have taken place since the SITE-94 project.

2.   SKI Systems Approach

The Systems Approach of SKI was developed during SITE-94. It is based on the definition of a Process System containing the majority of FEPs and the management of those (external) FEPs outside the Process System (EFEPs), so that they can be combined into useful scenarios which test and illustrate different aspects of disposal system response. A clear distinction is drawn between systems analysis, which is used for structuring the bulk of a PA, and scenario analysis, which draws on only one part of the systems analysis process. The systems analysis approach being developed is seen primarily as a means of demonstrating that an assessment is comprehensive.

In outline, the SKI approach involves the following principal steps:

1. Identify, define and evaluate those FEPs which describe the nature and the performance of the disposal system;

2. Structure the FEPs and their interactions, using a sensible distinction between system FEPs (in the Process System) and scenario generating or responsive FEPs (EFEPs), in a way that describes the behaviour of the evolving system and its environment ;

3. Ensure that there are adequate (and, where appropriate, alternative) conceptual models of the behaviour of each part of the system and that these encompass all the relevant FEPs and their interactions for that region: the Assessment Model Flowchart (AMF) concept of SITE-94 is used for this mapping of FEPs onto modelling and evaluation capabilities and tools;

4. Use these conceptual models to develop a logical group of calculation cases to assess the behaviour of parts of (and the complete) system, exploring the various types of uncertainty involved in the calculations, including scenarios of future system evolution.

Since the SITE-94 study, SKI has been developing improved software tools to facilitate the management of FEPs and the voluminous supporting information on state-of-the-art knowledge on FEPs and their interactions. A full description of the latter is the logical basis for justifying the safety of any waste management concept, and is a valuable tool for explaining issues to decision-makers and outside parties. Thus, apart from the obvious tools common to most PAs (databases, computer codes for modelling system behaviour and radionuclide fluxes), the SKI systems approach has developed two further tools:

*   a **software tool** (SPARTA) to manage FEPs and their interactions, and to allow investigation and manipulation of the Process System, the AMF and the impact of scenarios on the Process System;

*   an **encyclopaedia** which gives detailed descriptions of all the FEPs relevant to a specific disposal concept.

A prime purpose of these two tools is to provide a clear audit trail for future safety assessments. By showing how assessment decisions are made, and the information on which they are based, the tools allow subsequent assessments to develop more clearly, and parties not involved in the assessments to explore what has been done. With this purpose in mind, SKI intends that, in the future, these tools should be universally available on the Internet, to allow interested parties to review how PA issues are being addressed, and the information and assumptions on which they are based.

3.   The SPARTA Code

SPARTA stands for *Systematic Performance Assessment Review, Tracking and Auditing*. SKI is using it to replace and substantially develop beyond the capabilities of the Business Modeller software used in the SITE-94 project.

SPARTA can be used to construct and manipulate FEP influence diagrams and call up information from supporting databases. It is flexible in allowing a system to be represented at varying levels of complexity, either locally or in total, and will record decisions made on the importance of FEPs and influences, as well as the basis on which they are made. For example, FEPs can be represented at various levels of complexity, from the generality of a "super-FEP" (e.g. "engineered barrier decay") to fully disaggregated FEPs which, at the greatest level of detail, are nested within super-FEPs.

SPARTA thus enables the structured development of a system Process Influence Diagram (PID) via creation of a hierarchy of drawings. As one moves down this hierarchy, the diagrams tend towards more detail in terms of the number of FEPs displayed. However, there is also a corresponding decrease in the degree of embedded structure of individual FEPs in moving from top to bottom.

Influences between FEPs, between diagrams and between different hierarchic levels are bundled within connections which are visible with the FEPs on all drawings (see illustrative figures later in this paper). The influences themselves are hidden within the connections, but can be highlighted as required. Thus, using this approach, the complexity created by displaying dozens of separate influences in one diagram is avoided without the loss of any vital information. SPARTA allows interrogation of individual FEPs to establish what influences connect to it. Apart from producing and manipulating influence diagrams, SPARTA also records the decision bases for placing and ranking influences according to importance, using embedded protocol sheets.

SPARTA also allows colour coding of influences and can display simplified diagrams based on the level of importance attached to individual influences. Thus, for example, if certain features, events or processes have been identified but are deemed not to influence the system significantly, they may be screened out automatically from the visible drawing, although they are retained in the PID file.

The purpose of the application is thus to be able to draw multi-layer diagrams, representing the original, single sheet PID documents used in SITE-94, and to access the underlying information within the diagram. This information may be contained as data within the application and/or as links to files (HTML, Microsoft Word, Text, etc). It is intended to facilitate the quick and efficient production of PID diagrams with all the related data/files accessible through the diagram. The solution is also intended to be flexible enough that AMF diagrams can be created as well, and linked to the PID documents. SPARTA runs under the Visio drawing/object manipulation system on a PC and uses the Microsoft Access database engine for all data handling activities.

The intention of SPARTA is that, as well as acting as a review and audit tool, it should be used on a day-to-day basis by the Clearing Houses involved in an assessment. The concept of Clearing Houses was developed in SITE-94. They are small groups of people working together on a particular aspect of system behaviour (e.g. near-field chemistry, or waste degradation behaviour), to co-ordinate analysis work and to specify and develop calculation cases for the assessment. Access to the PID, the AMF and the underlying data will allow easier operational decisions by the Clearing Houses.

SPARTA is currently released and operational within SKI as Version 2. At present, it is being tested on the production of PIDs for the SFR repository. It will also be used to build Assessment Model Flowcharts which permit the structuring of PA consequence analyses. Clearly, an important application will be in the generation of scenarios by the imposition of EFEPs on the PID, as developed during SITE-94.

4.   The FEP Encyclopaedia

Despite many years of effort internationally on the production of FEP lists for PA purposes, the underlying descriptions of FEPs has remained rather sparse in many programmes. SKI is remedying this within its own projects by producing an encyclopaedia which provides a reasonably detailed statement of the definition and understanding of all the FEPs involved in an assessment. Each FEP entry comprises about three pages of text, diagrams and key references.

The objective of the encyclopaedia is that it provides, in one location, a comprehensive summary of the scientific basis for the disposal concept and the assessment. It is the first stop for any questions, particularly those which might arise from interested parties outside the waste management community (e.g. what is matrix diffusion?). It has thus been written in basic scientific language and, once written, should remain valid for many years.

At the time of writing, the encyclopaedia covered the majority of FEPs relevant to the Swedish SFR repository for L/ILW. It is currently being linked directly into SPARTA and, like SPARTA, will also be available on the internet. In the near future, it is to be extended to include additional FEPs relevant to the current SKB spent-fuel disposal system. Clearly, there are many FEPs common to both disposal systems.

5. Trial Application of SPARTA

During the Version 1.1 development phase of 1998-9, an initial trial application of SPARTA has been in constructing the PID for the SFR repository. The SFR system is more complex than the spent fuel (SFL2 repository) system which was evaluated in SITE-94, as it contains a wider range of materials and structures within the engineered barriers.

Five separate disposal regions exist in SFR (silo and four rock vaults, two of which have different designs) which makes the near-field PID rather complex. Whilst SPARTA was being developed, an initial SFR PID was constructed using the old SITE-94 software. A corresponding PID was then developed using SPARTA.

The starting point was a list of FEPs identified as relevant to the L/ILW repository. These were combined into a multi-level schematic diagram. At the top (system) level, the drawing comprises near field, far field and biosphere, with influences existing between the near-field and the far-field, and between the far-field and the biosphere. At the level below, each of the top-level FEPs ("super FEPs") is subdivided into sub-FEPs. In the same way, each of these sub-FEPs is further subdivided, and so on until the lowest level of the PID is reached which comprises a series of drawings, each of which is composed of "basic" FEPs, i.e. FEPs with no underlying structure. The figures at the end of this paper shows typical screen views from SPARTA for successively lower levels of such a diagram, from level 1 to 4.

6. Future Development

SPARTA will enable scenarios to be developed and their impacts evaluated both by superimposing EFEPs onto the PIDs produced (as in SITE-94) and by a bottom-up approach of tracking key sensitive influences from within the PID. During SITE-94, the scenario evaluation procedures with the systems methodology were not tested in depth. An obvious development of SPARTA will be to track the changing importance of FEP links within the Process System which result from the imposition of an EFEP: i.e. the propagation of the response to a scenario through the disposal system. The ability easily to display the parts of the system which change in response to external stresses, and to do this at a selection of ranges of complexity, will greatly facilitate presentation to reviewers and other audiences.

At the moment, the biosphere has not been incorporated into the SKI systems approach (being outside the chosen Process System, as the biosphere is outside the regulatory sphere of SKI) and is consequently not represented on the PIDs for any of the repositories under consideration. SPARTA would, of course, be capable of including biosphere FEPs and this may be considered for the future.

References

Chapman, N. A., Andersson, J., Robinson, P., Skagius, K., Wene, C-A, Wiborgh, M & Wingefors, S. 1995. Systems Analysis, Scenario Construction and Consequence Analysis Definition for SITE-94. SKI Technical Report 95:26

SKI, 1996. SKI SITE-94. Deep Repository Performance Assessment Project. SKI Technical Report 96:36, 2 volumes and Summary.

Figures 1 to 3: SPARTA screen images of part of the SFR PID showing three successive levels of detail. Figures 1 and 2 (above) show the near-field region (Level 2), then part of the BLA repository (Level 3), while Figure 3 (below) shows more detail of the waste package region in the BLA repository (Level 4). Level 1 (System Level) is not shown.

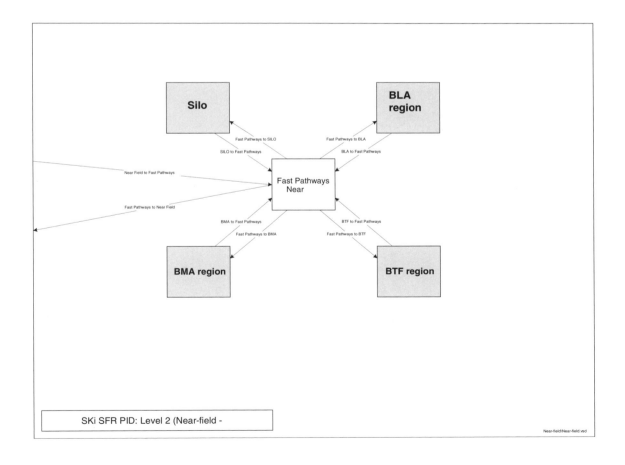

SKi SFR PID: Level 2 (Near-field -

Near-field\Near-field.vsd

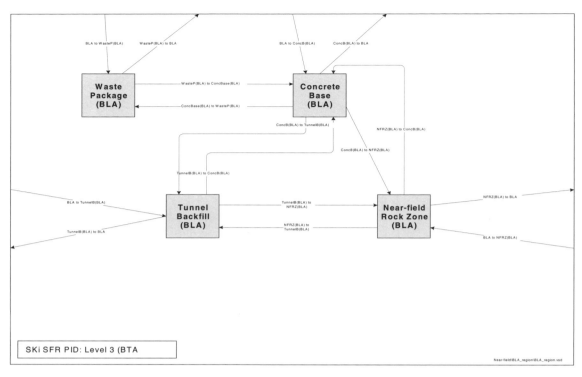

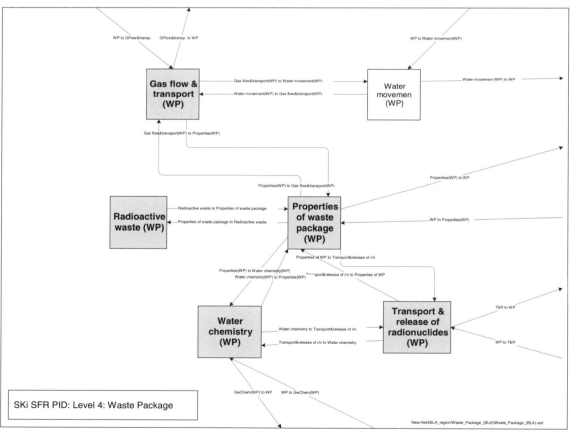

DEVELOPMENT OF SCENARIOS WITHIN A SYSTEMATIC ASSESSMENT FRAMEWORK FOR THE DRIGG POST-CLOSURE SAFETY CASE

Len Watts, Linda Clements[1], Mike Egan, Neil Chapman[2], Paul Kane[3] and Mike Thorne[4]
[1]Research & Technology, British Nuclear Fuels plc (BNFL), UK
[2]QuantiSci Limited, UK; [3]Kanvil Earth Sciences, UK
[4]Waste Environmental, AEA Technology plc, UK

1.   Introduction

The Drigg site, owned and operated by BNFL, is the UK's principal site for the disposal of low level radioactive waste. The site has operated since 1959 and receives wastes from a wide range of sources including nuclear power stations, nuclear fuel cycle facilities, isotope manufacturing sites, universities, general industry and clean-up of historically contaminated sites.

Disposals at Drigg are carried out under the terms of an authorisation granted under the Radioactive Substances Act. This authorisation is subject to periodic re-examination by the Environment Agency, with the next formal review to be conducted in 2002. BNFL is therefore currently concluding its strategy for development of the next iteration of the Drigg Post-Closure Safety Case (PCSC), to be submitted in support of the Company's application. It is planned that an interim safety case, including a description of the approach and illustrative calculations, should be presented in March 2000.

The UK authorising agencies have published principles and requirements for disposal facilities in their Guidance on Requirements for Authorisation (GRA) [Environment Agency *et al.*, 1997]. The GRA is explicit in its assertion that the numerical evaluation of risk alone cannot provide a sufficient basis to assure safety. Nevertheless, the central importance of potential long-term radiological impacts to the overall safety case for a disposal facility means that particular emphasis is inevitably attached to the derivation of quantitative measures of long-term safety performance, notably annual individual risk from exposure to radiation. Moreover, the expectation is that a comprehensive safety case should comprise an evaluation (although not necessarily a detailed computation) of all potential sources of radiological risk, rather than simply addressing in isolation particular areas of uncertainty or technical concern.

The uncertainties inherent in quantitative analyses of long-term performance mean that results are to be considered as representative indicators of safety, rather than definitive predictions of future radiological impact. The Post-Closure Radiological Assessment (PCRA) being developed for Drigg needs to deliver a comprehensive, quantitative appraisal of long-term safety performance, while also recognising the intrinsic limitations of the calculations on which it is based. The overall objective is to present a set of calculations that is sufficiently representative to provide an effective basis for decision making.

2. Accounting for Uncertainties – the Need for a Systematic Approach

UK regulatory guidance notes that "the treatment of uncertainty is central to the establishment of the post-closure safety case for a radioactive waste disposal system" (Environment Agency *et al.*, 1997). Such uncertainty may be associated with, inter alia, natural variability, the practical limitations on sampling of relevant processes and data, alternative interpretations of data and natural events and human activities that may affect radionuclide release, transport and exposure pathways. It is recognised that uncertainties will be addressed and assimilated into the safety case in a variety of ways, and that only some are likely to be amenable to quantitative treatment in a numerical assessment of risk.

It is useful here to identify two main groups of uncertainties: those corresponding to the state and behaviour of the disposal system and its environment at the start of the assessment calculations, and those relating to its future evolution. The former are sometimes known as "conceptual" uncertainties, the latter as "future" uncertainties. It is convenient to further divide these into uncertainties related to phenomena (i.e. whether or not all relevant features, events and processes (FEPs) are adequately represented) and those corresponding to parameters (i.e. limitations to the accuracy with which relevant FEPs can be quantitatively characterised). The structure of an assessment calculation will generally involve considering and justifying the approach taken to the treatment of phenomenological uncertainty first and then subsequently addressing parameter uncertainty within the context established by the selected conceptual models.

Against this background, the adoption of a systematic assessment framework is intended to provide a formal basis for exposing to scrutiny the logic of the underlying assumptions leading to the evaluation of a PCSC. This helps to provide assurance that the assessment has effectively addressed all potentially relevant FEPs and taken account of the ways in which combinations of these FEPs might produce qualitatively different outcomes. In addition, a systematic approach should provide the setting for demonstrating how uncertainties have been addressed and assimilated into the safety case.

3. Development of a Systematic Approach for the Drigg PCRA

Systematic approaches for PCRA, developed in the UK and internationally, have been reviewed by BNFL as a basis for the Drigg PCRA. There is only limited experience of the application of such methods in the context of shallow disposal facilities, and BNFL is therefore participating actively in the IAEA's ISAM programme [ISAM, 1997]. At the same time, the potential applicability of systematic and formal methods for the management of both future uncertainty and conceptual uncertainty, originally developed in the context of deep disposal (see, for example, [NEA, 1992; SKI, 1996; BIOMASS, 1998]), has been assessed.

The approach developed for the Drigg PCRA incorporates a range of activities required to deliver a comprehensive assessment, based on a clear identification and description of the underlying assessment context. This approach includes a framework for interpretation and assessment of risks from groundwater, gas and potential human intrusion pathways; a treatment of uncertainty; and an evaluation of the significance of optimisation in the context of PCRA. Systematic methods of acquiring and processing information are being developed and employed alongside traditional methods of scientific reasoning and expert judgement. These methods allow for a thorough evaluation of potential risks and for the identification of those risks that warrant detailed analysis using mathematical models. The assessment approach combines qualitative and quantitative studies and, by means of multiple and complementary lines of reasoning, provides for a comprehensive evaluation of the likely, long-term radiological performance of the Drigg disposal facility.

Because PCRA inevitably involves making assumptions and choices, the question arises as to how these choices may be justified. Scientifically-informed expert judgment is clearly fundamental to guiding the development of descriptions of the disposal facility and its future behaviour. However, judgments also need to be made in the context of certain fundamental premises of assessment.

One basic proposition is that the aim of the assessment should be to address as comprehensively as possible all those risks relevant to the disposal facility. These risks and their corresponding FEPs need to be prioritised and organised based on best scientific judgment regarding their potential significance. In accordance with international practice [BIOMASS, 1998; ISAM, 1998] the vehicle for this includes the systematic screening of an independent FEP list. Within such a framework, the principal basis for determining relevance is a set of arguments developed from the site context and overall assessment context (its purpose, the endpoints under consideration, etc). A FEP may be excluded on the basis that either its likelihood or impact is minimal. However, such FEPs may still need to be considered qualitatively, or by means of scoping calculations, in order to justify the position adopted. Alternatively, arguments may be developed to show that a relevant FEP can be subsumed within another for the purposes of PCRA. The systematic recording of how FEPs have been assessed through each stage of the procedure is an important element of the PCRA.

The framework proposed by BNFL and co-workers adopts a scenario-based approach to addressing future uncertainty. Scenarios are designed to correspond to "broad brush" descriptions of the future evolution of the system and associated environmental conditions, based on an analysis of how such futures might arise. It is emphasised that scenario analysis does not try to predict the future; rather, the aim is to identify salient changes, based on analysis of trends, within which variants are explored to investigate the importance of particular sources of uncertainty. The emphasis is therefore on providing meaningful *illustrations* to assist the decision process [Chapman *et al.*, 1995]. Moreover, although it is helpful to aim for plausibility in constructing scenarios, it is recognised that some deliberately "unrealistic" realisations (eg assuming no environmental change) are useful as aids to discussion.

A primary feature of the scenario-based approach is the classification of potentially relevant FEPs in two categories: those that are associated with the disposal system domain (the "Process System") and those that are treated as external, or scenario-generating FEPs (EFEPs). If an independent list of all potentially relevant FEPs is regarded as defining the overall scope of what needs to be addressed in the assessment, comprehensiveness will then be demonstrated within that framework. Fundamental considerations therefore include identification of the boundary of the Process System, the important components either side of that boundary and their interrelationships.

The management of conceptual uncertainty is then addressed through the development of model descriptions of the disposal facility and its environment. Systematic methods are necessary to demonstrate not only that all relevant FEPs are adequately represented in the assessment models, but that the modelling approach allows all potentially significant legitimate interpretations of the configuration of the Process System to be represented. For example, there may be uncertainties linked to the absence of a definitive final design (depth of cap, presence of cut-off walls, etc.) for the disposal facility. In addition, the limitations of available site characterisation information may be such that there are alternative interpretations of potential pathways from the waste to the accessible environment.

Based on the above considerations, the following elements of a systematic assessment framework for PCSC can be identified:

- Use of a comprehensive FEP list as the primary reference point for assuring coverage of issues that may be relevant to a PCSC. The subsequent augmentation, screening and categorisation of such a list generates an audit trail, allowing the logic of arguments supporting the definition of models and calculation cases to be scrutinised effectively.

- Clear definition of the overall assessment context (disposal system, assessment purpose, endpoints, etc), constituting the fundamental basis on which all other assumptions, simplifications and hypotheses relating to the assessment will be developed and justified.

- Definition of the extent, nature and content of the Process System to be analysed, thereby enabling all potentially relevant FEPs to be categorised either as "Process System" or "External" FEPs for the purposes of the assessment.

- Structured review of EFEPs, taking into account prescribed screening arguments and the overall assessment context, serving as the basis for distinguishing those external factors that represent significant controls on long-term evolution of the disposal system. Such a review, coupled with the output from modelling studies and simulations of the effects of, for example, climate change, then guides the systematic identification and development of scenarios for a PCSC.

- Development and justification of alternative conceptualisations of the Process System, based on its component features and characteristics, and an appraisal of potential pathways of release from the waste to the environment.

- Identification, screening and organisation of FEPs that are relevant to modelling the behaviour of the Process System, taking into account the disposal system context, the scenarios under consideration and the required indicators of safety performance. Mapping of the identified FEPs and FEP relationships onto those incorporated in conceptual and mathematical models for safety assessment.

- Derivation of representative sets of calculation cases from the selected conceptual models and scenarios, based on the assumed initial state and evolution of the system for each scenario. This also includes the identification of relevant data sources and methods for dealing with parameter uncertainty.

The overall framework for the Drigg PCRA is illustrated in Figure 1. In this Figure, the rectangular boxes represent the basic information used to identify and justify assumptions in relation to the comprehensive treatment of uncertainties associated with each stage of the assessment. The steps in the assessment framework via which such decisions are made and recorded are indicated by the octagonal boxes.

4. Basis for Scenario Identification

An important feature of the scenario-based approach is that necessary assumptions underlying the combination of quantitative analysis and qualitative judgment in the description of system evolution should be exposed and amenable to scrutiny [ISAM, 1997]. The aim is to present the assessment in a manner that is open to examination, confirming that the system has been comprehensively assessed and that choices and assumptions made in response to uncertainties are suitably coherent and properly justified. Within the selected scenarios, uncertainties in the indicated safety performance can then be investigated through alternative realisations based on the simulated effect of different timings, severities and durations of critical events and processes.

A schematic illustration of the systematic approach to scenario identification is presented in Figure 2. This begins with the definition of the Process System domain and subsequent categorisation of FEPs into Process System FEPs and EFEPs. The EFEPs list derived from a reference list (e.g. ISAM) may need to be elaborated and augmented for a site-specific assessment context. Then, based on defined screening arguments, those EFEPs that are deemed relevant to the disposal system environment and the overall assessment context are identified.

It is helpful to identify the basic arguments used in the process of screening EFEPs for their relevance to scenario identification. Screening is largely based on reference to a clear understanding and description of the assumed assessment basis (e.g. the site context, the approach taken to describing future human communities, etc.). For example, part of the basis for PCRA is that the disposal system is constructed, operated and completed as planned – it is for other aspects of the safety case to demonstrate that these are reasonable assumptions. The screening arguments currently anticipated for application to the Drigg PCRA include the following.

- Physically implausible given the timescale of the assessment (e.g. orogeny and volcanic activity).

- Physically implausible given the site context (e.g. geothermal effects).

- Rate or probability small relative to other EFEPs (e.g. large meteorite impact).

- Global disaster (e.g. extreme global warming creating a tropical/desert climate at Sellafield).

- Included elsewhere (e.g. human impacts on climate change).

- Excluded by regulatory guidance (e.g. technological development).

- Excluded by assessment basis (e.g. species evolution).

Outline scenario descriptions are then arrived at following consideration of interactions between FEPs within the EFEPs system. Such interactions need to be considered at an appropriate level of detail. At a high level, interactions can be represented as shown in Figure 3. However, to be useful, interactions need to be studied at a lower level. Generally, this will involve the characterising EFEPs by their attributes and the listing of the possible states for each attribute. A supporting programme of work provides the scientific and phenomenological understanding (relating to the potential magnitude, sequence of timing of changes) necessary to justify the development of illustrative scenarios and scenario variants in this way.

The approach taken in the disaggregation of EFEPs is illustrated by Figure 4. Here, climate change is represented in the form of a sequence of climate states defined according to a set of rules informed by modelling simulations and analogue studies tailored to the Drigg site. These rules relate to both the definition of climate states and their sequencing. The linkages between climate state and, for example, sea level, hydrology and land use are described such that postulated futures comprise self-consistent patterns of change. Figure 4 places the scenarios development study of Watts and Kane [1998] under a systematic framework of EFEP and scenario analysis.

The principle of subsuming is important in the process of scenario definition and selection. EFEPs may be excluded from detailed consideration because their significance in absolute terms is judged minimal, because they are implicitly included elsewhere, or because their substantial significance is similar to, or subsumed by, that of another. This involves making and documenting judgments regarding the relative importance of each included EFEP (e.g. by reference to scientific understanding of their likelihood or potential significance) in order to define a reduced list relevant to detailed scenario characterisation. Such judgments are particularly relevant in the context of assessing the multitude of possibilities associated with future human actions that could potentially compromise the integrity of the disposal system. However, they can also be pertinent in the broader context of system evolution. For example, the potential influence of human actions on climate is subsumed in the projections of future climate that support scenario development, through the use of research models that address changes in the composition of the atmosphere and albedo of the ground surface under alternative projections of future anthropogenic greenhouse-gas emissions, taking into account uncertainties in the response of the climate system to such emissions.

5. Scenarios for Future Evolution of the Drigg Site

The EFEPs model shown in simplified form in Figure 4 is capable of generating a very large number of possible futures. Although EFEP attribute states are discretised and the combinations of EFEP attributes are constrained by physically-based rules, the number of different possibilities is still very large. Fortunately, when the assessment context is taken into consideration, the number of qualitatively distinct classes of climate change futures is more limited. This is also true of corresponding landscape change futures at the level of detail required.

Drigg is a near-surface disposal facility located near to the coast, close to the Ravenglass estuary and more or less in line with the former path of the Wasdale valley glacier. As such, the analysis of futures for the site emphasises certain EFEPs (glaciation and coastal erosion) as being of particular interest because they provide convenient endpoints for qualitatively distinctive natural evolution scenarios. These are:

- Central Projection Scenario (CPS) of observed climatic variability with committed greenhouse warming, terminated by glaciation at 50ka;

- Coastal Erosion Scenario (CES) in which human influence on climate produces a rise in sea level and accelerated coastal erosion that eventually destroys the site.

The CPS starts with an initial period during which limited greenhouse warming produces a small rise in sea level and corresponding adjustments to the site water balance and agriculture. This is followed by a monotonically cooling climate sequence over tens of thousands of years, passing through boreal and tundra conditions and culminating in glaciation. Sea level falls substantially during this period causing the hydrogeological system to respond and completely changing the pattern of discharge of potentially contaminated groundwater. With a large fall in sea level, the landscape is transformed and all the attributes associated with it assume qualitatively different states. Short-term fluctuations in climate state and oscillations in sea level are not represented, on the basis that they are not directly relevant to an illustration of the significance of overall trends. The uncertainties associated with the response of the process system to this scenario are to be systematically investigated.

A variant on the CPS is the Deferred Glaciation Scenario (DGS). Here, the natural evolution of climate is perturbed by human influence to a greater extent than in the CPS, delaying the onset of glaciation until 100 ka or more into the future. The initial period of enhanced warmed climate is both more developed and longer lasting than in the CPS. The agricultural and hydrological responses are similarly greater than in the CPS. A cooling climate trend eventually sets in, but sea level fall and

138

corresponding discharges of contaminant to the terrestrial environment are deferred, as is the onset of glaciation.

With the CES, the initially enhanced warmed climate state gives rise to a sea level rise that results in the destruction of the site by coastal erosion. A quantitative model of coastal processes is not currently available and there is little guidance as to the timing of such an event, given a particular configuration of the EFEPs model. Variants on the CES, based on alternative assumptions regarding the rate of coastline regression will therefore allow the significance of this uncertainty to be reported on within the PCRA.

Superimposed on these basic descriptions of the likely natural evolution of the Process System, a number of alternative scenarios are being developed. These correspond to potentially significant, but rare, natural events and processes (e.g. major seismic events) as well as those EFEPs that are associated with future human actions (see Figure 3). Again, the emphasis is on using systematically derived scenarios as representative illustrations (rather than predictions) of alternative, qualitatively distinct, futures and their effects on a PCSC.

6.   Reference Case

Within the assessment framework developed for Drigg, the term "scenario" is associated solely with the consideration of EFEPs and their potential impacts on the Process System. Consideration of the anticipated natural evolution of the disposal system and its environment provides a necessary central theme in reporting on the radiological performance of the disposal facility within the PCSC. Nevertheless, an assessment of the safety performance for the Process System alone, independent of the influence of EFEPs, constitutes a useful benchmark against which the significance of other results can be compared. Moreover, although unrealistic in neglecting environmental change, the relative simplicity of such a calculation means that it represents a practical basis for exploring sensitivities to parameter and modelling uncertainties.

Analysis of such a "Reference Case" therefore provides a basis for evaluating the potential significance of conceptual model uncertainties or alternative engineering options. Variant realisations of the Reference Case can be envisaged, in which different initial conditions, or different representations of Process System FEPs, are used to investigate the effects of different assumptions on system performance. A series of Reference Case examples can therefore be anticipated as part of the overall suite of assessment calculations. The extent to which such calculations generate qualitative different outcomes in terms of post-closure safety performance will play a part in determining the detailed environmental evolution scenarios and scenario variants that are to be evaluated.

References

BIOMASS (1998). Long-term Releases from Solid Waste Disposal Facilities: The Reference Biosphere Concept. BIOMASS Theme 1, Working Document No.1, IAEA, Vienna.

Chapman N, Andersson J, Robinson P, Skagius K, Wene C-O, Wiborgh M and Wingefors S (1995). Systems Analysis, Scenario Construction and Consequence Analysis Definition for SITE-94. SKI TR 95:26, Swedish Nuclear Power Inspectorate, Stockholm.

Environment Agency, Scottish Environment Protection Agency and Department of the Environment for Northern Ireland (1997). Disposal Facilities on Land for Low and Intermediate Level Radioactive Wastes: Guidance on Requirements for Authorisation. HMSO, London.

ISAM (1997). ISAM – The International Programme for Improving Long-term Safety Assessment Methodologies for Near-surface Radioactive Waste Disposal Facilities. Objectives, Content and Work Programme. ISAM Document ISAM/G/0197, Final Version, International Atomic Energy Agency, Vienna.

ISAM (1998). Development of an Information System for Features, Events and Processes (FEPs) and Generic Scenarios for the Safety Assessment of Near-surface Radioactive Waste Disposal Facilities. Report of the Scenario Generation and Justification Working Group, ISAM Document SWG/0198, Version 0.1, June 1998.

NEA (1992). Safety Assessment of Radioactive Waste Repositories: Systematic Approaches to Scenario Development. A Report of the NEA Working Group on the Identification and Selection of Scenarios for Performance Assessment of Radioactive Waste Disposal. Nuclear Energy Agency, OECD, Paris.

SKI (1996). SKI SITE-94. Deep Repository Performance Assessment Project (2 volumes). SKI report 96:36. Swedish Nuclear Power Inspectorate, Stockholm.

Watts L and Kane P (1998). Development of Scenarios and Conceptual Models in Support of a Post-Closure Radiological Safety Assessment of the Drigg Near-Surface Low Level Waste Disposal Site. Proc of Int Conf on Radioactive Waste Disposal: Disposal Technologies and Concepts (DisTec'98). Hamburg, September 1998. 330-337.

Figure 1. Outline Framework for the Drigg Post-Closure Radiological Assessment

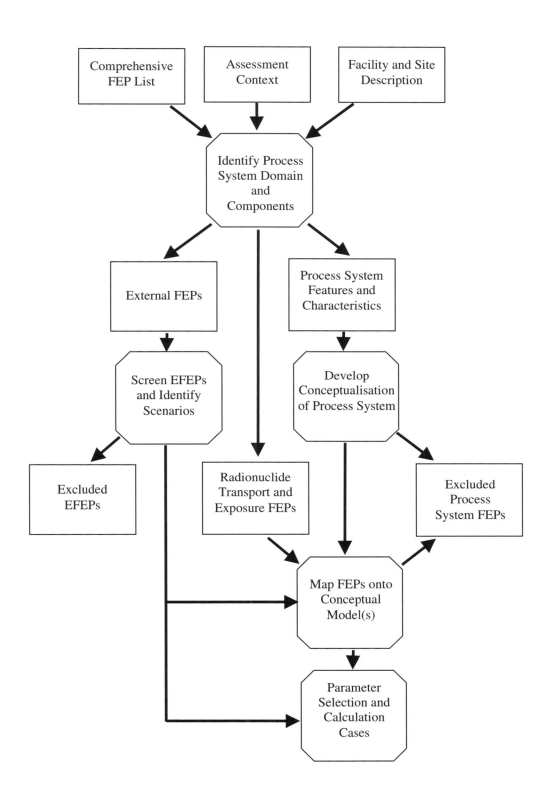

Figure 2. **Outline Framework for the Derivation of Futures**

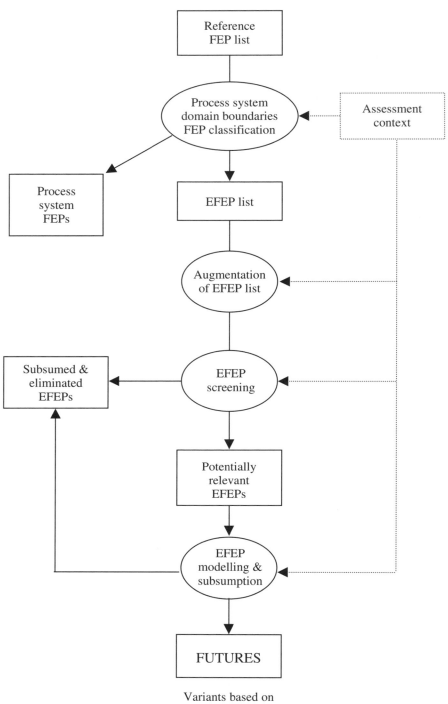

Variants based on
Magnitude / timing / sequencing

Figure 3. **External FEPs Overview**

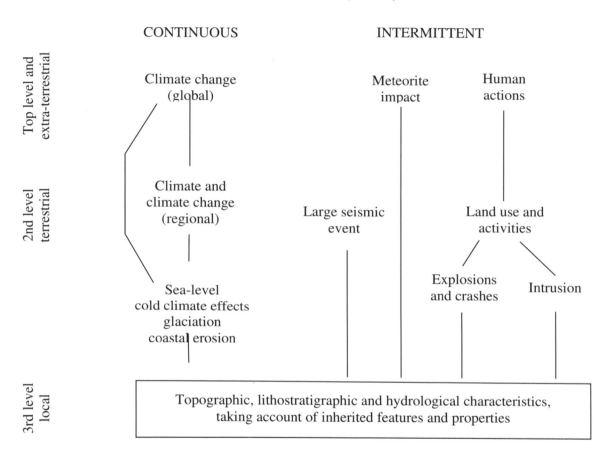

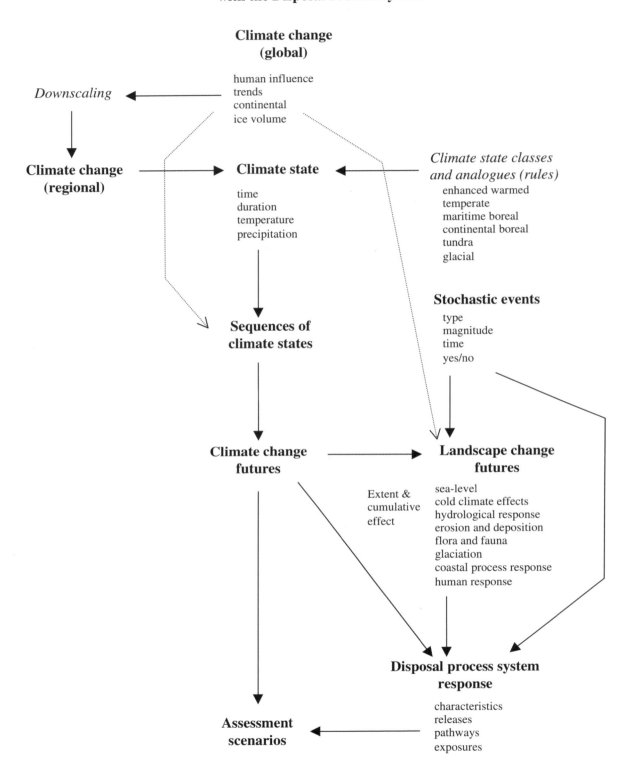

Figure 4. **Schematic Representation of the Drigg EFEPs Model and Interactions with the Disposal Process System**

Paper 7

SYSTEMATIC APPROACH TO SCENARIO DEVELOPMENT USING FEP ANALYSIS

L.E.F. Bailey[1] and D.A. Lever[2]
[1]United Kingdom Nirex Limited
[2]AEA Technology plc

1.   Introduction

UK regulatory requirements [1] require that the "assessed radiological risk … to a representative member of the potentially exposed group[1] at greatest risk should be consistent with a risk target of 10^{-6} per year" and that risks should be "summed over all situations that could give rise to exposure to the group". It is a further requirement that a repository performance assessment provides a "comprehen-sive record of the judgements and assumptions on which the risk assessments are based." In order to meet these requirements, Nirex, working with AEA Technology, has developed an approach to performance assessment based on the identification and analysis of features, events and processes (FEPs).

The objectives of the approach are to provide a comprehensive, traceable and clear presentation of a performance assessment for a deep geological radioactive waste repository. The approach to scenario development is fundamental to the overall Nirex strategy for performance assessment, eventually leading to a repository safety case for regulatory submission. This approach is described in Reference [2] and summarised in Figure 1. This paper outlines the main concepts of the approach, illustrated with examples of work undertaken by Nirex to demonstrate its practicality. Due to the current status of the Nirex repository programme, the approach has not yet been used to conduct a full performance assessment of a repository located at a specific site.

2.   Overview of the Approach

The Nirex disposal concept, a cementitious repository, historically considered to be located in a saturated, fractured hard rock site, forms the starting point for any assessment. It is then necessary to identify all the FEPs which are potentially relevant to the long-term performance of the disposal concept.

FEPs can be classified as either *system FEPs*, those that are certain to exist or occur during the timescale of the assessment, or *probabilistic FEPs*, whose occurrence can be characterised by a

---

1.   For a given radiation source, a potentially exposed group is any group of members of the public within which the potential exposure to radiation is reasonably homogeneous. UK regulatory guidance requires assessment of the risks to individual members of a range of potentially exposed groups in order to identify the group at greatest risk.

probability of less than one. The system FEPs, together with those probabilistic FEPs which are judged more likely than not to persist for a significant part of the assessment period, are used to define a *base scenario*. The base scenario is a broad-ranging representation of the natural evolution of the repository system and its surrounding environment. The remaining probabilistic FEPs are reviewed to identify those that potentially initiate a *variant scenario* (termed *scenario-defining FEPs*), and those which might follow the activation of a scenario-defining FEP (termed *scenario FEPs*).

An important feature of the Nirex approach is the focus on the base scenario and it is anticipated that the assessment of the base scenario would form the core of the presentation of a detailed performance assessment. The base scenario also forms the platform for the development of the variant scenarios, whose scope is defined by the addition of certain scenario-defining and scenario FEPs to the base scenario.

In considering which FEPs to carry forward into variant scenarios, it is recognised that some of the scenario-defining FEPs have similar characteristics. It has been found helpful to group the corresponding single-FEP variant scenarios together into a scenario class. A scenario class is defined as a set of scenarios with common characteristics relevant to the mathematical modelling of system performance. The scenario-defining FEPs have been categorised into the scenario classes listed in Table 1. This forms the basis for selecting representative variant scenarios defined by a single scenario-defining FEP.

This leads to a staged assessment approach (as illustrated in Figure 1), in which the base scenario is considered first, followed by variant scenarios defined by a single scenario-defining FEP, and finally assessment of the so-called *multi-FEP* variant scenarios.

The scenario development approach is based upon a cautious treatment of uncertain events, seeking to ensure that no contributions to overall risk are neglected. The approach is cautious because a weight[2] of unity is assigned to the base scenario. This cautious assumption means that any variant scenario which has a conditional risk not exceeding that of the base scenario can be subsumed into the base scenario without losing any contribution to the overall risk. As a result of this it is necessary only to carry out limited analysis, e.g. by simple scoping calculations or expert judgement, for those variant scenarios judged to give peak risks less than those associated with the base scenario. This enables resources to be focused on those areas most relevant to safety. In particular weights only need to be assessed for those variant scenarios giving rise to risks in excess of the base scenario.

3.   The MDD

The first stage in the identification of scenarios is the elicitation of relevant FEPs from expert group sessions and from any available international FEP lists. The aim of this stage is to develop a set of FEPs to a sufficient level of detail to form the basis of scenario identification and conceptual model development. This requires building a database describing the properties and potential impacts of all the identified FEPs. To facilitate considerations of the interactions between FEPs, they are structured using a directed diagram, known as the Master Directed Diagram (MDD) [3]. FEPs are decomposed to lower levels by asking the question "what do I need in order to know about this FEP?" The aim is to be comprehensive at each level, that is to include coverage of all relevant FEPs at an appropriate of detail. The top few levels of the MDD are illustrated in Figure 2. Below these levels the MDD

---

2. The term "weight" is preferred to "probability" because scenario weights are not constrained to obey the mathematical laws of probability.

branches to consider all areas relevant to the performance of a deep geological repository, for example, there are branches covering the engineered system, geosphere and biosphere. Many FEPs, such as those relating to radionuclide transport processes, are relevant to several areas of the disposal system and hence occur in more than one branch of the MDD. For this reason, although the MDD has a tree-structure at the higher levels, it is actually a network.

Nirex started its FEP analysis programme in 1994. The early stages of the work focused on a series of expert group meetings at which FEPs were elicited and structured on the MDD. In order to achieve the necessary breadth of expertise, this was a resource-intensive process, typically involving 6-8 experts per meeting. As the MDD took shape, it became appropriate for smaller groups of experts to develop particular areas of the MDD, typically in groups of 2-3. It is estimated that a total of around 1 000 man-days was spent in constructing the MDD and FEP database and identifying the scenario-defining FEPs. One of the challenges in constructing the MDD was maintaining a consistent level of detail across different components of the disposal system. It is important to have a common understanding of the appropriate level of detail to which the MDD should be developed; it was found that this was best achieved by involving at least one expert with high-level assessment experience of the overall system at each of the expert group sessions.

A computer program, FANFARE, has been developed by AEA Technology, to facilitate the handling of the MDD and the underlying FEP database. FANFARE is a tool which enables all decisions to be recorded "on-line" during expert-group meetings.

Development of the MDD is not an isolated activity; the MDD is an organic tool, to which changes and additions are made as it is used for the subsequent scenario analysis. To date, Nirex has used the MDD to define the scope of the base scenario [4] and to group the FEPs within the base scenario into identifiable sub-systems, defined as conceptual models.

Although the MDD illustrates the hierarchical interactions between FEPs, it does not display all the lateral interactions. For this purpose, an influence matrix is constructed. The diagonal elements of the matrix diagram represent the conceptual models and the off-diagonal elements describe their interactions. The MDD and matrix diagram are together used to record understanding of the FEPs and their interactions, in a structured framework that shows the impact on repository performance and form the basic building blocks for model development. Existing modelling capability was audited against the conceptual models to identify any areas requiring further model development [5].

4.   The Base Scenario

The base scenario represents the "natural" evolution of the system, including evolution of the engineered barriers and the effects of climate change. The base scenario represents potential pathways which may lead to exposures to repository-derived radiation as a result of the natural system evolution. These pathways include the groundwater pathway, with both natural discharge and discharge to small-size wells; and the gas pathway. Other potential exposure pathways may occur following the initiation of certain scenario-defining FEPs, which would be considered within the scope of appropriate variant scenarios.

Nirex has not performed a full assessment of the base scenario using the FEP analysis approach, however, the identified scope of the base scenario broadly encompasses the level of detail considered in the Nirex 97 assessment of the Sellafield site [6]. This assessment required around 2 000 man-days to complete the technical work. The proposed approach to scenario development places a strong focus on the base scenario. In a detailed performance assessment, such as would be required for a regulatory licensing application, it is envisaged that approximately half of the assessment resource would be expended on the base scenario.

5. Single-FEP Variant Scenarios

Having assessed the base scenario, the next stage is to identify single-FEP variant scenarios (see Figure 1). These scenarios are characterised by a sequence of events, initiated by a single scenario-defining FEP. The example considered here is that of drilling a large well. The sequence of events can be represented by a *timeline*. A timeline displays the scenario-defining FEP and the associated subsequent system characteristics (defined by the scenario FEPs), showing the order and timing of these characteristics relative to the initiation of the scenario-defining FEP. Figure 3 illustrates a timeline for a well drilling scenario and the first two columns of Table 2 describe the evolution of this scenario, it is described in more detail in Reference [7]. A timeline represents one possible evolution of the system following the initiation of the scenario-defining FEP. It may be possible to envisage alternative evolutions, for example, the well may be abandoned without pumping, leading to the definition of alternative timelines.

The aim is to identify a range of scenario timelines which represent all potential evolutions of the system which are relevant to its long-term performance. Peak conditional risks to members of the potentially exposed groups are calculated for each interval along the timeline, and weights are assigned. It may be appropriate to assign different weights to different time intervals, as the relevant question is not "What is the probability of this scenario?", but, for example, "What is the probability that a well is drilled in any one year?"

In the trial demonstration undertaken by Nirex to date [7], risks were estimated using scoping calculations and by comparison with the detailed calculations undertaken in the Nirex 97 assessment [6], see Table 2. This enables identification of those intervals which would require detailed calculation in a full performance assessment.

6. Multi-FEP Variant Scenarios

Having assessed scenarios developed from a single scenario-defining FEP, it is necessary to consider which potential combinations of scenario-defining FEPs could lead to scenarios which would make a significant contribution to the overall radiological risk associated with a repository. By definition, all scenario-defining FEPs are independent of each other (dependent FEPs would have been classified as scenario FEPs), hence it is only necessary to consider those combinations where co-existence could result in a conditional risk exceeding that from either of the underlying single-FEP scenarios. Multi-FEP variants which do not give rise to conditional risks exceeding that of the underlying single-FEP variants are subsumed into the single-FEP variants.

An initial demonstration of combining several scenario-defining FEPs to define a multi-FEP variant scenario has been undertaken. The first step is the construction of a joint timeline from the timelines for two scenario-defining FEPs. The example chosen is that of drilling a large-scale well, as discussed above, and the occurrence of a large seismic event.

For a large seismic event two possible scenario evolutions are envisaged. In the first, a significant volume of water is "shunted" through the system, and the distance moved by the water is small compared to the depth of the repository; however, flow-rates are enhanced for a period. Such an event is judged to occur once in every 10^5 years (i.e. an annual probability of 10^{-5}). In the second, a significant volume of water is moved from the depth of the repository along a transmissive fault into the near-surface aquifer. Such an event is judged to occur with an annual probability of 3×10^{-8}. An assessment of the evolution of a large seismic event scenario is described in Reference [7].

When combining timelines associated with two single-FEP variants, the total number of potential event sequences can be substantial. The event sequences are generated automatically by considering the two timelines "passing" each other (see Figure 4) and those which are not feasible are eliminated. Sequences are identified in an order such that adjacent sequences differ only in the ordering of a single pair of events. If the ordering of these events does not significantly affect the performance of the system, the sequences can be aggregated, by subsuming the one with the lower conditional risk into the more significant sequence. This process is summarised in Figure 5 and described in detail in Reference [7].

Each aggregated sequence defines a new timeline. By considering the characteristics of successive intervals in the sequence, it is possible to simplify the timeline. For example, in terms of the conditional risks to the "farmers and families" potentially exposed group, the short period of well drilling may be combined with the much longer period during which the well is pumped. The drilling period would be subsumed into the pumping period as the latter gives rise to the higher conditional risk. However, for "site workers", the drilling period has the higher conditional risk and hence cannot be subsumed into the pumping period. This demonstrates the importance of taking all decisions in relation to a defined potentially exposed group.

If two intervals on a timeline, each with an assigned conditional risk and weight, are merged, the conditional risk associated with the combined interval will be the higher conditional risk from the two intervals and the weight of the combined interval will be the sum of the weights of the merged intervals. This is a cautious approach which will over-estimate the overall risk contribution, but is adopted to make the assessment tractable and ensure resources are focused on areas most significant to safety. It is desirable to reduce the number of sequences as far as possible to minimise the number of timelines that have to be carried forward for combination with timelines associated with other scenario-defining FEPs.

Figure 6 illustrates how timelines may be simplified for the well drilling and seismic event scenarios. Further analysis of combinations of these simplified timelines leads to only two sequences that require further consideration, as shown in Table 3. Sequence "1AC3D5F" signifies well pumping during the plume-displacement period and sequence "AC13D5F" represents well pumping during the period of enhanced groundwater flow. It has been shown that all other potential sequences can be subsumed into one of these combined sequences or into one of the parent single-FEP scenarios [7].

Timelines for scenarios defined by more than two scenario-defining FEPs are constructed by repeating the above process, starting with the joint timelines developed from combining single-FEP variants.

The task of aggregating and simplifying timelines was performed by groups of 3-4 experts in performance assessment. To date, approximately 50 man-days have been spent trialling the process. The next step would involve undertaking detailed assessment calculations for the set of combined scenario timelines shown to encompass all significant aspects of the long-term performance of a repository.

7. Presentation of a Performance Assessment based on Scenario Analysis

The performance assessment strategy described leads to peak conditional risks and weights for scenario intervals for each of the identified potentially exposed groups. These conditional risks and weights can be displayed on a "weight-risk" diagram, as illustrated in Figure 7, to assess the relative importance of scenarios. The two axes of the diagram display the conditional risk associated with the scenario or scenario interval, and its estimated weight. The uncertainties in these two quantities are indicated by error bars. In practice, due to the cautious approach adopted throughout the assessment, the uncertainties will extend predominantly below the best estimates and hence it is considered appropriate to consider the best-estimate values within the assessment. Separate weight-risk diagrams are developed for each potentially exposed group.

The weight-risk diagram can be used as a decision-aiding tool throughout a performance assessment. In the initial stages, when scoping calculations are most likely to be used to obtain initial evaluations of the conditional risks and weights associated with scenarios, the uncertainties in these values may be considerable. The weight-risk diagram provides a clear presentation of whether it is the conditional risk, weight, or the uncertainty in either or both of these values that is of most significance to the repository safety case. Further research and assessment can then be focused on resolving those issues of most relevance to post-closure safety.

As the assessment progresses, conditional risks and weights associated with important scenarios are evaluated more carefully and the weight-risk diagram is refined appropriately.

Some scenarios may be eliminated from further detailed consideration at an early stage in an assessment because their conditional risk, even allowing for uncertainties, is less than that expected from the base scenario. Such scenarios will appear to the left of the base scenario on the weight-risk diagram and their effect can be subsumed into the base scenario. As the weight-risk diagram is refined, through more detailed calculations, uncertainties would be expected to be reduced and hence there should be scope for subsuming further scenarios.

The set of weight-risk diagrams, including their evolution over the assessment cycles, would form an important element of the presentation of the performance assessment. It is also expected that the presentation will include a number of risk-time curves, particularly for the base scenario, which will have been produced in order to calculate the peak conditional risks.

8. Conclusions

The described scenario approach to performance assessment seeks to consider at an appropriate level of detail all situations that could result in exposure to repository derived radionuclides. The advantages of the approach are as follows:

- The FEP analysis stage is comprehensive and leads to a structured database of FEPs relevant to the performance of the disposal system.

- All FEPs identified on the MDD are considered either within the scope of the base scenario or are associated with one or more of the scenario-defining FEPs. All scenario-defining FEPs are either developed into single-FEP variant scenarios or are subsumed within another scenario. This maintains the comprehensiveness achieved at the FEP analysis stage.

- The approach focuses on the assessment of the base scenario, which is defined to be broad-ranging, encompassing the natural evolution of the system. By cautiously assigning the base scenario a weight of unity, it is possible to subsume all scenarios with consequences not exceeding that of the base scenario into the base scenario, thus making the assessment task tractable.

- The development of the scenario timeline approach is believed to provide an efficient framework for assessing the impact of time-dependent event sequences. In effect, an assessment is performed for each interval along the timeline. This avoids the need for a full time-simulation of the system evolution and only those intervals leading to higher consequences than the base scenario require detailed assessment.

- A systematic approach has been developed for combining timelines. Potential event sequences are generated automatically and then systematically reviewed to aggregate intervals and simplify the timelines wherever possible. In the examples undertaken to date, it has been possible to identify a small number of simplified timelines which represent all significant impacts of the FEP combinations on the repository performance.

- The iterative approach and the use of scoping calculations and expert judgement in the early stages, ensures that resources are focused on those areas most relevant to the long-term safety of a repository, with less significant scenarios being subsumed prior to detailed calculations. However, the systematic recording of all subsuming decisions means a complete audit trail is maintained, detailing the treatment of each FEP.

- It is therefore believed that a tractable approach, addressing the UK regulatory requirement to consider all situations that could give rise to radiological exposures, has been achieved.

However, it is recognised that completing the task will require considerable resources, both in terms of expert group meetings and the development of computational models to represent FEP interactions at the appropriate level of detail. The main challenges presented by the approach are as follows:

- Heavy reliance is placed on expert groups, for the initial identification of FEPs and structuring of the MDD and the subsequent simplification of timelines for variant scenarios. Confidence in the output from the expert groups has been achieved by comparing the MDD with international FEP lists and by conducting independent peer reviews at key stages of the approach, culminating in a recent review of the complete methodology by an international team of experts under the auspices of the OECD/NEA.

- It is necessary to undertake a full assessment of the base scenario, including the impact of time-dependent effects such as climate change; and a full assessment of all scenario intervals which cannot be subsumed. It is also necessary to calculate appropriate weights for these scenario intervals. This represents a major assessment undertaking, however, it is believed that such an assessment would be required for a repository licensing application, whatever performance assessment methodology was followed. The advantages of the proposed approach is that it provides a framework for justifying the scenarios considered in an assessment.

References

1. Environment Agency, Scottish Environmental Protection Agency and Department of the Environment for Northern Ireland, *Disposal Facilities on Land for Low and Intermediate Level Radioactive Wastes: Guidance on Requirements for Authorisation (Radioactive Substances Act 1993)*, HMSO, London, 1997.

2. L.E.F. Bailey and D.E. Billington, *Overview of the FEP Analysis Approach to Model Development*, Nirex Science Report S/98/009, 1998.

3. M. Kelly and D.E. Billington, *Conceptual Basis of the Master Directed Diagram*, Nirex Science Report, S/98/010, 1998.

4. J. Locke and L.E.F. Bailey, *Overview Description of the Base Scenario Derived from FEP Analysis*, Nirex Science Report S/98/011, 1998.

5. J. Locke and L.E.F. Bailey, *Modelling Requirements for Future Assessments Based on FEP Analysis*, Nirex Science Report S/98/012, 1998.

6. *Nirex 97: An Assessment of the Post-closure Performance of a Deep Waste Repository at Sellafield*, Nirex Science Report S/97/012, 1997.

7. D.E. Billington and L.E.F. Bailey, *Development and Application of a Methodology for Identifying and Characterising Scenarios*, Nirex Science Report S/98/013, 1998.

Table 1. **Scenario-defining FEPs grouped by Scenario Class**

Wells and Boreholes for Resource Exploitation
HI: Agricultural Wells: Large Irrigation
HI: Commercial / Industrial Wells
HI: Wells for Fish Farm Supply
HI: Wells for Recreational Purposes
HI: Brine Abstraction during Borehole Operations
HI: Extraction of Cuttings from Boreholes
HI: Extraction of Drilling Cores from Boreholes
HI: Gas Abstraction during Borehole Operations
HI: NAPL Abstraction during Borehole Operations
HI: Solution Mining during Borehole Operations
Excavations of Large Underground Volumes
HI: Abandonment of Underground Excavations
HI: Construction & Abandonment of Underground Facilities
HI: Operation of Underground Facilities
Early Failure of Engineered Barriers
Container Fabrication Defect
Container Failure: Accidental Damage
Container Failure: Seal
Container Penetration before Closure
Criticality Incidents
Criticality in the ES
Disruption of the Geosphere and ES
Explosive Disruption of the ES
Magma: Deep Intrusion
Magma: Extrusion
Magma: Shallow Intrusion
Meteorite Impact: Repository Disruptive
Meteorite Impact: Repository Non-disruptive
Seismic Events (Note 1)

Notes

1. Very small seismic events occur regularly; their impact is taken into account in the base scenario. Larger, less frequent events are considered in variant scenarios.

HI   Human intrusion
NAPL   Non-aqueous phase liquids
ES   Engineered system

Table 2. Assessment of a Well Drilling Scenario

Interval	Characteristics	Weight (Note 2)	Peak Conditional Risk (yr^{-1}) (Note 1)					
			Farmers & families	Hunter/gatherers (Note 3)	Urban/suburban dwellers	Site developers	Drillers	Operator/Industrial workers
Before 1	Base scenario	1	**10^{-6}**	$5\,10^{-9}$	$<5\,10^{-8}$	$<10^{-10}$	–	–
1–2	Drill well	10^{-3}	**10^{-6}**	–	$<5\,10^{-8}$	$<10^{-10}$	$<10^{-10}$	–
2–3	Pump wells Maintain and refurbish wells as required.	10^{-1}	**$2\,10^{-6}$** (Note 4)	–	**$2\,10^{-6}$** (Note 5)	$\sim2\,10^{-8}$ (Note 6)	–	$\sim2\,10^{-8}$ (Note 6)
3–4	Abandon well, but hydrogeological memory of well retained	~1	**10^{-6}**	$5\,10^{-9}$	$<5\,10^{-8}$	$<10^{-10}$	–	–
4–5	Hydrogeological memory of well lost, return to base scenario	~1	**10^{-6}**	$5\,10^{-9}$	$<5\,10^{-8}$	$<10^{-10}$	–	–

Notes:
1. The potentially exposed group at greatest risk is indicated in bold.
2. Weights refer to the interval in question.
3. "Hunter/gatherers" would not be consistent with a society that drilled and pumped such wells.
4. Water with elevated radionuclide concentrations judged to enter well; scaling based on Nirex 97.
5. "Farmers and families" and "Urban/suburban dwellers" both make use of the well water for similar purposes.
6. Not taken to be a local resident.

Table 3. **Conditional Risks along the Two Simplified Sequences that Require Further Consideration**

(a)   1AC3D5F

Interval	1–A	A–C	C–3	3–D	D–5	5–F
Conditional Risk (yr^{-1}) (see Note 1)	$2\ 10^{-6}$	$5\ 10^{-6}$	10^{-5}	$5\ 10^{-6}$	10^{-6}	10^{-6}
Weight (see Note 2)	10^{-1}	10^{-4}	10^{-2}	10^{-1}	1	1

(b)   AC13D5F

Interval	A–C	C–1	1–3	3–D	D–5	5–F
Conditional Risk (yr^{-1}) (see Note 1)	$2\ 10^{-6}$	$5\ 10^{-6}$	10^{-5}	$5\ 10^{-6}$	10^{-6}	10^{-6}
Weight (see Note 2)	10^{-3}	10^{-1}	10^{-2}	10^{-1}	1	1

Notes
1.   The conditional risks are for the "Farmers and families" PEG.
2.   The weights are obtained as a product of the appropriate weights from the single FEP scenarios.

Figure 1. **Strategy for Scenario Assessment**

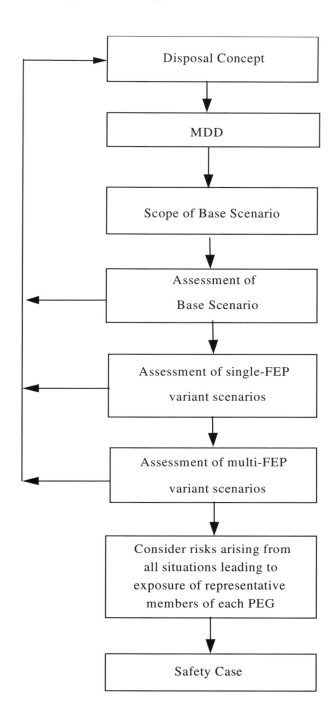

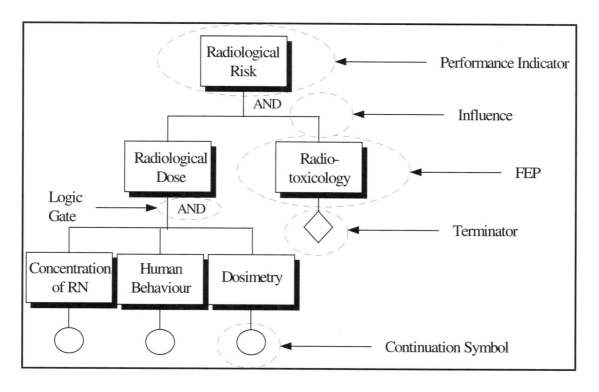

Figure 2. **Top Levels of the MDD**

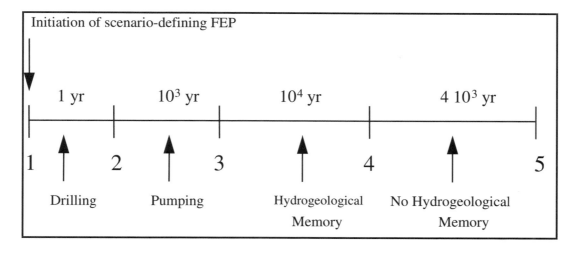

Figure 3. **Timeline for Well Drilling Scenario**

Figure 4. **Time Offset for Concurrent Timelines**

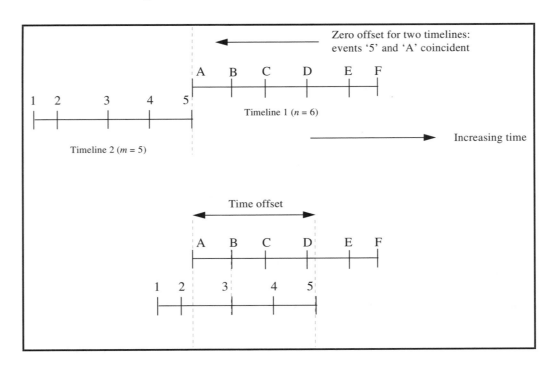

Figure 5. **Overview of Methodology for Combining Timelines**

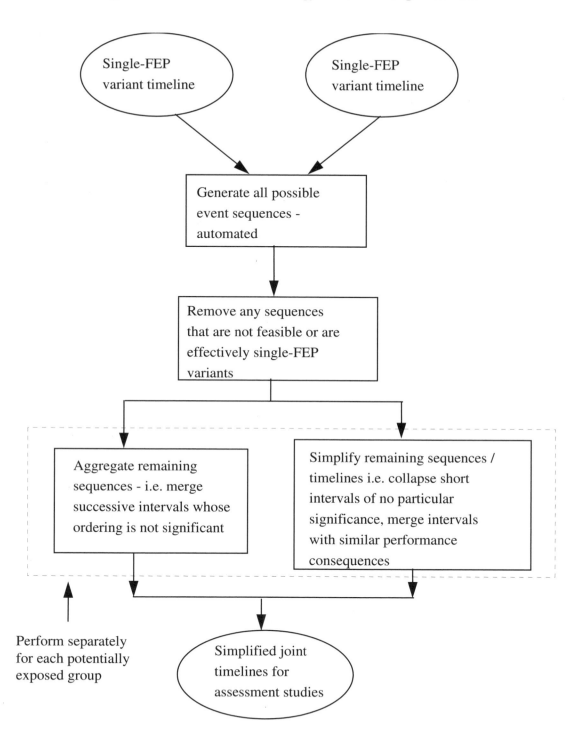

Figure 6. **Initial and Simplified Timelines for the Well Drilling and Seismic Event Scenarios**

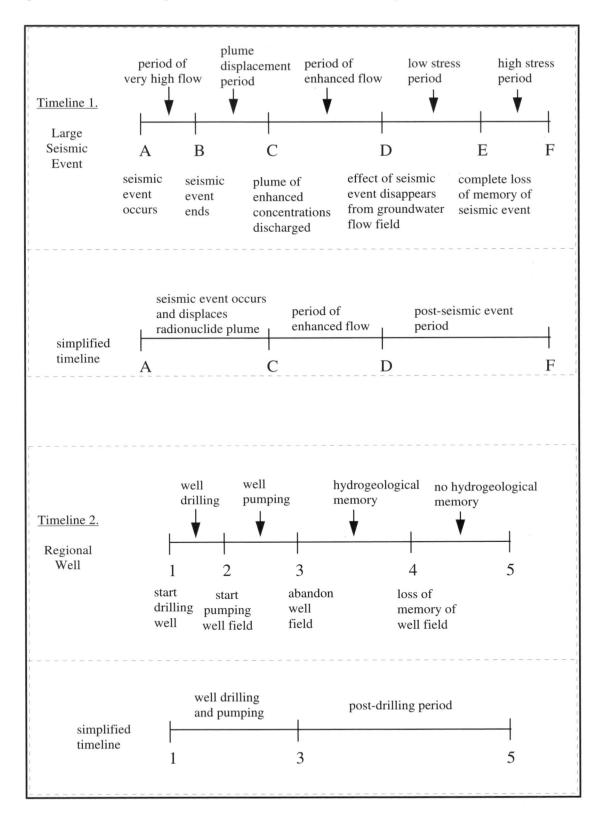

Figure 7. **An Illustrative Weight-Risk Diagram**

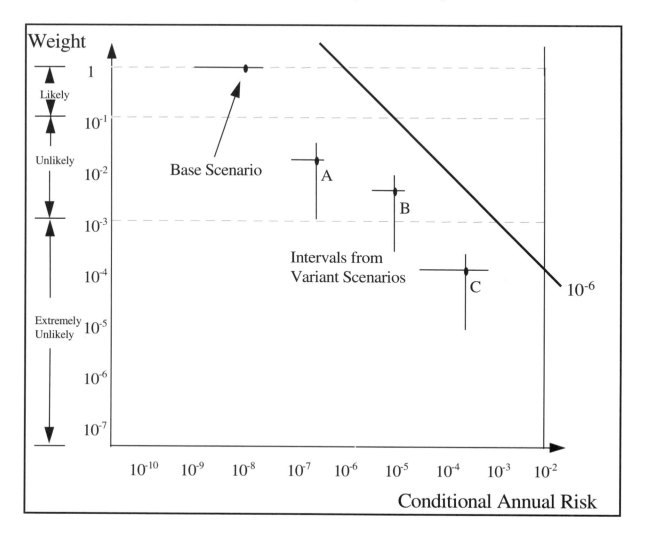

Paper 8

SCENARIO DEVELOPMENT FOR THE WASTE ISOLATION PILOT PLANT COMPLIANCE CERTIFICATION APPLICATION

D.A. Galson[1], P.N. Swift[2], D.R. Anderson[2], D.G. Bennett[1], M.B. Crawford[1], T.W. Hicks[1], R.D. Wilmot[1], and George Basabilvazo[3]
[1]Galson Sciences Limited, UK
[2]Sandia National Laboratories, USA
[3]United States Department of Energy, USA

(Also published in Reliability Engineering and System Safety, 2000, volume 69, p. 129-149)

Abstract

Demonstrating compliance with the applicable regulations for the Waste Isolation Pilot Plant (WIPP) requires an assessment of the long-term performance of the disposal system. Scenario development is one starting point of this assessment, and generates inquiry about the present state and future evolution of the disposal system. Scenario development consists of four tasks: (i) identifying and classifying features, events and processes (FEPs), (ii) screening FEPs according to well-defined criteria, (iii) forming scenarios (combinations of FEPs) in the context of regulatory performance criteria, and (iv) specifying of scenarios for consequence analysis. The development and screening of a comprehensive FEP list provides assurance that the identification of significant processes and events is complete, that potential interactions between FEPs are not overlooked, and that responses to possible questions are available and well documented. Two basic scenarios have been identified for the WIPP: undisturbed performance (UP) and disturbed performance (DP). The UP scenario is used to evaluate compliance with the Environmental Protection Agency's (EPA's) Individual Dose (40 CFR § 191.15) and Groundwater Protection (40 CFR § 191.24) standards and accounts for all natural and waste- and repository-induced FEPs that survive the screening process. The DP scenario is required for assessment calculations for the EPA's cumulative release standard (Containment Requirements, 40 CFR § 191.13) and accounts for disruptive future human events, which have an uncertain probability of occurrence, in addition to the UP FEPs.

1. Introduction

The Waste Isolation Pilot Plant (WIPP) will be used for the disposal of transuranic waste from defense programs of the U.S. Department of Energy (DOE). The WIPP facility is located 42 km east of the town of Carlsbad in southeastern New Mexico. The repository is located 655 m underground in a Permian bedded salt formation.

In October 1996, the DOE applied to the U.S. Environmental Protection Agency (EPA) for certification of the WIPP's compliance with the relevant radioactive waste disposal standards (40 CFR Part 191; EPA, 1993) and criteria (40 CFR Part 194; EPA, 1996) that govern post-closure safety (DOE, 1996). Demonstrating compliance with these standards and criteria requires an assessment of the long-term performance of the disposal system. For analysis, the universe of all possible occurrences within the 10 000-year regulatory time frame is divided into subsets of similar future occurrences, which are defined as scenarios.[1] Because a scenario is defined simply as a subset of futures with similar occurrences, it does not have a specific size. In general, applying the term scenario for larger subsets of futures is useful in discussions of concepts, whereas applying the term scenario for smaller subsets of futures is useful when presenting scenario consequences. This paper is concerned with concepts: see Helton *et al.* (2000) and other papers cited therein for a discussion of the treatment of scenario consequences.

The Containment Requirements of 40 CFR Part 191 (§ 191.13) set limits on the probability that cumulative releases of radionuclides to the accessible environment for 10,000 years after disposal will exceed certain values. The EPA defines the accessible environment to be (1) the atmosphere, (2) land surfaces, (3) surface waters, (4) oceans, and (5) all of the lithosphere that is beyond the controlled area (§ 191.12[k]). The definition of the controlled area plays an important role in scenario development, particularly in the consideration of future human actions. For the WIPP, the controlled area consists of a 41-km^2 area overlying the repository.

The EPA has provided criteria concerning the scope of performance assessments in 40 CFR Part 191 and in the WIPP-specific compliance criteria, 40 CFR Part 194:

- 40 CFR § 191.13(a) requires performance assessments to consider "all significant processes and events that may affect the disposal system"

- 40 CFR § 194.32(e) provides further detail for the WIPP, and states that:

Any compliance application(s) shall include information which:

(1) Identifies all potential processes, events or sequences and combinations of processes and events that may occur during the regulatory time frame and may affect the disposal system;

(2) Identifies the processes, events or sequences and combinations of processes and events included in performance assessments; and

(3) Documents why any processes, events or sequences and combinations of processes and events identified pursuant to paragraph (e)(1) of this section were not included in performance assessment results provided in any compliance application.

Evaluation of the consequences of scenarios begins with the determination of the scenarios to be analyzed. The DOE has determined scenarios through a formal process similar to that proposed by Cranwell *et al.* (1990), and used in preliminary performance assessments for the WIPP (WIPP

---

1. Note that scenarios would not necessarily have to be defined as subsets of similar future occurrences, but defining a scenario as a subset of similar futures confers a practical advantage because the consequences of futures falling within one scenario can be calculated with the same model configuration (Helton *et al.*, 2000).

Performance Assessment Division, 1991; WIPP Performance Assessment Department, 1992). This process has four steps:

(1) FEPs (features, events, and processes) potentially relevant to the WIPP are identified and classified.

(2) Certain FEPs are eliminated according to well-defined screening criteria because they are not important or not relevant to the performance of the WIPP.

(3) Scenarios are formed from the remaining FEPs in the context of regulatory performance criteria.

(4) Scenarios are specified for consequence analysis.

This paper illustrates the DOE's application of this methodology for the Compliance Certification Application (CCA) for the WIPP (DOE, 1996). Steps (1) and (2) of the scenario development process are described in Section 2; Steps (3) and (4) are described in Section 3.

Scenario development for a particular disposal concept depends on the purpose of the assessment and the barrier system that isolates the radioactive waste after disposal. For the WIPP, long-term containment of wastes will be provided by a multibarrier system that comprises three principal components (DOE, 1996):

(i) Engineered barriers (magnesium oxide [MgO] backfill, shaft, drift, and panel seal systems). Waste canisters will be crushed by salt creep relatively soon after the repository is decommissioned; other components of the repository system will evolve gradually, and will provide a barrier function over the regulatory period. In particular, long-term performance of the shaft seal systems, and chemical conditioning provided by the MgO backfill are important in limiting releases.

(ii) The 600 m thick halite host rock (Salado Formation). This unit has extremely low permeability when undisturbed, and will not provide a pathway for significant contaminant transport to the accessible environment.

(iii) The geologic units underlying and overlying the Salado. Given a breach of the Salado by a future borehole, significant delay and retardation of radionuclides will occur in units overlying or underlying this Formation. The historical focus of the project has been strongly on the Culebra Dolomite Member of the Rustler Formation, which is the most transmissive unit overlying the repository. However, the DOE accounts for additional hydrological units above and below the repository in performance assessment calculations.

2.   Identification and Screening of Features, Events, and Processes

2.1   *Identification of FEPs*

The first step of the scenario development procedure is the identification and classification of FEPs potentially relevant to the performance of the disposal system. In constructing a comprehensive list of FEPs for the WIPP, the DOE followed several avenues of inquiry, including (i) review of FEP lists developed in other disposal programs, (ii) review of WIPP project literature, and (iii) reviews by, and documented meetings with, WIPP project staff, WIPP project stakeholders,[2] and the EPA. This work is summarized here.

Catalogs of FEPs have been developed in several national radioactive waste disposal programs, as well as internationally. As a checklist for the development of a site-specific FEP list for the WIPP, the DOE assembled a list of potentially relevant FEPs using a set of nine existing FEP lists developed by different programs for different disposal concepts, including a bedded salt concept (see Table 1). The same set of FEP lists had been used by the Swedish Nuclear Power Inspectorate (SKI) in developing a FEP list in Sweden (Stenhouse *et al.*, 1993). This compilation of FEP lists formed the best documented and most comprehensive checklist available at the time the work was conducted.[3]

Table 1. FEP lists used in deriving a checklist for the WIPP

Study	Country	Number of FEPs
Atomic Energy of Canada Limited (AECL) study of disposal of spent fuel in crystalline rock (Goodwin *et al.* 1994)	Canada	275
SKI & Swedish Nuclear Fuel and Waste Management Company (SKB) study of disposal of spent fuel in crystalline rock (Andersson 1989)	Sweden	157
National Cooperative for the Storage of Radioactive Waste (NAGRA) Project Gewähr study (NAGRA 1985)	Switzerland	44
UK Department of the Environment Dry Run 3 study of deep disposal of low- and intermediate-level waste (L/ILW) (Thorne 1992)	UK	305
UK Department of Environment assessment of L/ILW disposal in volcanic rock at Sellafield (Miller and Chapman 1992)	UK	79
UK Nuclear Industry Radioactive Waste Executive (NIREX) study of the deep disposal of L/ILW (Hodgkinson and Sumerling 1989)	UK	131
Sandia National Laboratories (SNL) study of deep disposal of spent fuel (Cranwell *et al.* 1990)	US	29
NEA Working Group on Systematic Approaches to Scenario Development (OECD 1992)	International	122
International Atomic Energy Agency (IAEA) Safety Series (IAEA 1981)	International	56

2. WIPP project stakeholders contributing to the process included the Enviromental Evaluations Group, the State of New Mexico Attorney General's office, the Southwest Research and Information Center, Citizens for Alternatives to Radioactive Dumping, Concerned Citizens for Nuclear Safety, and members of the public.

3. The Nuclear Energy Agency (NEA) of the Organization for Economic Cooperation and Development (OECD) is in the process of establishing a broadly based international FEP database, consisting of the various national FEP lists. When available, this international database will form a useful tool for future FEP analysis. The CCA FEP list forms part of this international database.

166

This checklist was used as a starting point to derive the comprehensive site-specific CCA FEP list. The following steps were taken:

- To ensure comprehensiveness, other FEPs specific to the WIPP were added to the checklist based on review of key project documents, and examination of the checklist by project participants, stakeholders, and the EPA (Galson *et al.,* 1995). The final checklist is contained in Attachment 1 of Appendix SCR of the CCA.

- The checklist was then substantially restructured, revised, and initially screened, with the number of FEPs reduced to approximately 240, as follows:

    - Duplicate FEPs were eliminated. Duplicate FEPs arose in the checklist because individual FEPs can act in different subsystems. FEPs have a single entry in the CCA FEP list whether they are applicable to several parts of the disposal system or to a single part only.

    - FEPs that are not relevant to the WIPP design or inventory were eliminated. Examples include FEPs related to high-level waste, copper canisters, and bentonite backfill.

    - FEPs related to engineering design changes were eliminated because they are not relevant to a compliance application based on the DOE's design for the WIPP.

    - FEPs related to constructional, operational, and decommissioning errors were eliminated. The DOE has administrative and quality control procedures to ensure that the WIPP facility will be constructed, operated, and decommissioned properly.

    - Detailed FEPs related to processes in the surface environment were aggregated into a small number of generalized FEPs.

    - FEPs related to the containment of hazardous metals, volatile organic compounds (VOCs), and other chemicals that are not regulated by 40 CFR Part 191 were not included on the CCA FEP list.

    - Several FEPs were renamed to be consistent with terms used to describe specific WIPP processes.

    - Additional detail was added to the FEP list in some areas where it was felt necessary to increase the clarity of the analysis. For example, the single FEP "dissolution" was replaced by the FEPs "deep dissolution," "lateral dissolution," and "shallow dissolution," all of which represent distinct processes at the WIPP.

    - FEPs were reclassified under the major headings Natural, Waste- and Repository-Induced, and Human-Initiated, with each of these major headings being given consistent subheadings according to a top-down structured breakdown of knowledge about the WIPP (see Table 2).

Finally, as part of the revisions to produce the final CCA FEP list, the draft CCA list was reviewed by project staff, stakeholders, and the EPA, as part of the DOE's efforts to ensure comprehensiveness and clarity of the final list. The CCA FEP list is included in Chapter 6 and Appendix SCR of the CCA (DOE, 1996).

Table 2. **Categorization scheme for the CCA FEP list. The endpoint of the scheme, the detailed FEPs, are not shown here. The categorization hierarchy is up to four levels deep for each FEP. The entire FEP list, containing approximately 240 FEPs, is documented in DOE (1996); the FEPs accounted for in PA calculations are listed in Tables 3 and 4 of this paper.**

NATURAL	Geological	Stratigraphy	
		Tectonics	
		Structural FEPs	Deformation
			Fracture development
			Fault movement
			Seismic activity
		Crustal processes	Igneous activity
			Metamorphism
		Geochemical FEPs	Dissolution
			Mineralization
	Subsurface hydrological	Groundwater characteristics	
		Changes in groundwater flow	
	Subsurface geochemical	Groundwater geochemistry	
		Changes in groundwater chemistry	
	Geomorphological	Physiography	
		Meteorite impact	
		Denudation	Weathering
			Erosion
			Sedimentation
		Soil development	
	Surface hydrological	Fluvial	
		Lacustrine	
		Groundwater recharge and discharge	
		Changes in surface hydrology	
	Climatic	Climate	
		Climate change	Meteorological
			Glaciation
	Marine	Seas	
		Marine sedimentology	
		Sea level changes	
	Ecological	Flora & fauna	
		Changes in flora & fauna	
WASTE AND REPOSITORY-INDUCED	Waste and repository characteristics	Repository characteristics	
		Waste characteristics	
		Container characteristics	
		Seal characteristics	
		Backfill characteristics	
		Postclosure monitoring	
	Radiological	Radioactive decay	
		Heat from radioactive decay	
		Nuclear criticality	

Table 2.   **Categorization scheme for the CCA FEP list. The endpoint of the scheme, the detailed FEPs, are not shown here. The categorization hierarchy is up to four levels deep for each FEP. The entire FEP list, containing approximately 240 FEPs, is documented in DOE (1996); the FEPs accounted for in PA calculations are listed in Tables 3 and 4 of this paper.**

	Geological and mechanical	Radiological effects on material properties	
		Excavation-induced fracturing	
		Rock creep	
		Roof falls	
		Subsidence	
		Effects of fluid pressure changes	
		Effects of explosions	
		Thermal effects	
		Mechanical effects on material properties	
	Subsurface hydrological and fluid dynamical	Repository-induced flow	
		Effects of gas generation	
		Thermal effects	
	Geochemical/chemical	Gas generation	Microbial gas generation
			Corrosion
			Radiolytic gas generation
		Chemical speciation	
		Precipitation/dissolution	
		Sorption	
		Reduction-oxidation chemistry	
		Organic complexation	
		Exothermic reactions	
		Chemical effects on material properties	
	Contaminant transport mode	Solute transport	
		Colloid transport	
		Particulate transport	
		Microbial transport	
		Gas transport	
	Contaminant transport process	Advection	
		Diffusion	
		Thermochemical transport phenomena	
		Electrochemical transport phenomena	
		Physicochemical transport phenomena	
	Ecological	Plant, animal and soil uptake	
		Human uptake	
HUMAN INITIATED	Geological	Drilling	
		Excavation activities	
		Subsurface explosions	Resource recovery

Table 2. **Categorization scheme for the CCA FEP list. The endpoint of the scheme, the detailed FEPs, are not shown here. The categorization hierarchy is up to four levels deep for each FEP. The entire FEP list, containing approximately 240 FEPs, is documented in DOE (1996); the FEPs accounted for in PA calculations are listed in Tables 3 and 4 of this paper.**

			Underground nuclear device testing
	Subsurface hydrological and geochemical	Borehole fluid flow	Drilling-induced flow
			Fluid extraction
			Fluid injection
			Flow through abandoned boreholes
		Excavation-induced flow	
		Explosion-induced flow	
	Geomorphological	Land use and disturbances	
	Surface hydrological	Water control and use	
	Climatic	Anthropogenic climate change	
	Marine	Marine activities	
	Ecological	Agricultural activities	
		Social and technological developments	

2.2   *Criteria for screening FEPs and categorizing retained FEPs*

The purpose of FEP screening was to identify those FEPs on the CCA FEP list that should be accounted for in performance assessment calculations, and those FEPs that need not be considered further. The DOE's process of removing FEPs from consideration in performance assessment calculations involved the structured application of three screening criteria. The criteria used to screen out FEPs were explicit regulatory exclusion (SO-R), probability (SO-P), and/or consequence (SO-C). As discussed in Section 2.2.1, all three criteria are derived from regulatory requirements. FEPs not screened as SO-R, SO-P, or SO-C were retained for inclusion in performance assessment calculations and were classified as undisturbed performance (UP) or disturbed performance (DP) FEPs. These screening criteria and FEP classifiers are discussed in this section, and FEP screening is briefly discussed in Sections 2.3-2.5 under the headings Natural FEPs, Waste- and Repository-Induced FEPs, and Human-Initiated FEPs. Detailed screening discussions for FEPs are not presented here, but are contained in Appendix SCR of the CCA. This Appendix is several hundreds of pages in length, and is supported by numerous WIPP project references.

2.2.1   *Elimination of FEPs based on regulation (SO-R), probability (SO-P), and/or consequence (SO-C)*

Regulation (SO-R). The EPA provides specific FEP screening criteria in 40 CFR Part 191 and 40 CFR Part 194. These screening criteria represent screening decisions made by the EPA. That is, in the process of developing and demonstrating the feasibility of the 40 CFR Part 191 standard and the 40 CFR Part 194 criteria, the EPA considered and made conclusions on the relevance, consequence, and/or probability of occurrence of particular FEPs and, in so doing, allowed for some

FEPs to be eliminated from consideration. Section 2.5 describes the regulatory screening criteria that pertain to the human-initiated events and processes that need to be considered.

Probability *of occurrence of a FEP leading to significant release of radionuclides (SO-P).* Low-probability events can be excluded on the basis of the criterion provided in 40 CFR § 194.32(d), which states that "performance assessments need not consider processes and events that have less than one chance in 10 000 of occurring over 10 000 years." In practice, for most FEPs screened out on the basis of low probability of occurrence, it has not been possible for the DOE to estimate a meaningful quantitative probability. In the absence of quantitative probability estimates, a qualitative argument was provided in the CCA.

Potential *consequences* *associated with the occurrence of the FEPs (SO-C).* The DOE recognized two uses for this criterion:

(1) FEPs can be eliminated from performance assessment calculations on the basis of insignificant consequence. Consequence can refer to effects on the repository or site or to radiological consequence. In particular, 40 CFR § 194.34(a) states that "The results of performance assessments shall be assembled into complementary, cumulative distribution functions (CCDFs) that represent the probability of exceeding various levels of cumulative release caused by all *significant* processes and events." (emphasis added). The DOE has omitted events and processes from performance assessment calculations where there is a reasonable expectation that the remaining probability distribution of cumulative releases would not be significantly changed by such omissions.

(2) FEPs that are potentially beneficial to subsystem performance may be eliminated from performance assessment calculations if necessary to simplify the analysis. This argument has been used when there is uncertainty as to exactly how the FEP should be incorporated into assessment calculations or when incorporation would incur unreasonable difficulties.

In some cases the effects of the occurrence of a particular event or process, although not necessarily insignificant, can be shown to lie within the range of uncertainty of another FEP already accounted for in the performance assessment calculations. In such cases the event or process may be considered to be included in performance assessment calculations implicitly, within the range of uncertainty associated with the included FEP.

The distinctions between the SO-R, SO-P, and SO-C screening classifications are summarized in Figure 1. Although some FEPs could be eliminated from performance assessment calculations on the basis of more than one criterion, the most practical screening criterion was used for classification. In particular, a regulatory screening classification was used in preference to a probability or a consequence screening classification, as illustrated in Figure 1. FEPs that have not been screened out based on any one of the three criteria have been accounted for in performance assessment calculations.

2.2.2   *Undisturbed performance (UP) FEPs*

FEPs classified as UP are accounted for in calculations of undisturbed performance of the disposal system (see Section 3.1). Undisturbed performance is defined in 40 CFR § 191.12 as "the predicted behavior of a disposal system, including consideration of the uncertainties in predicted behavior, if the disposal system is not disrupted by human intrusion or the occurrence of unlikely natural events." The UP FEPs are accounted for in evaluating compliance with the individual dose criterion in 40 CFR § 191.15 and the groundwater protection requirements in 40 CFR § 191.24. The UP FEPs are also accounted for in the performance assessment calculations to evaluate compliance with the Containment Requirements in 40 CFR § 191.13.

2.2.3   *Disturbed performance (DP) FEPs*

FEPs classified as DP are accounted for only in the assessment calculations for disturbed performance, required to evaluate compliance with the Containment Requirements (see Section 3.2). The DP FEPs that remain following the screening process relate to the potential disruptive effects of future drilling and mining events in the WIPP controlled area.

Figure 1. **Screening process based on screening classifications.**

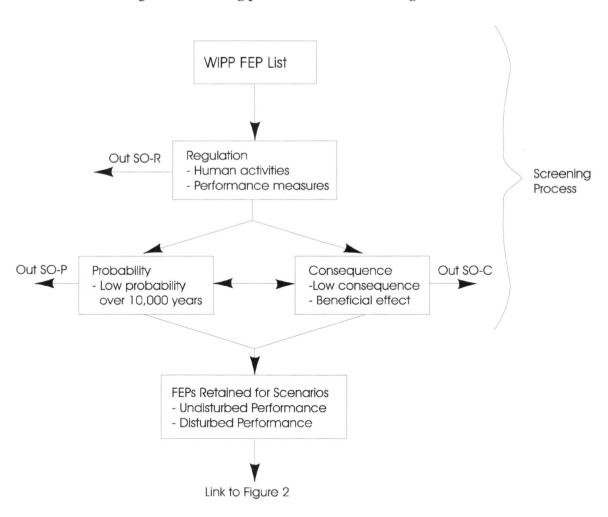

CCA-117-2

172

2.3   Screening of natural FEPs

Consistent with 40 CFR § 194.32(d), the DOE screened out several natural FEPs from performance assessment calculations on the basis of a low probability of occurrence at or near the WIPP site. In particular, natural events for which there is no evidence of occurrence within the Delaware Basin were screened out on this basis. In this analysis, the probabilities of occurrence of these events was assumed to be zero. Quantitative, nonzero probabilities for such events, based on numbers of occurrences, cannot be ascribed without considering regions much larger than the Delaware Basin, thus neglecting established geological understanding of the events and processes that occur within particular geographical provinces. No disruptive natural FEPs that could result in the creation of new pathways or significant alteration of existing pathways have a probability of greater than 10^{-4} of occurring during the 10 000-year regulatory time frame. For the WIPP setting, this is also true over much longer periods (10^5–10^6 years).

In considering the overall geological setting of the Delaware Basin, the DOE eliminated many FEPs from performance assessment calculations on the basis of low consequence. Events and processes that have had little effect on the characteristics of the region in the past are expected to be of low consequence for the period of regulatory interest.

2.4   Screening of waste- and repository-induced FEPs

The waste- and repository-induced FEPs are those that relate specifically to the waste material, waste containers, shaft seals, MgO backfill, panel closures, repository structures, and investigation boreholes. All FEPs related to radionuclide chemistry and radionuclide migration have been included in this category. FEPs related to radionuclide transport resulting from future borehole intersections of the WIPP excavation have also been included in this category.

The DOE screened out many FEPs in this category on the basis of low consequence to the performance of the disposal system. For example, the DOE has shown that the heat generated by radioactive decay of the emplaced RH- and CH-TRU waste will not result in significant thermal convection, thermal stresses and strains, or thermally induced chemical perturbations within the disposal system. Also, hydration of the emplaced concrete seals and MgO chemical conditioner will be exothermic, but the DOE has shown that the heat generated will not have a significant effect on the performance of the disposal system.

Other waste- and repository-induced FEPs were eliminated from performance assessment calculations on the basis of beneficial effect on the performance of the disposal system, when necessary to simplify the analysis.

Waste- and repository-induced FEPs eliminated on the basis of low probability of occurrence over 10,000 years are generally those for which no mechanisms have been identified that could result in their occurrence within the disposal system. Such FEPs include explosions resulting from nuclear criticality, and the development of large-scale reduction-oxidation fronts.

2.5   Screening of human-Initiated events and processes

Assessments of compliance with the Containment Requirements in 40 CFR § 191.13 require consideration of "all significant processes and events" including human-initiated FEPs. For the WIPP, human-initiated events and processes drive the identification of disturbed performance scenarios.

The scope of performance assessments is clarified with respect to human-initiated events and processes in 40 CFR § 194.32. At 40 CFR § 194.32(a) the EPA states that "Performance assessments shall consider natural processes and events, mining, deep drilling, and shallow drilling that may affect the disposal system during the regulatory time frame." Thus, performance assessments must include consideration of human-initiated FEPs relating to mining and drilling activities that might take place during the 10 000-year regulatory time frame. In particular, performance assessments must consider the potential effects of such activities that might take place within the controlled area at a time when institutional controls cannot be assumed to eliminate completely the possibility of human intrusion.

Further criteria concerning the scope of performance assessments are provided at 40 CFR § 194.32 (c):

> Performance assessments shall include an analysis of the effects on the disposal system of any activities that occur in the vicinity of the disposal system prior to disposal and are expected to occur in the vicinity of the disposal system soon after disposal. Such activities shall include, but shall not be limited to, existing boreholes and the development of any existing leases that can be reasonably expected to be developed in the near future, including boreholes and leases that may be used for fluid injection activities.

Thus, performance assessments must include consideration of all human-initiated FEPs relating to activities that have taken place or are reasonably expected to take place outside the controlled area in the near future.

In order to implement the criteria in 40 CFR § 194.32 relating to the scope of performance assessments, the DOE divided human activities into three categories. Distinctions are made between (1) human activities that are currently taking place and those that took place prior to the submission of the CCA, (2) human activities that might be initiated in the near future after submission of the CCA, and (3) human activities that might be initiated after repository closure. The first two categories of FEPs are considered under undisturbed performance, and FEPs in the third category lead to disturbed performance conditions.

(1) Historical and current human activities include resource extraction activities that have historically taken place and are currently taking place outside the controlled area. These activities are of potential significance insofar as they could affect geological, hydrological, or geochemical conditions within or outside the disposal system. Current human activities taking place within the controlled area are essentially those associated with development of the WIPP repository. Historical activities include existing boreholes.

(2) Near-future human activities include resource extraction activities that may be expected to occur outside the controlled area based on existing plans and leases. Thus, the near future includes the expected lives of existing mines and oil and gas fields, and the expected lives of new mines and oil and gas fields that the DOE anticipates will be developed based on existing plans and leases. These activities are of potential significance insofar as they could affect geological, hydrological, or geochemical conditions within or outside the disposal system. The only human activities that are expected to occur within the controlled area in the near future are those associated with development of the WIPP repository. The DOE assumes that any activity that is expected to be initiated in the near future, based on existing plans and leases, will be initiated prior to repository closure. Activities initiated prior to repository closure are assumed to continue for their expected economic lifetime.

174

(3) Future human activities include activities that might be initiated within or outside the controlled area after repository closure. This includes drilling and mining for resources within the disposal system at a time when institutional controls cannot be assumed to eliminate completely the possibility of such activities. Future human activities could influence the transport of contaminants within and outside the disposal system by directly removing waste from the disposal system, or altering the geological, hydrological, or geochemical conditions within or outside the disposal system.

For the WIPP, performance assessments must consider the potential effects of historical, current, near-future, and future human activities on the performance of the disposal system. The EPA requires that performance assessments "shall assume that the characteristics of the future remain what they are at the time the compliance application is prepared." This criterion was applied to eliminate the following human-initiated FEPs from performance assessment calculations:

- Drilling associated with geothermal energy production, hydrocarbon storage, and archaeological investigations.

- Excavation activities associated with tunneling and construction of underground facilities (for example, storage, disposal, and accommodation).

- Changes in land use.

- Anthropogenic climate change.

- Changes in agricultural practices.

- Demographic change, urban developments, and technological developments.

2.5.1   Screening of historical, current, and near-future human activities

The observational data obtained as part of WIPP site characterization reflect any effects of historical and current human activities in the vicinity of the WIPP, such as groundwater extraction and oil and gas production. Historical and current human activities were either modeled or found to be of low consequence to long-term performance.

Historical, current, and near-future human activities could affect WIPP site characteristics subsequent to the submission of the CCA, and could influence the performance of the disposal system. The hydrogeological impacts of historical, current and near-future potash mining outside the controlled area were accounted for in calculations of the undisturbed performance of the disposal system. Other human-initiated FEPs expected to occur in the Delaware Basin were eliminated from assessment calculations on the basis of low consequence to the performance of the disposal system.

2.5.2   Screening of future human activities

Performance assessments must consider the effects of future human activities on the performance of the disposal system. The EPA has provided criteria relating to future human activities in 40 CFR § 194.32(a), which limits the scope of consideration of future human actions in performance assessments to mining and drilling.

Criteria concerning future *mining:* The EPA provides additional criteria concerning the type of future mining that should be considered by the DOE in 40 CFR § 194.32 (b):

> Assessments of mining effects may be limited to changes in the hydraulic conductivity of the hydrogeologic units of the disposal system from excavation mining for natural resources. Mining shall be assumed to occur with a one in 100 probability in each century of the regulatory time frame. Performance assessments shall assume that mineral deposits of those resources, similar in quality and type to those resources currently extracted from the Delaware Basin, will be completely removed from the controlled area during the century in which such mining is randomly calculated to occur. Complete removal of such mineral resources shall be assumed to occur only once during the regulatory time frame.

Thus, consideration of future mining may be limited to mining within the controlled area at the locations of resources that are similar in quality and type to those currently extracted from the Delaware Basin. Potash is the only resource that has been identified within the controlled area in quality similar to that currently mined from underground deposits elsewhere in the Delaware Basin. Within the controlled area, the McNutt Member of the Salado Formation provides the only potash of appropriate quality to justify mining. The hydrogeological impacts of future potash mining within the controlled area were accounted for in calculations of the disturbed performance of the disposal system. Consistent with 40 CFR § 194.32(b), all economically recoverable resources in the vicinity of the disposal system (outside the controlled area) were assumed to be extracted in the near future.

Criteria concerning future drilling: With respect to consideration of future drilling, in the preamble to 40 CFR Part 194, the EPA "reasoned that while the resources drilled for today may not be the same as those drilled for in the future, the present rates at which these boreholes are drilled can nonetheless provide an estimate of the future rate at which boreholes will be drilled." Criteria concerning the consideration of future deep and shallow drilling[4] in performance assessments are provided in 40 CFR § 194.33. These criteria require that, to calculate future drilling rates, the DOE should examine the historical rate of drilling for resources in the Delaware Basin. Historical drilling for purposes other than resource exploration and recovery (such as WIPP site investigation) need not be considered in determining future drilling rates.

In particular, in calculating the frequency of future deep drilling, 40 CFR § 194.33(b)(3)(i) states that the DOE should "Identify deep drilling that has occurred for each resource in the Delaware Basin over the past 100 years prior to the time at which a compliance application is prepared." Oil and gas are the only known resources below 655 meters (2,150 feet) that have been exploited over the past 100 years in the Delaware Basin. However, some potash and sulfur exploration boreholes have been drilled in the Delaware Basin to depths in excess of 655 meters (2,150 feet) below the surface relative to where the drilling occurred. Thus, consistent with 40 CFR § 194.33(b)(3)(i), the DOE has used the historical record of deep drilling associated with oil, gas, potash and sulfur exploration, and oil and gas exploitation in the Delaware Basin in calculations to determine the rate of deep drilling within the controlled area and throughout the basin in the future. Deep drilling may occur within the controlled area after the end of the period of active institutional control (100 years after disposal).

In calculating the frequency of future shallow drilling, 40 CFR § 194.33(b)(4)(i) states that the DOE should "Identify shallow drilling that has occurred for each resource in the Delaware Basin

---

4. The EPA defined two types of drilling in 40 CFR § 194.2: deep drilling is defined as "drilling events in the Delaware Basin that reach or exceed a depth of 2 150 feet below the surface relative to where such drilling occurred"; shallow drilling is defined as "drilling events in the Delaware Basin that do not reach a depth of 2 150 feet below the surface relative to where such drilling occurred."

over the past 100 years prior to the time at which a compliance application is prepared." An additional criterion with respect to the calculation of future shallow drilling rates is provided in 40 CFR § 194.33(b)(4)(iii): "In considering the historical rate of all shallow drilling, the Department may, if justified, consider only the historical rate of shallow drilling for resources of similar type and quality to those in the controlled area."

As an example of the use of the criterion in 40 CFR § 194.33(b)(4)(iii), the EPA states in the preamble to 40 CFR Part 194 that "if only non-potable water can be found within the controlled area, then the rate of drilling for water may be set equal to the historical rate of drilling for non-potable water in the Delaware Basin over the past 100 years". Thus, the DOE may limit the rate of future shallow drilling based on a determination of the potential resources in the controlled area. Shallow drilling associated with exploration and extraction of water, potash, sulfur, oil, and gas has taken place in the Delaware Basin over the past 100 years. However, of these resources, only water and potash are present at shallow depths (less than 655 meters [2 150 feet] below the surface) within the controlled area. Thus, consistent with 40 CFR § 194.33(b)(4), the DOE used the historical record of shallow drilling associated with water and potash exploitation in the Delaware Basin in calculations to determine the rate of shallow drilling within the controlled area.

The EPA also provides a criterion in 40 CFR § 194.33(d) concerning the use of future boreholes subsequent to drilling: "With respect to future drilling events, performance assessments need not analyze the effects of techniques used for resource recovery subsequent to the drilling of the borehole." Thus, performance assessments need not consider the effects of techniques used for resource extraction and recovery, that would occur subsequent to the drilling of a borehole in the future.

The EPA provides an additional criterion that limits the severity of human intrusion scenarios that must be considered in performance assessments. In 40 CFR § 194.33(b)(1) the EPA states that "Inadvertent and intermittent intrusion by drilling for resources (other than those resources provided by the waste in the disposal system or engineered barriers designed to isolate such waste) is the most severe human intrusion scenario." Thus, human intrusion scenarios involving deliberate intrusion need not be considered in performance assessments.

Summary: Future human-initiated FEPs accounted for in performance assessment calculations for the WIPP are those associated with mining and deep drilling within the controlled area at a time when institutional controls cannot be assumed to eliminate completely the possibility of such activities. All other future human-initiated FEPs, if not eliminated from performance assessment calculations based on regulation, have been eliminated based on low consequence or low probability. For example, the effects of future shallow drilling within the controlled area have been eliminated from performance assessment calculations on the basis of low consequence to the performance of the disposal system.

3.   Scenario Development and Selection

This section addresses the formation of scenarios from FEPs that have been retained for performance assessment calculations, and introduces the specification of scenarios for consequence analysis. Scenarios are formed from combinations of FEPs that survive the screening process. The language and requirements of the regulations have a significant influence on the scenario development process. For example, as noted in Section 2.2, the EPA has defined undisturbed performance to mean "the predicted behavior of a disposal system, including consideration of the uncertainties in predicted behavior, if the disposal system is not disrupted by human intrusion or the occurrence of unlikely natural events."

Logic diagrams can be used to illustrate the formation of scenarios for consequence analysis (Figure 2). Each scenario shown in Figure 2 is defined by a combination of occurrence and nonoccurrence of all potentially disruptive FEPs. Disruptive FEPs are defined as those FEPs that result in the creation of new pathways, or significant alteration of existing pathways, for fluid flow and, potentially, radionuclide transport within the disposal system. Each of these scenarios also contains a set of features and nondisruptive FEPs that remain after FEP screening. As shown in Figure 2, undisturbed performance and disturbed performance scenarios are considered in consequence modeling for the WIPP performance assessment. Important aspects of undisturbed and disturbed performance are summarized in this section.

3.1   *Undisturbed performance*

No potentially disruptive natural FEPs are likely to occur during the regulatory time frame. All of the natural FEPs retained for scenario construction are nondisruptive and, with the exception of the FEP "brine reservoirs", are considered as part of undisturbed performance. Brine reservoirs may be present in the Castile Formation, which underlies the Salado and, although they are not relevant to undisturbed performance, brine reservoirs could play a role in certain disturbed performance scenarios that account for the potential effects of future deep drilling within the controlled area (see Section 3.2).

Similarly, the majority of waste- and repository-induced FEPs retained for scenario construction are considered as part of the undisturbed performance scenario. Again, the only exceptions are four FEPs exclusively related to the potential effects of future deep drilling within the controlled area.

Several FEPs relating to human activities that are retained for scenario construction are not disruptive to the disposal system and are, therefore, considered in undisturbed performance. For example, potash mining outside the controlled area does not constitute a disruption of the disposal system. However, the retained future human-initiated FEPs occurring inside the controlled area do present potential disruptions to the disposal system and have been used to develop disturbed-performance scenarios.

Figure 2. **Logic diagram for scenario analysis. FEPs accounted for in all performance assessment calculations have a probability of occurrence of one. Disruptive events used to form disturbed performance scenarios have an uncertain probability of occurrence.**

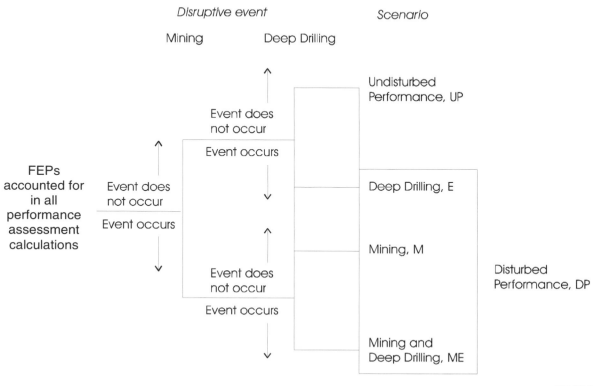

CCA-118-2

In total, 67 undisturbed performance FEPs have been identified (Table 3). Among the most significant FEPs that will affect the undisturbed performance within the disposal system are excavation-induced fracturing, gas generation, salt creep, and MgO backfill in the disposal rooms:

- The excavation of the repository and the consequent changes in the stress field in the rock surrounding the excavated opening will create a disturbed rock zone (DRZ) immediately adjacent to excavated openings. The DRZ will exhibit mechanical and hydrological properties different than those of the intact rock.

- Organic material in the waste may degrade because of microbial activity, and brine will corrode metals in the waste and waste containers. Gas generation from either or both processes may result in pressures sufficient to both maintain or develop fractures and change the fluid flow pattern around the waste disposal region.

- At the repository depth, salt creep will tend to heal fractures and reduce the permeability of the DRZ and the crushed salt component of the long-term shaft seals to near that of the host rock salt.

- MgO backfill to be emplaced in the disposal rooms will react with carbon dioxide (CO_2) and maintain mildly alkaline conditions. Corrosion of metals in the waste and waste containers will maintain reducing conditions. These effects will control radionuclide solubility.

Table 3. **Undisturbed performance FEPs and their treatment in performance assessment calculations**

FEP Categorization	FEP Incorporation[a]	FEP Treatment[b]
NATURAL FEPs		
Geological FEPs		
Stratigraphy		
Stratigraphy	P	Accounted for in the BRAGFLO model geometry
Structural FEPs		
Seismic activity		
Seismic activity	P	Accounted for in the DRZ permeability used by BRAGFLO
Geochemical FEPs		
Dissolution		
Shallow dissolution	P	Accounted for in the Culebra transmissivity fields
Subsurface hydrological FEPs		
Groundwater characteristics		
Saturated groundwater flow	C	Accounted for in BRAGFLO treatment of two-phase flow, and in SECOFL2D representation of flow in the Culebra
Unsaturated ground-water flow	C	Accounted for in BRAGFLO treatment of two-phase flow
Fracture flow	C	Accounted for in SECOTP2D treatment of flow in the Culebra
Effects of preferential pathways	P	Accounted for in the Culebra transmissivity fields
Subsurface geochemical FEPs		
Groundwater geochemistry		
Groundwater geochemistry	P	Accounted for in the actinide source term model, and in the actinide transport and retardation model used by SECOTP2D
Geomorphological FEPs		
Physiography		
Physiography	P	Accounted for in BRAGFLO model geometry
Surface hydrological FEPs		
Groundwater recharge and discharge		
Groundwater discharge	P	Accounted for in specification of boundary conditions to SECOFL2D
Groundwater recharge	P	Accounted for in specification of boundary conditions to SECOFL2D
Infiltration	P	Accounted for in specification of boundary conditions to SECOFL2D
Changes in surface hydrology		
Changes in ground-water recharge and discharge	P	Accounted for by the climate change model
Climatic FEPs		
Climate		
Precipitation (for example, rainfall)	P	Accounted for by the climate change model
Temperature	P	Accounted for by the climate change model
Climate change		

Table 3. **Undisturbed performance FEPs and their treatment in performance assessment calculations**

FEP Categorization	FEP Incorporation[a]	FEP Treatment[b]
Meteorological		
Climate change	P	Accounted for by the climate change model
WASTE- AND REPOSITORY-INDUCED FEPs		
Waste and repository characteristics		
Repository characteristics		
Disposal geometry	P	Accounted for in BRAGFLO model geometry
Waste characteristics		
Waste inventory	P	Accounted for in the actinide source term model
Container characteristics		
Container material inventory	P	Accounted for in cumulative distribution functions (CDFs) for gas generation rates used by BRAGFLO
Seal characteristics		
Seal geometry	P	Accounted for in BRAGFLO model geometry
Seal physical properties	P	Accounted for in seal parameter values used by BRAGFLO
Backfill characteristics		
Backfill chemical composition	P	Accounted for in the actinide source term model
Radiological FEPs		
Radioactive decay		
Radionuclide decay and ingrowth	C	Accounted for in NUTS, PANEL and SECOTP2D
Geological and mechanical FEPs		
Excavation-induced fracturing		
Disturbed rock zone	P	Accounted for in BRAGFLO parameter values and materials definition
Excavation-induced changes in stress	P	Accounted for in the creep closure model in BRAGFLO
Rock creep		
Salt creep	P	Accounted for in the creep closure model in BRAGFLO
Changes in the stress field	P	Accounted for in the creep closure model in BRAGFLO
Roof falls		
Roof falls	P	Accounted for in the permeability of the DRZ used by BRAGFLO
Effects of fluid pressure changes		
Disruption due to gas effects	C	Accounted for in BRAGFLO fracture model for Salado interbeds
Pressurization	C	Accounted for in BRAGFLO fracture model for Salado interbeds
Effects of explosions		
Gas explosions	P	Accounted for in the permeability of the DRZ used by BRAGFLO
Mechanical effects on material properties		

Table 3. **Undisturbed performance FEPs and their treatment in performance assessment calculations**

FEP Categorization	FEP Incorpor- ation[a]	FEP Treatment[b]
Consolidation of waste	P	Accounted for in the creep closure model in BRAGFLO
Consolidation of seals	P	Accounted for in seal parameters used by BRAGFLO
Mechanical degradation of seals	P	Accounted for in seal parameters used by BRAGFLO
Underground boreholes	P	Accounted for in the permeability of the DRZ used in BRAGFLO
Subsurface hydrological and fluid dynamical FEPs		
Repository-induced flow		
Brine inflow	C	Accounted for in BRAGFLO treatment of two-phase flow
Wicking	P	Accounted for in BRAGFLO gas generation model
Effects of gas generation		
Fluid flow due to gas production	C	Accounted for in BRAGFLO treatment of two-phase flow
Geochemical and chemical FEPs		
Gas generation		
Microbial gas generation		
Degradation of organic material	C	Accounted for in BRAGFLO gas generation model
Effects of temperature on microbial gas generation	P	Accounted for in CDFs for gas generation rates used by BRAGFLO
Effects of biofilms on microbial gas generation	P	Accounted for in CDFs for gas generation rates used by BRAGFLO
Corrosion		
Gases from metal corrosion	C	Accounted for in BRAGFLO gas generation model
Chemical effects of corrosion	P	Accounted for in CDFs for gas generation rates used by BRAGFLO
Chemical speciation		
Speciation	P	Accounted for in the actinide source term model, and in actinide transport and retardation model in SECOTP2D
Precipitation and dissolution		
Dissolution of waste	P	Accounted for in the actinide source term model
Sorption		
Actinide sorption	C	Accounted for in actinide retardation model in SECOTP2D
Kinetics of sorption	P	Accounted for in actinide retardation model in SECOTP2D
Changes in sorptive surfaces	P	Accounted for in actinide retardation model in SECOTP2D
Reduction-oxidation chemistry		
Effect of metal corrosion	P	Accounted for in the actinide source term model
Reduction-oxidation kinetics	P	Accounted for in the actinide source term model
Organic complexation		

Table 3. **Undisturbed performance FEPs and their treatment in performance assessment calculations**

FEP Categorization	FEP Incorpor-ation[a]	FEP Treatment[b]
Humic and fulvic acids	P	Accounted for in estimates of the colloidal actinide source term
Chemical effects on material properties		
Chemical degradation of seals	P	Accounted for in seal parameters in BRAGFLO
Microbial growth on concrete	P	Accounted for in seal parameters in BRAGFLO
Contaminant transport mode FEPs		
Solute transport		
Solute transport	C	Accounted for by NUTS in the Salado and SECOTP2D in the Culebra
Colloid transport		
Colloid transport	C	Advection and diffusion of humic colloids in the Culebra is estimated with SECOTP2D.
Colloid formation and stability	P	Accounted for in the colloidal actinide source term model.
Colloid filtration	C	Accounted for in treatment of transport for microbial and mineral fragment colloidal particles.
Colloid sorption	C	Accounted for in estimates of humic colloid retardation used by SECOTP2D.
Microbial transport		
Microbial transport	C	Accounted for by treatment of microbes as colloids.
Contaminant transport processes		
Advection		
Advection	C	Accounted for by NUTS in the Salado and SECOTP2D in the Culebra
Diffusion		
Diffusion	C	Accounted for by SECOTP2D in the Culebra
Matrix diffusion	C	Accounted for by SECOTP2D in the Culebra
HUMAN-INITIATED FEPs		
Excavation activities		
Excavation activities		
Potash mining	P	Potash mining outside the controlled area is accounted for by modifying the Culebra transmissivity fields used by SECOFL2D
Subsurface hydrological and geochemical FEPs		
Borehole fluid flow		
Drilling-induced flow		
Drilling-induced geochemical changes	P	Accounted for in SECOPT2D in the Culebra
Fluid injection		
Fluid injection-induced geochemical changes	P	Accounted for in SECOTP2D in the Culebra
Flow through abandoned boreholes		

Table 3. **Undisturbed performance FEPs and their treatment in performance assessment calculations**

FEP Categorization	FEP Incorporation[a]	FEP Treatment[b]
Borehole-induced geochemical changes	P	Accounted for in SECOTP2D in the Culebra
Excavation-induced flow		
Changes in groundwater flow due to mining	P	Potash mining outside the controlled area is accounted for by modifying the Culebra transmissivity fields used by SECOFL2D

Notes: a. C FEP treated through explicit representation in the equations implemented in the performance assessment code.
P FEP treated through the specification of parameters values.

b. BRAGFLO, SECOFL2D, SECOTP2D, NUTS, and PANEL are codes used directly in performance assessment calculations. These codes and their inter-relationships are described in Froehlich *et al.,* (2000).

Radionuclides can become mobile as a result of waste dissolution and colloid generation following brine flow into the disposal rooms. Colloids may be generated from the waste (humics, mineral fragments, and actinide intrinsic colloids) or from other sources (humics, mineral fragments, and microbes).

Conceptually, there are several pathways for radionuclide transport within the undisturbed disposal system that may result in releases to the accessible environment (Figure 3). Contaminated brine may move away from the waste-disposal panels if pressure within the panels is elevated by the generation of gas from corrosion or microbial degradation. Radionuclide transport may occur laterally, through the anhydrite interbeds toward the subsurface boundary of the accessible environment in the Salado, or through access drifts or anhydrite interbeds, primarily Marker Bed 139 (MB139), to the base of the shafts. In the latter case, if the pressure gradient between the panels and overlying strata is sufficient, then contaminated brine may move up the shafts. As a result, radionuclides may be transported directly to the ground surface, or they may be transported laterally away from the shafts, through permeable strata (such as the Culebra Member of the Rustler Formation), toward the subsurface boundary of the accessible environment. These conceptual pathways are shown in Figure 3.

Figure 3. **Conceptual release pathways for the undisturbed performance scenario**

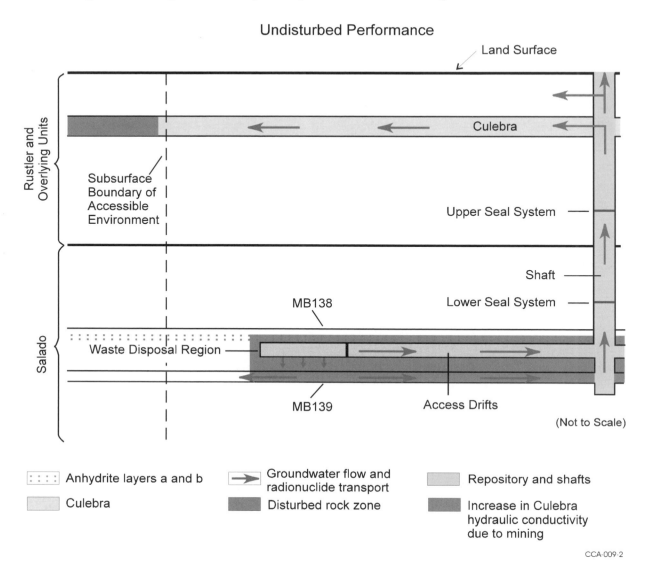

3.2 *Disturbed performance*

Assessments for compliance with 40 CFR § 191.13 need to consider the potential effects of future disruptive natural and human-initiated FEPs on the performance of the disposal system. No potentially disruptive natural FEPs are considered to be sufficiently likely to require inclusion in analyses of either undisturbed or disturbed performance. The only future human-initiated FEPs retained after FEP screening were those associated with mining and deep drilling (but not the subsequent use of a borehole) within the controlled area at a time when institutional controls cannot be assumed to eliminate the possibility of such activities. In total, 21 disturbed performance FEPs associated with future mining and deep drilling were identified (Table 4).

185

Table 4. Disturbed performance FEPs and their treatment in performance assessment calculations

FEP Categorization	Scenario[a]	FEP Incorporation[b]	FEP Treatment[c]
ALL UNDISTURBED PERFORMANCE FEPs (see Table 3)			
NATURAL FEPs			
Geological FEPs			
Stratigraphy			
Brine reservoirs	E1	C	Accounted for in BRAGFLO
WASTE- AND REPOSITORY-INDUCED FEPs			
Waste and repository characteristics			
Waste characteristics			
Heterogeneity of waste forms	E1, E2	P	Accounted for in the waste activity probabilities used by CCDFGF
Contaminant transport mode FEPs			
Particulate transport			
Suspensions of particles	E1, E2	C	Accounted for in CUTTINGS_S treatment of releases through boreholes
Cuttings	E1, E2	C	Accounted for in CUTTINGS_S treatment of releases through boreholes
Cavings	E1, E2	C	Accounted for in CUTTINGS_S treatment of releases through boreholes
Spallings	E1, E2	C	Accounted for in CUTTINGS_S treatment of releases through boreholes
HUMAN-INITIATED FEPs			
Geological FEPs			
Drilling			
Oil and gas exploration	E1, E2	P	Drilling of deep boreholes[d] is accounted for in estimates of drilling frequency used by CCDFGF
Potash exploration	E1, E2	P	Drilling of deep boreholes is accounted for in estimates of drilling frequency used by CCDFGF
Oil and gas exploitation	E1, E2	P	Drilling of deep boreholes is accounted for in estimates of drilling frequency used by CCDFGF
Other resources	E1, E2	P	Drilling of deep boreholes is accounted for in estimates of drilling frequency used by CCDFGF
Enhanced oil and gas recovery	E1, E2	P	Drilling of deep boreholes is accounted for in estimates of drilling frequency used by CCDFGF
Excavation activities			
Potash mining	M	P	Potash mining inside the controlled area is accounted for by modifying the Culebra transmissivity fields used by SECOFL2D
Subsurface hydrological and geochemical FEPs			
Borehole fluid flow			

Table 4. **Disturbed performance FEPs and their treatment in performance assessment calculations**

FEP Categorization	Scenario[a]	FEP Incorporation[b]	FEP Treatment[c]
Drilling-induced flow			
Drilling fluid flow	E1, E2	C	Accounted for in spallings and direct brine release models
Drilling fluid loss	E2	P	Accounted for in the BRAGFLO treatment of brine flow
Blowouts	E1, E2	C	Accounted for in spallings and direct brine release models
Drilling-induced geochemical changes	E1, E2	P	Accounted for by SECOTP2D in the Culebra
Flow through abandoned boreholes			
Natural borehole fluid flow	E1, E2	C	Accounted for in BRAGFLO treatment of long-term releases through boreholes
Waste-induced borehole flow	E1, E2	C	Accounted for in BRAGFLO treatment of long-term releases through boreholes
Borehole-induced geochemical changes	E1, E2	P	Accounted for by SECOTP2D in the Culebra
Excavation-induced flow			
Changes in groundwater flow due to mining	M	P	Potash mining inside the controlled area is accounted for by modifying the Culebra transmissivity fields used by SECOFL2D
Ecological FEPs			
Social and technological developments			
Loss of records	M, E1, E2	P	Accounted for in estimates of the probability of inadvertent human intrusion.

Notes: a. M Mining within the controlled area.
E1 Deep drilling that intersects the waste disposal region and a brine reservoir in the Castile.
E2 Deep drilling that intersects a waste disposal panel.

b. C FEP treated through explicit representation in the equations implemented in the performance assessment codes.
P FEP treated through the specification of parameters values.

c. BRAGFLO, CCDFGF, CUTTINGS_S, SECOFL2D, and SECOTP2D are codes used directly in performance assessment calculations. These codes and their inter-relationships are described in Froehlich *et al.,* (2000).

d. Deep drilling means those drilling events in the Delaware Basin that reach or exceed a depth of 2 150 feet below the surface relative to where such drilling occurred.

For evaluation of the consequences of disturbed performance, the DOE defined the mining scenario, M, the deep drilling scenario, E, and a mining and drilling scenario, ME. These scenarios are described in the following sections.

187

3.2.1   The disturbed performance mining scenario (M)

The disturbed performance mining scenario, M, involves future mining within the controlled area. Consistent with the criteria stated by the EPA in 40 CFR § 194.32 (b), for performance assessment calculations, the effects of potential future mining within the controlled area are limited to changes in hydraulic conductivity of the Culebra that result from subsidence. Radionuclide transport may be affected in the M scenario if a head gradient between the waste-disposal panels and the Culebra causes brine contaminated with radionuclides to move from the waste-disposal panels to the base of the shafts and up the shafts to the Culebra. The changes in the Culebra transmissivity field may affect the rate and direction of radionuclide transport within the Culebra. Features of the M scenario are illustrated in Figure 4.

The three disturbed performance FEPs labeled M in Table 4 relate to the occurrence and effects of future mining. The modeling system used for the M scenario is similar to that developed for the undisturbed performance scenario, but with a modified Culebra transmissivity field within the controlled area to account for the effects of mining.

3.2.2   The disturbed performance deep drilling scenario (E)

The disturbed performance deep drilling scenario, E, involves at least one deep drilling event that intersects the waste disposal region. The EPA provides criteria concerning analysis of the consequences of future drilling events in performance assessments in 40 CFR § 194.33(c):

> Performance assessments shall document that in analyzing the consequences of drilling events, the Department assumed that:
>
> (1) Future drilling practices and technology will remain consistent with practices in the Delaware Basin at the time a compliance application is prepared. Such future drilling practices shall include, but shall not be limited to: the types and amounts of drilling fluids; borehole depths, diameters, and seals; and the fraction of such boreholes that are sealed by humans; and
>
> (2) Natural processes will degrade or otherwise affect the capability of boreholes to transmit fluids over the regulatory time frame.

Consistent with these criteria, there are several pathways for radionuclides to reach the accessible environment in the E scenario. During the period before any deep drilling intersects the waste, potential release pathways are identical to those in the undisturbed performance scenario.

If a borehole intersects the waste in the disposal rooms, releases to the accessible environment may occur as material entrained in the circulating drilling fluid is brought to the surface. Particulate waste brought to the surface may include cuttings, cavings, and spallings. Cuttings are the materials cut by the drill bit as it passes through waste. Cavings are the materials eroded by the drilling fluid in the annulus around the drill bit. Spallings are the materials that may be forced into the circulating drilling fluid if there is sufficient pressure in the waste disposal panels. During drilling, contaminated brine may flow up the borehole and reach the surface, depending on fluid pressure within the waste disposal panels.

Figure 4. **Conceptual release pathways for the disturbed performance mining scenario M**

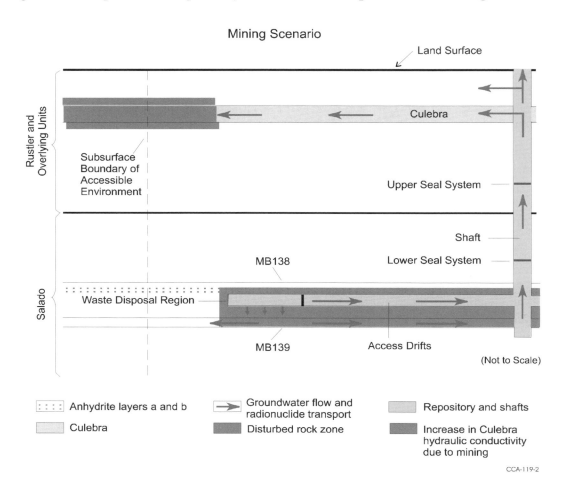

When abandoned, the borehole is assumed to be plugged in a manner consistent with current practice in the Delaware Basin. An abandoned intrusion borehole with degraded casing and/or plugs may provide a pathway for fluid flow and contaminant transport from the intersected waste panel to the ground surface if the fluid pressure within the panel is sufficiently greater than hydrostatic. Additionally, if brine flows through the borehole to overlying units, such as the Culebra, it may carry dissolved and colloidal actinides that can then be transported laterally to the accessible environment by natural groundwater flow in the overlying units.

The units intersected by an intrusion borehole may provide sources for brine flow to a waste panel during or after drilling. For example, in the northern Delaware Basin, the Castile, which underlies the Salado, contains isolated volumes of brine at fluid pressures greater than hydrostatic. Such a borehole could provide a connection for brine flow from the Castile to the waste panel, thus increasing fluid pressure and brine volume in the waste panel.

Also, a borehole that is drilled through a disposal room pillar, but does not intersect waste, could penetrate the brine reservoir underlying the waste disposal region. Such an event would, to some extent, depressurize the brine reservoir, and thus would affect the consequences of any subsequent intersections of the reservoir. The possibility for boreholes that do not penetrate the waste to depressurize a brine reservoir underlying the waste disposal region is accounted for in the consequence analysis of the WIPP.

The DOE has distinguished two types of deep drilling events by whether or not the borehole intersects a Castile brine reservoir. A borehole that intersects a waste disposal panel and penetrates a Castile brine reservoir has been designated an E1 event. The 18 disturbed performance FEPs labeled E1 in Table 4 relate to the occurrence and effects of an E1 drilling event. A borehole that intersects a waste panel but does not penetrate a Castile brine reservoir has been designated an E2 event. The 18 disturbed performance FEPs labeled E2 in Table 4 relate to the occurrence and effects of an E2 drilling event.

In order to evaluate the consequences of future deep drilling, the DOE has divided the E scenario into three drilling subscenarios, E1, E2 and E1E2, distinguished by the number of E1 and E2 drilling events that are assumed to occur in the regulatory time frame. These subscenarios are described in order of increasing complexity in the following sections.

The E2 Scenario: The E2 scenario is the simplest scenario for inadvertent human intrusion into a waste disposal panel. In this scenario, a panel is penetrated by a drill bit; cuttings, cavings, spallings, and brine flow releases may occur; and brine flow may occur in the borehole after it is plugged and abandoned. Sources for brine that may contribute to long-term flow up the abandoned borehole are the Salado or, under certain conditions, the units above the Salado. An E2 scenario may involve more than one E2 drilling event. Features of the E2 scenario are illustrated in Figure 5. A modeling system has been developed to evaluate the consequences of an E2 scenario during which single or multiple E2 events occur.

The E1 Scenario: Any scenario with a single inadvertent penetration of a waste panel that also penetrates a Castile brine reservoir is called E1. Features of this scenario are illustrated in Figure 6. Sources of brine in the E1 scenario are the brine reservoir, the Salado and, under certain conditions, the units above the Salado. However, the brine reservoir is conceptually the dominant source of brine in this scenario. The model configuration developed for the E1 scenario is used to evaluate the consequences of futures that have only one E1 event per panel. A future during which more than one E1 event occurs in a single panel is described as an E1E2 scenario.

The E1E2 Scenario: The E1E2 scenario is defined as all futures that have multiple penetrations of a waste panel of which at least one intrusion is an E1 type. One case of this scenario, with a single E1 event and a single E2 event penetrating the same panel, is illustrated in Figure 7. However, the E1E2 scenario can include many possible combinations of intrusion times, locations, and types of event (E1 or E2). The sources of brine in this scenario are those listed for the E1 scenario, and multiple E1-type sources may be present. The E1E2 scenario potentially has a flow path not present in the E1 or E2 scenarios: flow from an E1 borehole through the waste to another borehole. This flow path has the potential to (i) bring large quantities of brine in direct contact with waste and (ii) provide a less restrictive path for this brine to flow to the units above the Salado (via multiple boreholes) compared to either the E1 or E2 individual scenarios. Both the presence of brine reservoirs and the potential for flow through the waste to other boreholes make this scenario different in terms of potential consequences from combinations of E2 boreholes. The extent to which flow occurs between boreholes, as estimated by modeling, determines whether combinations of E1 and E2 boreholes at specific locations in the repository should be treated as E1E2 scenarios or as independent E1 and E2 scenarios in the consequence analysis. Because of the number of possible combinations of drilling events, the modeling configuration for the E1E2 scenario differs in significant ways from the model configuration used for evaluating E1 and E2 scenarios.

Figure 5. **Conceptual release pathways for the disturbed performance deep drilling scenario E2**

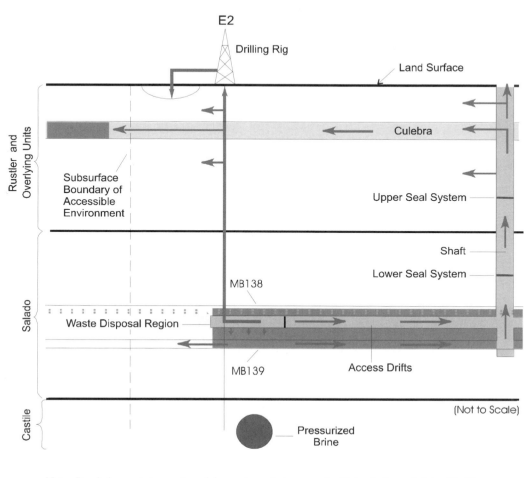

Note: Borehole penetrates waste and does not penetrate pressurized brine in the underlying Castile
Formation. Arrows indicate hypothetical direction of groundwater flow and radionuclide transport.

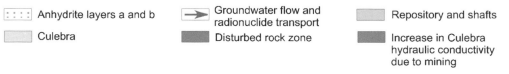

Anhydrite layers a and b	Groundwater flow and radionuclide transport	Repository and shafts
Culebra	Disturbed rock zone	Increase in Culebra hydraulic conductivity due to mining

CCA-011-2

Figure 6. **Conceptual release pathways for the disturbed performance deep drilling scenario E1**

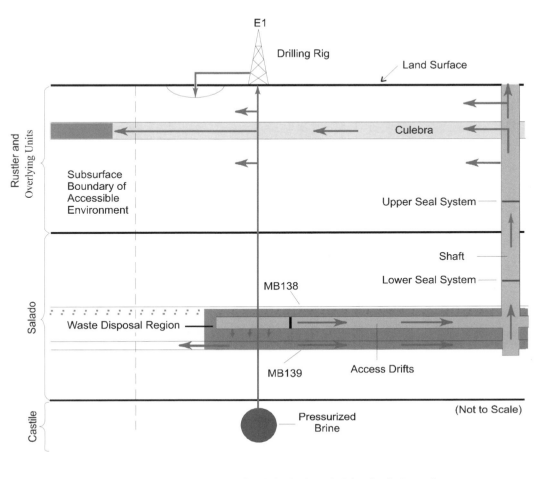

Note: Borehole penetrates waste and pressurized brine in the underlying Castile Formation.
Arrows indicate hypothetical direction of groundwater flow and radionuclide transport.

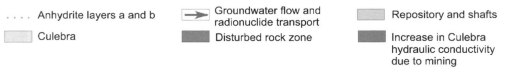

CCA-010-2

Figure 7. Conceptual release pathways for the disturbed performance deep drilling scenario E1E2

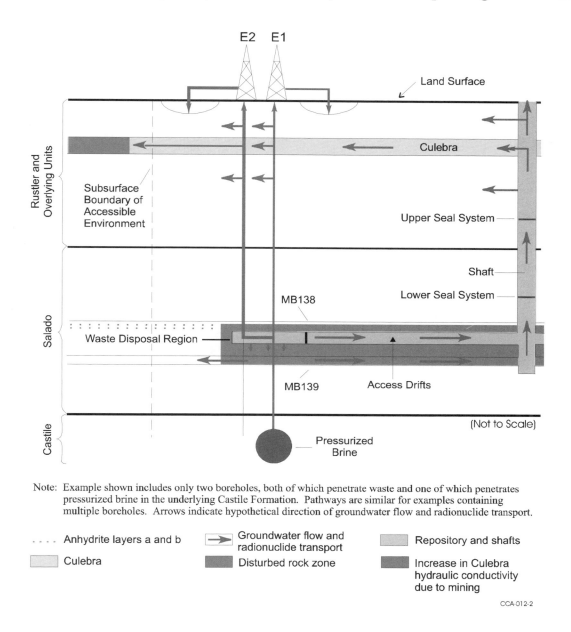

Note: Example shown includes only two boreholes, both of which penetrate waste and one of which penetrates pressurized brine in the underlying Castile Formation. Pathways are similar for examples containing multiple boreholes. Arrows indicate hypothetical direction of groundwater flow and radionuclide transport.

CCA-012-2

3.2.3 *The disturbed performance mining and deep drilling scenario (ME)*

Mining in the WIPP site (the M scenario) and deep drilling (the E scenario) may both occur in the future. The DOE calls a future in which both of these events occur the ME scenario. The occurrence of both mining and deep drilling does not create processes in addition to those already described separately for the M and E scenarios. For example, the occurrence of mining does not influence any of the interactions between deep boreholes and the repository or brine reservoirs. As well, the occurrence of drilling does not impact the effects of mining on Culebra hydrogeology. The difference between the M and E scenarios considered separately and the ME scenario is that the combination of borehole transport to the Culebra (E) and a transmissivity field impacted by mining (M) may result in more rapid transport of radionuclides to the accessible environment. For example, because the M scenario does not include drilling, the only pathway for radionuclides to reach the Culebra is up the sealed shafts. For clarity in describing computational results, the ME scenario was subdivided in the CCA according to the types of deep drilling subscenarios into the ME1 scenario (M and E1), the ME2 scenario (M and E2), and the ME1E2 scenario (M and E1E2).

The system used for modeling flow and transport in the Culebra for the ME scenario is similar to that used for the E scenario. However, in the ME scenario the Culebra transmissivity field is modified to account for the effects of mining within the controlled area.

3.3   *Scenarios retained for performance assessment*

The FEPs that remain after screening are accounted for in performance assessment calculations either through explicit representation in the equations that form the mathematical models or implicitly through the specification of parameter values used as input to the performance assessment codes. Tables 3 and 4 list the FEPs accounted for in calculations of disposal system performance under undisturbed and disturbed conditions, respectively. In these tables, FEPs treated through explicit representation in the equations on which the performance assessment codes are based are designated C (for code), and FEPs treated through the specification of parameter values are designated P (for parameter). FEPs designated C generally require specification of parameter values as well. In some cases, a submodel is used to generate parameter values that are necessary for the solution of the basic governing equations. FEPs incorporated by such submodels are generally denoted P. For example, a model of creep closure of the disposal rooms has been used to generate values of room porosity for use in the performance assessment code BRAGFLO, and this creep closure model accounts for several FEPs designated P.

The modeling systems used to evaluate the consequences of the undisturbed and disturbed performance scenarios are discussed by Helton *et al.* (2000) and other papers cited therein. For consequence analysis, the scenarios and subscenarios described here were further subdivided into modeling scenarios (termed S_i, see Helton *et al.*, (2000). The modeling scenarios are distinguished by, for example, the time of occurrence of disruptive events, and are generated by probabilistic sampling of selected processes and events.

3.4   *Conclusions*

A robust and tested methodology has been applied for identifying and screening FEPs, and for combining FEPs to form scenarios for consequence analysis. This paper has described the methodology and its application to the WIPP. The methodology consists of (i) identifying and classifying FEPs, (ii) screening FEPs according to well-defined criteria, (iii) forming scenarios (combinations of FEPs) in the context of regulatory performance criteria, and (iv) specification of scenarios for consequence analysis.

The procedure used to derive and build confidence in the comprehensiveness and relevance of the CCA FEP list included the use of available international experience in assembling FEP lists, combined with extensive documented review of the WIPP FEP list within the project, and by stakeholders and the EPA. FEPs were eliminated from performance assessment calculations using criteria defined by regulation, including explicit regulatory exclusion, probability of occurrence over 10 000 years, and/or consequence to the performance of the disposal system. The development and screening of a comprehensive FEP list provides assurance that the identification of significant processes and events is complete, that potential interactions between FEPs are not overlooked, and that responses to possible questions are available and well documented.

The FEPs remaining after screening were combined to form two main scenarios: undisturbed performance and disturbed performance. Two means of accounting for screened-in FEPs were identified: through explicit representation in the equations of the assessment codes, or through parameter values used by the codes. The undisturbed performance scenario formed the basis of calculations to evaluate compliance with the EPA's Individual Dose (40 CFR §191.15) and Groundwater Protection (40 CFR §191.24) criteria, and accounted for all natural and waste- and repository induced FEPs that survived the screening process. Disturbed performance scenarios, along with the undisturbed performance scenario, formed the basis of calculations to evaluate compliance with the EPA's Containment Requirements (40 CFR § 191.13). The disturbed performance scenarios accounted for future human-initiated events and processes, which have an uncertain probability of occurrence, in addition to the undisturbed performance FEPs.

The scenario development work formed an important focus of the review of the CCA by the EPA and by project stakeholders. This work has stood up well to the scrutiny received. Review did not lead to the identification of any fundamentally new FEPs or scenarios, but did lead to the introduction of greater detail in the analysis of certain human-initiated FEPs and in the consequence modeling of disturbed performance scenarios, and to the development of more comprehensive, clearer and more detailed screening documentation. The EPA's Certification Decision of May 18, 1998 (EPA, 1998), which approved disposal of radioactive wastes at the WIPP, shows that the EPA has accepted the DOE's scenario development methodology and its site-specific application as part of the performance assessment for the WIPP CCA.

When the WIPP opens in 1998, it will be the world's first specially mined deep geologic disposal system for long-lived radioactive wastes. In no other country is a similar type of repository due to open for at least another decade. The techniques and approaches used within the WIPP project deserve close examination by other disposal projects as they design their performance assessment and site characterization programs, and move toward licensing.

Acknowledgments

This work has been performed by the United States Department of Energy under Contract DE-AC04-94-AL8500 with Sandia National Laboratories (SNL), and Contract AP-2278 between Galson Sciences Limited and SNL. SNL is operated by Sandia Corporation, a Lockheed Martin Company.

References

Andersson, J., Ed. 1989. *The Joint SKI/SKB Scenario Development Project*. SKB Technical Report 89-35, Authors: J. Andersson, T. Carlsson, T. Eng, F. Kautsky, E. Söderman, and S. Wingefors. Swedish Nuclear Fuel and Waste Management Co., Stockholm, Sweden.

Cranwell, R.M., Guzowski, R.V., Campbell, J.E., and Ortiz, N.R. 1990. *Risk Methodology for Geologic Disposal of Radioactive Waste: Scenario Selection Procedure*. NUREG/CR-1667, SAND80-1429. Sandia National Laboratories, Albuquerque, NM.

DOE (Department of Energy). 1996. *Title 40 CFR Part 191 Compliance Certification Application for the Waste Isolation Pilot Plant.* DOE/CAO-1996-2184. DOE Carlsbad Area Office, Carlsbad, NM.

EPA (Environmental Protection Agency). 1993. "40 CFR Part 191: Environmental Radiation Protection Standards for the Management and Disposal of Spent Nuclear Fuel, High-Level and Transuranic Radioactive Wastes; Final Rule." *Federal Register,* Vol. 48, No. 242, pp. 66398-66416, December 20, 1993. Office of Radiation and Indoor Air, Washington, D.C.

EPA (Environmental Protection Agency), 1996. "40 CFR Part 194: Criteria for the Certification and Re-Certification of the Waste Isolation Pilot Plant's Compliance with the 40 CFR Part 191 Disposal Regulations; Final Rule." *Federal Register*, Vol. 61, No. 28, pp. 5224-5245, February 9, 1996. Office of Radiation and Indoor Air, Washington, D.C.

EPA (Environmental Protection Agency), 1998. "40 CFR Part 194: Criteria for the Certification and Re-Certification of the Waste Isolation Pilot Plant's Compliance with the 40 CFR Part 191 Disposal Regulations: Certification Decision; Final Rule." *Federal Register*, Vol. 63, No. 95, pp. 27353-27406. Office of Radiation and Indoor Air, Washington, D.C.

Froehlich, G.K., Williamson, C.M., and Ogden, H.C., 2000. "Computational Environment and Software Configuration Management of the 1996 Performance Assessment for the Waste Isolation Pilot Plant." *Reliability Engineering and System Safety*, Vol. 69, p. 421-427.

Galson, D.A., Hicks, T.W., Wilmot, R.D., and Swift, P.N. 1995. Systems Prioritization Method – Iteration 2 Baseline Position Paper: Scenario Development for Long-Term Performance Assessments of the WIPP. Sandia National Laboratories, Albuquerque, NM. WPO 28726.

Goodwin, B.W., Stephens, M.E., Davison, C.C., Johnson, L.H., and Zach, R. 1994. *Scenario Analysis for the Postclosure Assessment of the Canadian Concept for Nuclear Fuel Waste Disposal.* AECL-10969, COG-94-247. Whiteshell Laboratories, Pinawa, Manitoba.

Hodgkinson, D.P. and Sumerling, T.J. 1989. "A Review of Approaches to Scenario Analysis for Repository Safety Assessment." In *Proceedings of the IAEA/CEC/NEA (OECD) Symposium on Safety Assessment of Radioactive Waste Repositories* (Paris, 1989). OECD/NEA, Paris.

Helton, J.C., Anderson, D.R., Basabilvazo, G., Jow, H.-N., and Marietta, M.G., 2000. "Conceptual Structure of the 1996 Performance Assessment for the Waste Isolation Pilot Plant," *Reliability Engineering and System Safety*, Vol. 69, p. 151-165.

IAEA (International Atomic Energy Agency). 1981. *Safety Assessment for the Underground Disposal of Radioactive Wastes.* IAEA Safety Series No. 56, Vienna.

Miller, W.M. and Chapman, N.A., Ed. 1992. *Identification of Relevant Processes, System Concept Group Report,* UKDOE/HMIP Report TR-ZI-11. DOE, London.

NAGRA. 1985. Nuclear Waste Management in Switzerland: Feasibility Studies and Safety Analyses (Project Gewahr, 1985). NAGRA Project Report NGB 85-09 (English Summary). NAGRA, Wettingen.

OECD Nuclear Energy Agency. 1992. *Systematic Approaches to Scenario Development.* Organisation for Economic Co-Operation and Development, Paris.

Stenhouse, M.J., Chapman, N.A., and Sumerling, T.J. 1993. *SITE-94 Scenario Development FEP Audit List Preparation: Methodology and Presentation.* SKI Technical Report 93:27. Swedish Nuclear Power Inspectorate, Stockholm.

Thorne, M.C. 1992. Dry Run 3 - A Trial Assessment of Underground Disposal of Radioactive Wastes Based on Probabilistic Risk Analysis – Volume 8: Uncertainty and Bias Audit. United Kingdom Department of Environment Report DOE/HMIP/RR/92.040. DOE, London.

WIPP Performance Assessment Division. 1991. *Preliminary Comparison with 40 CFR Part 191, Subpart B for the Waste Isolation Pilot Plant, December 1991.* SAND91-0893. Sandia National Laboratories, Albuquerque, NM. Vols. 1-4.

WIPP Performance Assessment Department. 1992. *Preliminary Performance Assessment for the Waste Isolation Pilot Plant, December 1992.* SAND92-0700. Sandia National Laboratories, Albuquerque, NM. Vols. 1-5.

Paper 9

FEATURE, EVENT, AND PROCESS SCREENING AND SCENARIO DEVELOPMENT FOR THE YUCCA MOUNTAIN TOTAL SYSTEM PERFORMANCE ASSESSMENT

SAND98-2831C

Peter Swift[1], George Barr[1], Ralston Barnard[1], Rob Rechard[1], Al Schenker[2], Geoffrey Freeze[3] and Peter Burck[3]
[1]Sandia National Laboratories[2]; Los Alamos Technical Associates
[3]Duke Engineering and Services, USA

1.   Introduction

Scenario development has two primary purposes in the design and documentation of post-closure performance assessments in a regulatory setting. First, scenario development ensures a sufficiently comprehensive consideration of the possible future states of the system. Second, scenario development identifies the important scenarios that must be considered in quantitative analyses of the total system performance assessment (TSPA).

To ensure clear documentation of the treatment of potentially relevant future states of the system in the Yucca Mountain license application (LA), the US Department of Energy (DOE) has chosen to adopt a scenario development process based on the methodology developed by Cranwell *et al.* (1990) for the US Nuclear Regulatory Commission (NRC). Although the process, described below, has been modified somewhat as a result of experience gained in the last decade, the underlying methodology is consistent with that outlined by the DOE in the 1988 Site Characterization Plan for the Yucca Mountain Project (YMP) (U.S. DOE, 1988). The approach is fundamentally the same as that used in many performance assessments, including the most recent analysis of the Yucca Mountain repository by the NRC (Wescott *et al.*, 1995). The approach has also been used by the DOE for the Waste Isolation Pilot Plant (WIPP) (U.S. DOE, 1996), by the Nuclear Energy Agency (NEA) of the Organisation for Economic Co-Operation and Development (OECD), and by other radioactive waste programs internationally (e.g., Skagius and Wingefors, 1992).

Section 2.0 of this report describes the scenario development process. Steps in the process are described in Section 2.1, and terms introduced in this section are defined in Section 2.2. The electronic database used to document the process is described in Section 3, and Section 4 provides a summary of the current status of the YMP scenario development work. Section 5 contains acknowledgments, and Section 6 contains a list of the references cited.

2. The Scenario Development Process

There are five principal steps to the scenario development process, as outlined in Section 2.1 and illustrated in Figure 1. Documentation of the scenario development process will include documentation of each of these steps.

2.1 The five steps of scenario development

1. Identify and classify features, events, and processes (FEPs) potentially relevant to the long-term performance of the disposal system.

2. Screen the FEPs using well-defined criteria to distinguish between those FEPs that can be excluded from the TSPA and those that should be included in the analysis.

3. Use the retained FEPs to construct scenarios, or scenario classes (which are defined as sets of related scenarios), as appropriate.

4. Screen the scenarios (or scenario classes) using the same criteria applied to the FEPs to identify any scenarios that can be excluded from the TSPA.

5. Specify the implementation of the scenarios (or scenario classes) in the computational modeling for the TSPA, and document the treatment of included FEPs.

Figure 1. **The Five Steps in Scenario Development**

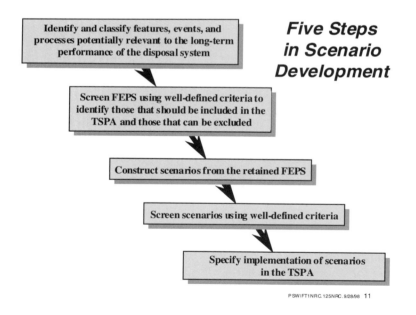

These five steps differ slightly from those identified by Cranwell *et al.* (1990), in that FEP classification, which was the second step in their procedure, has been included with the first step, and the final step has been modified to clarify the linkage between scenario development and the TSPA analysis.

2.1.1   Step 1: Identifying FEPs and building the initial FEP list

The NRC's proposed rule for the Yucca Mountain repository, 10 CFR part 63, defines performance assessment to be:

… a probabilistic analysis that:

(1)   Identifies the features, events, and processes that might affect the performance of the geologic repository; and

(2)   Examines the effects of such features, events, and processes on the performance of the geologic repository; and

(3)   Estimates the expected annual dose to the average member of the critical group as a result of releases from the geologic repository. (Proposed 10 CFR § 63.2)

Step 1 of the scenario development process, the identification of FEPs potentially relevant to the performance of the Yucca Mountain repository, will help meet NRC expectations regarding the scope of the performance assessment.

The initial set of FEPs has been created for the Yucca Mountain TSPA by combining lists of FEPs previously identified as relevant to the YMP (e.g., by Wilson *et al.*, 1994, CRWMS M&O, 1995, and other documents) with a draft FEP list compiled by an NEA working group. The NEA list is the most comprehensive list available internationally, and currently contains 1261 entries from Canadian, Swiss, and Swedish spent-fuel programs, intermediate and low-level waste programs of the UK, and the US WIPP program. The YMP initial FEP list currently (as of November 1998) contains 1573 entries.

The FEP list is open, and will continue to grow as additional FEPs are identified. Because one of the major goals of the process is to address the comprehensiveness of the TSPA, no FEPs are removed from the list at this stage. Consistent with the diverse backgrounds of the programs contributing to the NEA list, FEPs currently on the list were identified by a variety of methods, including expert judgement, informal elicitation, event tree analysis, stakeholder review, and regulatory stipulation. For the purposes of the Yucca Mountain scenario development effort, no specific technique is identified as a preferred method of FEP identification. All potentially relevant FEPs are included, regardless of origin.

This approach leads to considerable redundancy in the FEP list, because the same FEPs are frequently identified by multiple sources. To eliminate this redundancy and to create a more useful FEP list to carry forward into the screening process in Step 2, FEPs are identified in this stage as either Primary FEPs or Secondary FEPs. Primary FEPs are those FEPs for which the project proposes to develop detailed screening arguments. Secondary FEPs are either FEPs that are completely redundant (for example, the NEA list contains as many entries for meteorite impact as there were participating programs), or FEPs that can be aggregated into a single primary FEP for the purposes of the Yucca Mountain TSPA. Examples of secondary FEPs that can be aggregated into a single primary FEP for Yucca Mountain include almost all FEPs related to human disruption of the disposal system, given the proposed regulatory requirement regarding the treatment of human intrusion through a prescribed drilling scenario.

FEPs that are unarguably irrelevant to the Yucca Mountain system, such as those that are specific to repositories in salt host rock, are also identified at this stage, and are not carried through into Step 2 for the development of specific screening arguments.

Documentation is maintained at this stage of all mapping of FEPs into the primary and secondary categories, and of any FEPs identified as irrelevant. Screening work in Step 2 focuses on the primary FEPs. For comprehensiveness, traceability is maintained from the secondary FEPs to the related primary FEPs.

2.1.2 *Step 2: Screening the FEP list.*

Each FEP is screened for inclusion or exclusion in the TSPA on the basis of three basic criteria. First, each FEP is examined to determine whether or not it is of regulatory concern, given the specific regulatory requirements applicable to the Yucca Mountain TSPA. If the FEP is potentially of concern, it is then screened on the basis of its probability of occurrence or its consequence.

As described in Section 2.1.2.1, each of these screening criteria have their basis in regulatory requirements contained in the NRC's proposed rule 10 CFR part 63. FEPs are excluded from the TSPA only if they are specifically ruled out by regulation (e.g., deliberate human disruption of the site), if they can be shown to have a probability of occurrence less than 10^{-4} in 10^4 yr, or if their occurrence can be shown to have no significant effect on the overall performance of the system. Because the regulatory requirements allow exclusion of FEPs on any one of these criteria, a FEP need not be shown to be both of low probability and low consequence to be excluded. The order in which the criteria are applied is, therefore, not essential.

In practice, FEPs are screened as shown in Figure 2: regulatory criteria are examined first, and then either probability or consequence may be examined next at the discretion of the analyst. This application of the analyst's judgment regarding the order in which to apply the criteria does not affect the final decision: FEPs that are retained on one criterion will then be considered against the other. Allowing the analyst to chose the most appropriate criteria to apply at this step prevents needless work developing quantitative probability arguments for low consequence events or complex consequence models for low probability events. For example, there is no need to develop detailed models of the response of the disposal system to the impact of a large meteorite if it can be shown that this event has a probability below the regulatory cutoff.

Probability estimates for FEPs may be based on technical analysis of the past frequency of similar events (such as seismic events), or, in some cases, on expert elicitation. Probability arguments, in general, require including some information about the magnitude of the event in its definition. For example, the probability of meteorite impacts depends on the size of the meteorite of interest. Impacts of meteorites sufficiently large to create large craters at Yucca Mountain are much less probable than smaller impacts. Thus, meteorites large enough to affect the disposal system may be screened out on the basis of low probability (if a sufficiently low probability can be established), but small impacts that have no effect are more appropriately screened out on low consequence. Probability arguments are also sensitive to the spatial and temporal scales at which FEPs are defined (meteorite impacts are less likely in shorter time intervals and at smaller locations), and probability arguments should therefore be made at reasonably coarse scales.

Figure 2. **Schematic illustration of the FEP screening process**

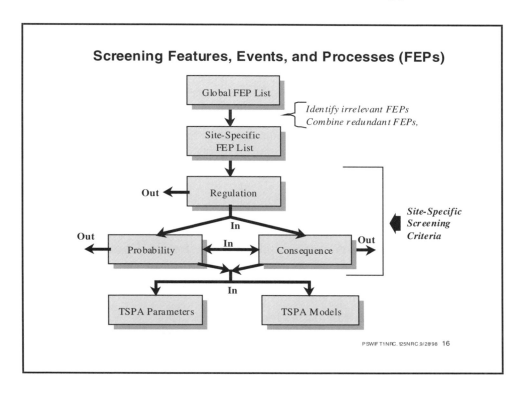

The quantitative basis for consequence-based screening arguments can be established in a variety of ways, including TSPA sensitivity analyses, modeling studies outside of the TSPA, or, in the case of relatively straightforward arguments, through the use of reasoned arguments based on literature research. For example, consequences of many geomorphic processes such as erosion and sedimentation can be evaluated by considering bounding rates reported in geologic literature. More complicated processes such as criticality require detailed analyses conducted specifically for the Yucca Mountain Project. Low-consequence arguments are often made by demonstrating that a particular FEP has no effect on the distribution of an intermediate performance measure in the TSPA. For example, demonstrating that including a particular waste form has no effect on the concentrations of radionuclides transported from the repository in the aqueous phase may be sufficient to demonstrate that including this waste form would not change the overall performance measure. Explicit modeling of the characteristics of this waste form could therefore be excluded from the TSPA.

Documentation of the FEP screening step in the scenario development process will include a statement of the screening decision for each FEP (retained or excluded). For excluded FEPs, documentation will include the criterion on which it was excluded and the technical basis for the screening argument. Documentation of the treatment of retained FEPs in the models and parameters of the TSPA, as shown in the last steps of Figure 2, will be provided by Step 4.

2.1.2.1   *Regulatory screening criteria in proposed 10 CFR part 63*

Proposed 10 CFR part 63 contains regulatory screening criteria relevant to many FEPs. Examples include the explicit requirements regarding assumptions about the critical group to be considered in the dose assessment (at § 63.115), and the specification of the treatment of human intrusion (at § 63.113(d)).

The probability criterion is explicitly stated at § 63.114:

(d) Consider only events that have at least one chance in 10 000 of occurring over 10 000 years.

Because the probability of any specific event depends strongly on how it is defined, the probability criterion can only be applied at an appropriately broad scale. For example, the probability of seismic events should be evaluated over the entire 10 000-year period, rather than being artificially lowered by defining 10 000 different seismic events each occurring in a different year.

Consequence criteria are provided at § 63.114(e) and § 63.114(f):

(e) Provide the technical basis for either inclusion or exclusion of specific features, events, and processes of the geologic setting in the performance assessment. Specific features, events, and processes of the geologic setting must be evaluated in detail if the magnitude and time of the resulting expected annual dose would be significantly changed by their omission.

(f) Provide the technical basis for either inclusion or exclusion of degradation, deterioration, or alteration processes of engineered barriers in the performance assessment, including those processes that would adversely affect the performance of natural barriers. Degradation, deterioration, or alteration processes of engineered barriers must be evaluated in detail if the magnitude and time of the resulting expected annual dose would be significantly changed by their omission.

2.1.3   *Step 3: Constructing scenarios*

The NRC has not defined the term "scenario" in draft proposed 10 CFR part 63. The Yucca Mountain TSPA has chosen to define a scenario as a subset of the set of all possible futures of the disposal system that contains futures resulting from a specific combination of features, events, and processes.

The primary reason for adopting this definition is pragmatic: one of the goals of scenario development is to define a limited set of scenarios that can reasonably be analyzed quantitatively while still maintaining comprehensive coverage of the range of possible future states of the system. There are an essentially infinite number of possible future states, and for scenario development to be useful, it must generate scenarios that are representative of the range of futures that are potentially relevant to the licensing of the facility.

Under the definition adopted for the Yucca Mountain TSPA, a scenario is not limited to a single, deterministic future of the system, and instead is a set of similar futures that share common FEPs. The number and breadth of scenarios depend on the resolution at which the FEPs have been defined: coarsely defined FEPs result in fewer, broad scenarios, whereas narrowly defined FEPs result in many narrow scenarios. There is no uniquely correct level of detail at which to define scenarios: decisions regarding the appropriate level of resolution for the analysis are made based on consideration of the importance of the scenario in its effect on overall performance and the resolution desired in the results. For efficiency, both FEPs and scenarios should be aggregated at the coarsest level at which a technically sound argument can be made that is adequate for the purposes of the analysis.

More coarsely defined scenarios may be referred to as scenario classes (sets of closely related scenarios), and more narrowly defined scenarios may be referred to as subscenarios. Mathematically, scenario classes and subscenarios share the same definition as scenarios: all are subsets of the set of all possible futures of the system. In practical application, however, distiguishing between coarsely defined scenario classes and more narrowly defined scenarios and subscenarios is useful. For example, both the DOE and the NRC have identified "igneous activity occurs at Yucca Mountain" as one of the most important disruptive scenario classes for the repository. Within this class, consequence analyses have focussed on specific scenarios and subscenarios involving processes such as ash plume eruption and lava intrusion.

Before scenarios are constructed, FEPs retained from Step 2 are identified as either expected FEPS (EFEPs) or disruptive FEPs (DFEPs). Expected FEPs are those that can be assumed, for the purposes of the TSPA, to have a probability of occurrence equal to 1.0 (although they may have uncertain consequences). DFEPs are those that have a probability less than 1.0 (but greater than the lower cutoff prescribed by the NRC) and have a significant effect on overall performance. All EFEPs are included in a nominal scenario, which is simulated by the base case model described in the TSPA documentation. Disruptive scenarios are constructed from all EFEPs and combinations of DFEPs, with the probability of each disruptive scenario calculated as the product of the probabilities of the included DFEPs.

Scenario construction can be displayed graphically using logic diagrams (Figure 3). Note that these diagrams do not imply any ordering of the events: they are simply a graphical way of displaying the possible combinations of the retained DFEPs. Documentation of this step in the scenario development process will include demonstration that scenarios incorporate all combinations of retained DFEPs, and that probabilities of the scenarios have been correctly calculated based on FEP probabilities.

2.1.4   Step 4: Screening scenarios

Scenarios constructed in step 3 are screened using the same regulatory, probability, and consequence criteria defined in step 2. For example, the probability criterion may be used to exclude scenarios that include some combinations of low probability FEPs.

If scenarios are to be screened out on the basis of low probability, the probability must be taken at an appropriately coarse level. Scenarios should not be defined artificially narrowly to reduce their probability below the NRC cutoff.

Documentation of this step in the scenario development process will include identification of any scenarios that have been screened from the analysis, and the technical basis for that screening decision.

205

Figure 3. **Logic Diagram for the Yucca Mountain TSPA for the 1998 Viability Assessment, showing the construction of scenarios using combinations of disruptive FEPs. Note that this figure is provided for illustration only. The scenarios shown here may not be the final set analyzed for the Yucca Mountain license application.**

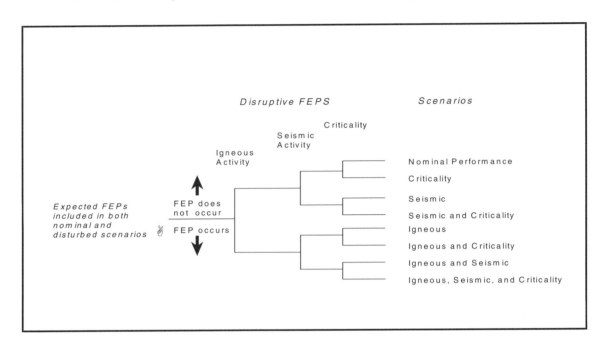

2.1.5   Step 5: Specifying scenarios for TSPA analysis

All retained FEPs must be included in TSPA analyses either in the nominal scenario or in disruptive scenarios. EFEPs may be included in the nominal scenario either through explicit modeling or through the selection of parameter values. DFEPs are included explicitly in modeling of disruptive scenarios.

Documentation of step 5 will include identification of how each retained FEP has been treated in the TSPA. As shown in Figure 2, retained FEPs will be treated either through explicit incorporation in TSPA models or through uncertainty included in the assignment of parameter values used in the TSPA models.

2.2   Definitions

FEP: a feature, event, or process.

Feature: an object, structure, or condition that has a potential to affect disposal system performance.

Event: a natural or anthropogenic phenomenon that has a potential to affect disposal system performance and that occurs during an interval that is short compared to the period of performance.

Process:	a natural or anthropogenic phenomenon that has a potential to affect disposal system performance and that operates during all or a significant part of the period of performance.
Future:	a single, deterministic representation of the future state of the system. An essentially infinite set of futures can be imagined for any system.
Scenario:	a subset of the set of all possible futures of the disposal system that contains futures resulting from a specific combination of features, events, and processes.
Scenario class:	a set of scenarios that share sufficient similarities that they can usefully be aggregated for the purposes of a specific analysis.
Subscenario:	a subset of a scenario (or a scenario class) created by defining one or more of the component FEPs more narrowly.
Retained FEP:	a FEP that is identified by the screening process as requiring analysis in the quantitative total system performance assessment.
Expected FEP (EFEP):	a retained FEP that, for the purposes of the total system performance assessment, is assumed to occur with a probability equal to 1.0 during the period of performance.
Disruptive FEP (DFEP):	a retained FEP that has a probability of occurrence during the period of performance less than 1.0 (but greater than the cutoff of $10^{-4}/10^4$ yr defined by the NRC at 10 CFR § 63.114(d)).
Nominal scenario:	the scenario that contains all expected FEPs and no disruptive FEPs.
Disruptive scenario:	any scenario that contains all expected FEPs and one or more disruptive FEPs.

3.   The Electronic FEP Database

The YMP performance assessment team is constructing an electronic database of FEPs. Each FEP identified in Step 1 of the process will be entered as a separate record in the database. Fields within each record will provide a description of the FEP, unique identification numbers, the origin of the FEP, identification as a primary or secondary FEP for the purposes of the YMP TSPA, and mapping to related FEPs. Fields will also provide summaries of the screening arguments, with references to supporting documentation, and, for all retained FEPs, statements of the disposition of the FEP within the TSPA modeling system.

The current YMP electronic FEP database has 1737 FEPs entered in preliminary form. The database has been developed in Claris Filemaker Pro Version 4.0, which is the same software adopted by the NEA working group for their FEP database. Working copies of the YMP FEP database are also available in Microsoft Access 97.

4.   Current Status of the YMP Scenario Development Work

Work done for the viability assessment and previous preliminary TSPAs has identified igneous activity, seismic activity, and criticality as potentially important disruptive FEPs, and quantitative analyses have focussed on the nominal scenario and the major disturbed scenarios associated with these events.

Scenario development work for the Yucca Mountain license application is primarily focussed on documentation of Steps 1 and 2 of the five-step process at this time. This documentation may confirm that the scenarios selected for preliminary analysis are appropriate and sufficiently comprehensive to support the LA. However, ongoing work may identify FEPs for which additional analyses are needed to support a screening decision (either in or out), and additional EFEPs or DFEPs could be identified that will require modification of the scenarios analyzed in the TSPA.

Once the TSPA modeling system for the LA is mature, FEP work will focus on Step 5, providing the documentation for how all retained FEPs have been treated in the TSPA.

Scenario development is an iterative process, because new FEPs may be added to the initial list and screening decisions for existing FEPs may change as new information becomes available. Regulatory requirements that form the essential basis for all FEP screening may also change when the US Environmental Protection Agency (EPA) promulgates 40 CFR part 197 and when the NRC promulgates the final rule for 10 CFR part 63. FEP screening decisions and the resulting scenarios considered in the TSPA-VA are therefore preliminary. Screening arguments for excluded FEPs will continue to be developed during the preparation of the LA, and the treatment of the included EFEPs and DFEPs will change as the TSPA models and parameters are refined.

5. Acknowledgements

Kate Trauth and Jack Gauthier provided valuable technical reviews of this report. Work was done at Sandia National Laboratories for the Civilian Radioactive Waste Management System Management and Operating Contractor and for the US Department of Energy Yucca Mountain Site Characterization Project. Sandia is a multiprogram laboratory operated by Sandia Corporation, a Lockheed Martin Company, for the United States Department of Energy under contract DE-AC04-94AL8500.

6. References

Cranwell, R.M., Guzowski, R.V., Campbell, J.E., and Ortiz, N.R. 1990. *Risk Methodology for Geologic Disposal of Radioactive Waste: Scenario Selection Procedure*. NUREG/CR-1667, SAND80-1429. Prepared for the Division of High Level Waste Management, Office of Nuclear Material Safety and Safeguards, U.S. Nuclear Regulatory Commission, Washington, D.C. NNA.19900611.0073.

CRWMS M&O (Civilian Radioactive Waste Management System Management and Operating Contractor). 1995. *Total System Performance Assessment – 1995: An Evaluation of the Potential Yucca Mountain Repository*. B00000000-01717-2200-00136, Rev. 01. TRW Environmental Safety Systems Inc., Las Vegas, NV for U.S. Department of Energy, Office of Civilian Radioactive Waste Management, Washington, D.C. TIC Catalog Number 224028.

Skagius, K., and Wingefors, S. 1992. *Alligator Rivers Analogue Project Final Report, Volume 16: Application of Scenario Development Methods in Evaluation of the Koongarra Analogue*. ISBN 0-642-59942-4, DOE/HMIP/RR/92/086, SKI TR 92:20-16. Australian Nuclear Science and Technology Organisation. TIC Catalog Number: 231268.

U.S. DOE. 1988. *Consultation Draft Site Characterization Plan Overview, Yucca Mountain Site, Nevada Research and Development Area, Nevada.* DOE/RW-0161. U.S. Department of Energy, Office of Civilian Radioactive Waste Management, Washington, D.C. TIC Catalog Number: 203432.

U.S. DOE. 1996. *Title 40 CFR Part 191 Compliance Certification Application for the Waste Isolation Pilot Plant.* DOE/CAO-1996-2184. United States Department of Energy, Waste Isolation Pilot Plant, Carlsbad Area Office, Carlsbad, NM. Vols. I-XXI. TIC Catalog Number: 240511.

U.S. NRC. 1999. *Title 10 CFR Parts 2, 19, 20, 21, 30, 40, 51, 60, 61, and 63, Disposal of High-Level Radioactive Wastes in a Proposed Geologic Repository at Yucca Mountain; Proposed Rule.* February 22, 1999. United States Nuclear Regulatory Commission. Federal Register, Vol. 64, no. 34, p. 8640-8679.

Wescott, R.G., Lee, M.P., Eisenberg, N.A., McCartin, T.J., and Baca, R.G., Editors. 1995. *NRC Iterative Performance Assessment Phase 2: Development of Capabilities for Review of a Performance Assessment for a High-Level Waste Repository.* NUREG-1464. Southwest Research Institute, Center for Nuclear Waste Regulatory Analyses, San Antonio, TX for Nuclear Regulatory Commission, Washington, DC. TIC Catalog Number: 221527.

Wilson, M.L., Gauthier, J.H., Barnard, R.W., Barr, G.E., Dockery, H.A., Dunn, E., Eaton, R.R., Guerin, D.C., Lu, N., Martinez, M.J., Nilson, R., Rautman, C.A., Robey, T.H., Ross, B., Ryder, E.E., Schenker, A.R., Shannon, S.A., Skinner, L.H., Halsey, W.G., Gansemer, J.D., Lewis, L.C., Lamont, A.D., Triay, I.R., Meijer, A., and Morris, D.E. 1994. *Total-System Performance Assessment for Yucca Mountain-SNL Second Iteration (TSPA-1993).* SAND93-2675. Sandia National Laboratories, Albuquerque, NM. TIC Catalog Number: 102773.

SCENARIO DEVELOPMENT FOR SAFETY ASSESSMENT OF RADIOACTIVE WASTE REPOSITORIES IN SWITZERLAND

Trevor Sumerling[1] and Frits von Dorp[2]
[1] Safety Assessment Management Ltd., Reading, UK.
[2] Nagra, Wettingen, Switzerland.

1. Introduction

Radioactive waste in Switzerland arises from the operation of nuclear power plants,[1] from the management of nuclear fuel waste, and from medicine, industry and research. Wastes are stored at the sites of origin and also at the ZWILAG central facility for interim storage, opened in 1998(?). Two types of repository are foreseen for the long-term underground storage, and eventual disposal, of radioactive waste:

- a repository for low-level and short-lived intermediate-level waste (L/ILW), which will consist of mined caverns with horizontal access located in a suitable host rock. Wellenberg, in North-central Switzerland, has been proposed as the location for this repository, where the potential host rock is a Valanginian Marl (a calcareous, argillaceous sediment).

- a repository for spent fuel, vitrified high-level waste and long-lived intermediate level waste (SF/HLW/ILW), which will consist of deep underground tunnels and caverns. In the past, crystalline basement rocks of Northern Switzerland have been investigated as a potential host rock, and attention is currently being given to bringing assessments of an argillaceous sediment – the Opalinus Clay – also in Northern Switzerland, to a similar standard.

Nagra is responsible for research and development work associated with the development of such facilities and, in particular, the assessment of their long-term safety. Since 1985, Nagra has carried out a series of safety assessments of possible disposal systems in Switzerland, in which scenario development has played as increasingly central role, see Table 1.

As described in Sumerling *et al.* (1993), the scenario development procedure identifies and provides the logical framework for the safety calculations to be made in the immediate phase of assessments and, also, identifies and keeps track of issues which may affect safety but cannot be fully dealt with at the present stage of site data, scientific understanding or model development, see Figure 1.

---

1. Switzerland has an operating nuclear capacity of 3 GW electrical power.

2. Objectives for Scenario Development

The aim of safety assessments by Nagra is to provide a simple but unequivocal demonstration of safety. As discussed in McCombie *et al.* (1991), to provide a robust safety case, an assessment should comprise:

- a detailed description of all key features of the disposal system and of the events and processes which will operate upon them;

- the representation of selected features, events and processes (FEPs) by means of models and parameter values (or ranges of values) that are either conservative or are well supported by direct evidence;

- an examination of the uncertainty associated with selection of FEPs and with their representation in models by means, for example, of a hierarchy of deterministic calculations.

Figure 2 illustrates the general approach. In moving from detailed understanding of the system to a robust safety concept, progressively reduced or simplified models are used and conservative (pessimistic) model assumptions and data are adopted. The reduction process cannot reduce the uncertainty that is inherent in the problem. Rather, the uncertainty is replaced by conservatism. The resulting model estimates are not precise forecasts of the system performance but, rather, provide an upper bound on the potential radiological consequences. This simplification of reality increases the prospects for validation of models and obtaining supportable data. Attention can be focused on processes which have been observed in laboratory, field or analogue studies; other less well characterised processes are treated conservatively.

The objectives for scenario development within this context are detailed in Table 2.

3. The Scenario Development Procedure

The Nagra scenario development procedure, developed from that presented by Sumerling *et al.* (1993), is summarised in Figure 3. It consists of the following stages, although, during a practical application, there may be substantial iteration between the stages.

1. Define the disposal system, including waste allocation and design options. Identify the key features and processes that are expected to provide for the long-term safety – termed the *Safety Concept*. This will include, for example, favourable waste, engineered barrier and host rock properties, and the processes which can be expected to ensure the longevity of favourable properties and prevent, or minimise, release of radionuclides. If necessary, iterate on the design with the aim of ensuring reliable functioning and performance of the various safety barriers.

2. Develop a catalogue of all the potentially relevant features, events and processes (FEPs) based on detailed understanding of the system and related experimental and field evidence. First, record the scientific knowledge and understanding of each FEP, evaluate the importance and, then, add information on how the process could or will be treated in the safety assessment. This catalogue may be expanded by iteration among project staff and, also, audited against international experience as a means to improve completeness.

3. Develop a description of the behaviour of the disposal system (the wastes, repository and its environment) incorporating scientific understanding and indicating the interactions of all relevant FEPs – termed the **System Concept**. First, develop a description of the expected behaviour, respecting the various design functions set out in the safety concept, then alternative behaviours, e.g. due to less likely events or evolutions, can be explored. Influence diagrams can be used to illustrate the interactions. In Nagra work, these have been used to show the main dependencies for the whole disposal system and also build up understanding of the interactions within sub-elements of the disposal system, e.g. the waste form, the buffer/backfill, particular host rock domains, etc. In these more detailed diagrams each FEP of the catalogue can be represented and the importance of FEPs and interactions indicated.

4. Compare the system understanding, e.g. as illustrated by influence diagrams, with the available models and data and use this to define the set of safety assessment calculations. In the Nagra methodology, this consists of:

   a) a Reference Case,[2] which consists of a Reference Scenario, Reference Model Assumptions and Reference Data;

   b) alternative models and data which are used to explore uncertainty in the representation and data related to the Reference Scenario;

   c) alternative scenarios, which investigate alternative evolutions of the disposal system or the effect of additional FEPs not included in the Reference Scenario;

   d) if necessary, alternative models and data can also be applied within important alternative scenarios.

In addition, FEPs that may be important but are not included in current assessment models should also be identified. These fall into two categories:

   e) *reserve FEPs* – are FEPs that are expected to be beneficial to safety but are not included in current analyses because of lack of data or for reasons of modelling convenience. Exclusion of a reserve FEP from model will tend to make the model conservative, although the degree of conservatism may be difficultt to estimate.

   f) *open questions* – are issues that may adversely affect safety, but are not adequately dealt with at present. Usually these are discussed qualitatively and design changes or additional research required to resolve the issue are suggested.

5. Finally, a *robust safety calculation case* is defined, including only those FEPs that can be relied on to enhance safety, plus the most conservative interpretation of current uncertainties. For example, in the Kristallin-I assessment, the robust case considered normal functioning of the engineered barriers with conservative parameter selection, plus a very pessimistic treatment of the geosphere in which radionuclides were assumed to be transported from the engineered barriers to the biosphere with no delay or attenuation.

---

2. The Reference Case is devised as a calculationally convenient case within the Reference Scenario. It will usually incorporate the most conservative of alternative models for key processes and parameter values will tend to be conservatively selected. Hence, the result will be a moderately conservative.

Figure 4 summarises the handling of FEPs in the Kristallin-I scenario development. All FEPs are first screened and then categorised as: unimportant, reserve, open question or included in the safety assessment calculations. Those included are represented in the Reference Scenario, which includes alternative model assumptions and parameter variations (see points a) and b) in 4., above) or in alternative scenarios (see points c) and d) in 4.) that cover the realistically expected future conditions and also unexpected or unlikely conditions.

4.   Experience with Scenario Development

The Nagra scenario development procedures have been developed iteratively, and experience has been gained, over a number of safety assessments, see Table 1. Key features of this experience are as follows:

1. It is important to use the scientific and technical experience of the various project staff and find methods (e.g. via meetings, written report by experts and review of draft scenario-related material) to mobilise and incorporate this experience.

2. It is necessary to present and explain the scenario methodology to project staff as the vehicle by which individual experts will be able to contribute to developing the safety assessment.

3. Meetings of experts from various disciplines are a good tool to expand the common understanding of system behaviour and give individuals a better feel for where their contribution fits within an overall framework and what is, and is not, important to safety.

4. Thorough documentation of FEPs, initially by subject experts, provides the scientific and technical information basis. This must then be synthesised into a coherent whole, and decisions on how to treat various FEPs made by experts with overall understanding of system performance and model capabilities.

5. Given the relatively long time needed to develop new models and the relatively short time sometimes available for an assessment, it is clear that assessment calculations may be constrained by existing capability. The identification of reserve FEPs and open questions is a valuable way to keep track of limitations within current models and calculations and give pointers for future model development and data collection.

6. Audit against international FEP lists and experience can give broad assurance on completeness, but key processes are generally design and/or host rock specific. More detailed assurance of completeness must come from good understanding of the relevant processes in their design, host rock and site-specific context.

7. The discipline of creating a comprehensive FEP catalogue and ensuring traceability to calculations is valuable and gives considerable confidence to reviewers, e.g. in regulatory review, who often focus on issues of completeness.

8. Formal scenario development methods also give a logical framework to safety assessments which is valuable in communicating both to outside audiences and within an assessment project.

References

McCombie C., McKinley I. G. and Zuidema P. 1991: Sufficient Validation: The Value of Robustness in Performance Assessment and System Design. In GEOVAL-1990, Symposium on Validation of Geosphere Flow and Transport Models, pp. 598-610. OECD/NEA, Paris, France.

Nagra 1985. Project Gewähr 1985: Nuclear Waste Management in Switzerland: Feasibility Studies and Safety Analyses. Nagra Project Report NGB 85-09, Baden, Switzerland.

Nagra 1994: Kristallin-I Safety Assessment Report, NTB 93-22, Wettingen, Switzerland.

Nagra 1994b: Bericht zur Langzeitsicherheit des Endlagers SMA am Standort Wellenberg. Nagra Technisher Bericht NTB 94-06, Wettingen, Switzerland

Sumerling T.J., Zuidema P., Grogan H.A. and von Dorp F. 1993: Scenario development for safety demonstration for deep geological disposal in Switzerland. Proc. 4th International Conference on High Level Radioactive Waste Management, Las Vegas.

Sumerling T.J., Grogan H.A and Smith P.A. 1999: Scenario Development for Kristallin-I, Nagra Technical Report NTB 93-13, Wettingen, Switzerland.

Table 1. **Safety assessments carried out in Switzerland – their objectives and the increasing role of scenario development**

Title (reference)	Purpose and scope of assessment	Scope and method of scenario development
Project Gewähr 1985 (Nagra 1985)	Demonstration of feasibility of safe disposal of radioactive waste in Switzerland. Considered (1) deep geological disposal of vitrified HLW and long-lived ILW in crystalline basement of Northern Switzerland, and (2) disposal of L/ILW in caverns with horizontal access in low permeability host rock.	A list of relevant "scenario mechanisms" were identified, classified and indications given of how these were accommodated in various models. Most could be considered as parameter variations on a groundwater transport scenario (base case). Other cases were mainly low probability scenarios.
Kristallin-I (Nagra 1994)	Post-closure radiological safety assessment of disposal of vitrified HLW in the crystalline basement of Northern Switzerland, taking account of a synthesis of information from regional geological investigations and four deep boreholes in the crystalline basement.	A formal scenario development method was applied including development of a FEP catalogue, screening, auditing, construction of influence diagrams and mapping to model capability. Time pressures predicated that the latter part of the exercise was carried out as a "back-fitting" exercise with attention given to justification of selected scenarios and identification and discussion of reserve FEPs and open questions.
Wellenberg (Nagra 1994b)	Post-closure radiological safety assessment in support of an application for a general licence for a repository for L/ILW at Wellenberg. Disposal in large cross-section concrete-lined caverns with cement backfill excavated in Valanginian Marl.	Scenario development method similar to Kristallin-1, although a detailed FEP catalogue was not developed. The most important FEPs affecting the various elements of the system plus future geological and climatic processes, and human activities, were identified and their implications considered. This led to definition of a Reference scenario treated with alternative models and alternative scenarios.

Table 2. The objectives for scenario development within the Nagra safety assessment approach

1. To identify and document all those features, events and processes (FEPs) that could be relevant to the performance and/or safety of the disposal system, and to examine the FEPs to determine which should be accounted for in safety assessment calculations.

2. To organise the selected FEPs into scenarios consistent with the safety assessment models that are available.

3. To provide traceable technical arguments for the phenomenological scope and basis of the scenarios defined for quantitative analysis, and to document arguments for the exclusion of those FEPs that are not included.

4. To identify any FEPs that are not being adequately addressed within the current structure of models and scenarios and are the cause of unacceptable uncertainties or have the potential to undermine significant elements of the safety assessment. These are termed "open questions".

5. To identify any FEPs that are not accounted for within the current models but which are expected to be beneficial to safety. These are termed "reserve FEPs" 1.

6. To provide guidance for model development, detailed modelling or data gathering to support future phases of safety assessment calculations and, in particular, to recommend paths by which open questions may be resolved, or reserve FEPs taken into account, to improve the final safety demonstration.

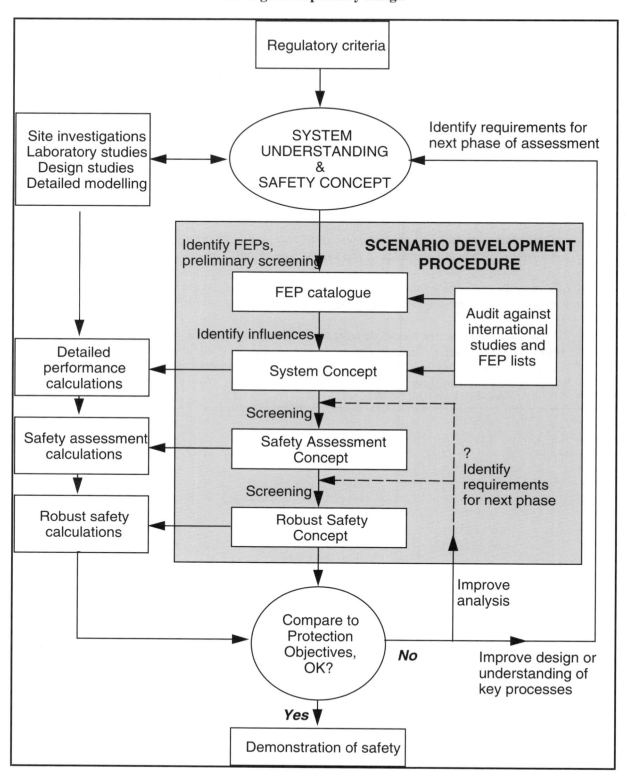

Figure 1. **The central role of the Nagra scenario development procedure for a given repository design**

Figure 2. **Development of a robust safety concept by progressive simplification of models and adoption of conservative model assumptions and data**

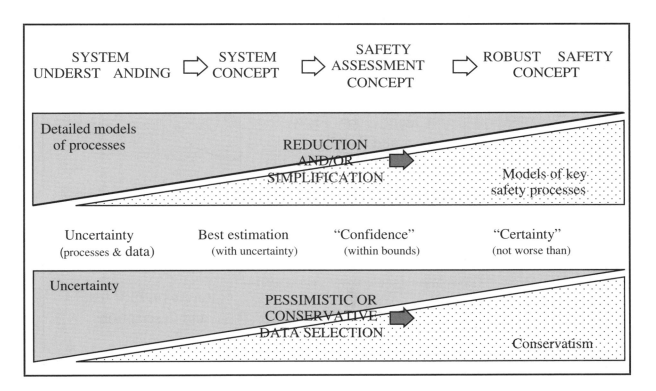

Figure 3. **The Nagra scenario development procedure**

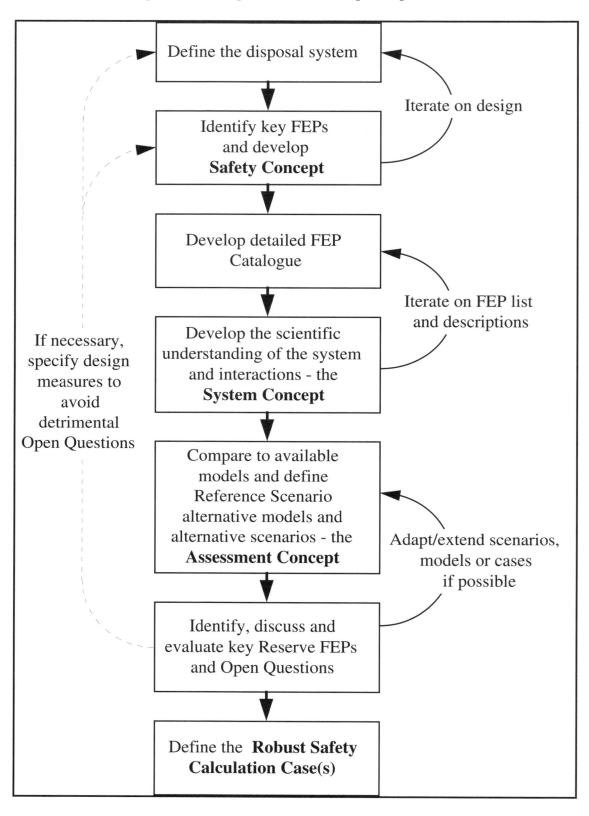

Figure 4. The treatment of FEPs in the Kristallin-I scenario development

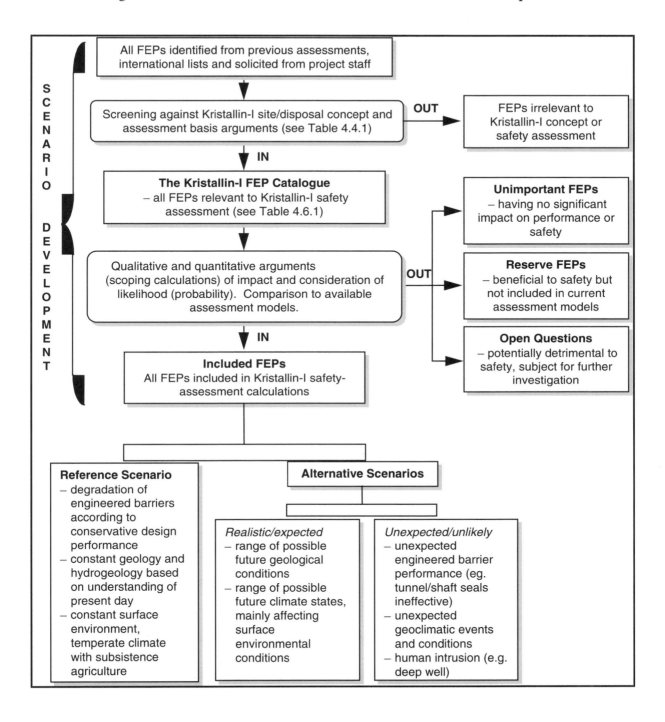

Tables A and B are to be used in the NEA Scenario Workshop report appendix. Similar information will be requested from other organisations.

Table A. **Summary of scenarios evaluated in the Kristallin-I safety assessment (Nagra 1994)**

Scenarios	Main characteristics
Reference Scenario	• conservative near-field evolution according to design • expected long-term performance of buffer and chemical controls • radionuclide release and transport in groundwater • constant hydrogeology and biosphere based on present-day • exfiltration to gravel aquifer in the Rhine Valley • agricultural subsistence exposed group The Reference Scenario is represented by Reference and alternative models which consider: radionuclide transport in a major water-conducting-fault, alternative geometries of water-conducting features in the host rock, limited and unlimited matrix diffusion, heterogeneous distribution of groundwater flow in water-conducting features, transport of radionuclides with colloids.
Continuation of Alpine Orogeny	Uplift, erosion and southward movement of the Rhine lead to changed flow path in HPD and changed groundwater flow in the LPD. These changes are covered by parameter variations within the Reference Scenario.
Exfiltration to Small Valley	Possible for a repository in 'Area East'. Exfiltration to gravel aquifer of small tributary valley. Covered by additional biosphere calculations within the Reference Scenario.
Deep Groundwater Well	Water abstracted directly from the crystalline basement. Exposure by drinking water only.
Tunnel/Shaft Seal Failure	Tunnel/shaft seals ineffective after repository closure. Radionuclide movement along tunnels and shafts and/or associated excavation disturbed zone.
Alternative Climate-Related Scenarios	
Dry Climate State	Increased evapotranspiration and decreased precipitation. Increased irrigation. Agricultural subsistence group.
Humid Climate State	Increased precipitation and evapotranspiration. Agricultural subsistence group.
Periglacial Climate State	Decreased temperature, precipitation and evapotranspiration. Reduced flow in local aquifer. Subsistence group based on grazing and herding. Continuous permafrost developed.
Rhine Gravels Absent	Rhine gravels eroded. No local aquifer. Exfiltration to river Rhine or to soil directly over the basement.

Note: Because of the simplifications of the assessment models, the Reference Scenario as represented by the models and parameter variations is sufficiently broad to represent a range of scenarios for future evolution.

Abbreviations: LPD = low permeability domain of the crystalline basement.

                    HPD = higher permeability domain of the crystalline basement.

Table B. Summary of scenarios evaluated in the Wellenberg safety assessment (Nagra 1994b)

Scenario	Main Characteristics
Reference Scenario	• considers four waste groups with different characteristics • rapid saturation of caverns, dissolution of radionuclides into cavern pore water and transport in the EBS by advection, dispersion • different degrees of displacement of contaminated water by repository generated gas • transport in the geosphere by advection-dispersion in cataclastic zones and limestone beds • long-term increase in host rock permeability due to erosion of overburden • exfiltration to valley floor (most likely) or to hill slopes (low probability) The Reference Scenario is represented by Reference and alternative models which consider, for example, alternative waste characteristics, gas-induced radionuclide release, release influenced by near-field colloids, geosphere transport in limestone beds, geosphere colloids, exfiltration to hill sides, increased permeability due to erosion, arid climate.
Release along Connecting Tunnel	Tunnel seals are ineffective. Radionuclide release occurs along connecting tunnel. (No plausible reason identified; scenario evaluated to investigate the importance of repository sealing).
Erosive Uncovering of the Repository	Erosion leading to early uncovering of the repository and direct release of radionuclides into the biosphere at 100 000 years after closure.
Release of Gaseous Volatile Nuclides	Gas formation in the repository near field and the transport of volatile nuclides from the near-field to the biosphere in gas phase.

SCENARIO DEVELOPMENT AND ANALYSIS IN JNC'S SECOND PROGRESS REPORT

H. Umeki, H. Makino, K. Miyahara and M. Naito
Japan Nuclear Cycle Development Institute (JNC)

Abstract

Scenario development and analysis is an integral part of the performance assessment in the JNC's second progress report which will be issued by the end of November 1999. A systematic approach has been elaborated to ensure traceability and transparency in overall context of the scenario development and set up of calculation cases for assessment of the repository performance.

In this approach, the hierarchical FEP matrix was designed to flexibly identify FEPs at different level of detail. The reasoned argument with clearly defined criteria was then applied for screening and grouping of FEPs to define scenarios in the form of influence diagrams. Scenarios and calculation cases were developed based on the expected safety functions of disposal system and relationships with potential detrimental/favorable factors and perturbation factors. The process to develop scenarios and calculation cases are recorded and managed in a computer system.

1.   Introduction

Safety assessments of geological disposal consider time scales that surpass those relevant to ordinary social or technological activities. In addition, assessments need to consider large spatial domains of geosphere whose properties are heterogeneous. These large spatio-temporal scales and the uncertainties associated with them are key characteristics of safety assessments for geological disposal. It is therefore impossible to demonstrate safety by a direct method, as in conventional engineering practice, in which a system is created and confirmed through and optimized direct testing.

As a result of extensive discussion of approaches to this problem by different national and international organizations, a general approach to the safety assessment of geological disposal has been developed and practical methodologies for conducting safety assessments have been implemented (e.g. OECD/NEA, 1991). The process starts by defining a repository concept (based, at least partly, on the waste type), collecting information on the geological environment to be considered and designing the repository design on the basis of this information. The safety functions of the geological disposal system are then defined, and the future behavior of the system is assessed based on scenarios, models and data.

The primary objective of scenario analysis is to define an unambiguous scope for the safety assessment. This is achieved by identifying potential future situations where radionuclides in the waste could give rise to radiological impacts to future generations. These situations are then analyzed in order to assess their likely consequences and the implications to repository performance.

A key stage in developing scenarios is to compile a comprehensive list of Features, Events and Processes (FEPs) which could affect the safety and performance of a geological disposal system. Combinations of FEPs are used to build scenarios, which cover a wide spectrum of possible future behavior of a geological disposal system, providing the foundation for a comprehensive safety assessment. Information on FEPs is derived from the international scientific knowledge base augmented by relevant laboratory and field experiments. Clearly, it is impossible to make precise predictions of the future evolution of the geological disposal system, because of an incomplete understanding of the relevant FEPs. However, an international consensus has been reached that scenarios which are fit for the purpose of safety assessment can be developed for geological disposal systems in individual countries on the basis of the FEP lists prepared through international cooperation (OECD/NEA, 1991) and expert judgment.

In the second progress report of JNC (entitled H12), scenarios are developed based on a systematic approach proposed internationally but the following features have been introduced:

- FEPs are linked to expected safety functions, potential detrimental/favorable factors and perturbation factors of disposal system.

- Performance assessment starts with a discussion of the FEPs which are language-based descriptions of the experts' view on the system's behavior. This leads to quantitative analyses for a set of calculation cases. In many assessments, scenario analysis covers only a part of this procedure and there is a risk of introducing inconsistency and of losing traceability at the interface between scenarios and calculation cases. In order to avoid this, the scope of the scenario analysis is expanded to include the development of a number of calculation cases corresponding alternative geological disposal systems and uncertainties in scenarios, models and data.

- A site for geological disposal in Japan and the associated repository design have yet to be decided and this therefore expands the scope of the safety assessment for H12.

The safety assessment in H12 is performed in accord with the guidelines published in 1997 ("Guidelines on Research and Development Relating to Disposal of High-Level Radioactive Waste in Japan", hereafter the AEC Guidelines) (the Advisory Committee on Nuclear Fuel Cycle Backend Policy, AEC, 1997).

2.   Procedures for Scenario Analysis

2.1   General procedure for scenario development

Scenarios are developed by taking the following steps based on a systematic approach which was proposed by several international organizations (e.g. OECD/NEA, 1991; 1992; 1997) and reviewed by a working group coordinated by the NEA (Hodgkinson and Sumerling, 1990):

- Preparing a comprehensive FEP list relevant to the performance of the system, which must meet the objectives and scope of geological disposal in Japan;

- Repeated screening of FEPs according to a set of well-defined criteria to ensure that all possibilities are examined;

226

- Developing scenarios taking into account interactions among FEPs and preparing a final list of FEPs to be considered in calculations that are deemed to adequately cover all likely evolutions of repository behavior.

2.2 *Scenario analysis procedure in H12*

A "bottom-up" approach represented by the above steps is combined with a "top-down" approach, in which expected safety functions, potential detrimental/favorable factors or perturbation factors are defined and are subdivided to components (corresponding to FEPs or groups of FEPs and their interaction) to describe their possible impact on long-term safety in more detail. Table 1 shows expected safety functions and factors to affect system performance considered in H12. In this approach, a list of FEPs is used to represent views of experts from a wide range of subjects, and scenarios are developed regarding these FEPs and their interactions as the building blocks, which are integrated based on a top-down view concerning their possible impact on long-term safety. Thus a comprehensive set of scenarios can be developed that is also linked with the body of scientific expertise.

Following the scenario development, calculation cases for the safety assessment are developed by taking the following steps:

- Definition of groups of calculation cases based on the following variations and uncertainties that need to be considered in the safety assessment :

  - Alternative geological environments in Japan;

  - Design options for the EBS and other repository components;

  - Uncertainty due to incomplete understanding of possible future behavior of the geological disposal system (*scenario uncertainty*);

  - Uncertainty in models used to describe the nuclide transport processes and/or the repository evolution (*model uncertainty*);

  - Uncertainty in the data used in the models (*data uncertainty*).

- Definition of the detailed contents of the calculation cases for each group mentioned above.

Figure 1 summarizes the procedure in scenario analysis mentioned above.

3. Scenario Development

3.1 *Preparation of a comprehensive FEP list*

When developing scenarios for H12, a comprehensive list of FEPs was generated to describe the expected safety functions in more detail, and to discuss potential detrimental/favorable or potential perturbation factors which may impact the system performance. Generic FEP lists, prepared as part of international collaborative projects (OECD/NEA, 1992; 1997), as well as expert scientific opinion, were included in order to avoid the omission of any important FEPs. FEPs not relevant to the assessment context of H12 were screened out (e.g. FEPs relevant only to the disposal of spent fuel or intentional human intrusion into the repository).

FEPs are allocated in the matrix, which is structured into six zones representing components of the disposal system and seven line-items representing relevant features and phenomena (hereafter called the hierarchical FEP matrix, see Figure 2). The merits of introduction of this structure for scenario development are as follows.

- Possible to identify FEPs at different levels of detail;

- Helpful to elicit a wide spectrum of expert opinion and encode these opinions in structured fashion;

- Easy to lump FEPs and record lumping process;

- Easy to develop a relational database system based on this hierarchical structure.

A comprehensive FEP list developed in this project is shown in Table 2. The comprehensiveness of the FEP list has been systematically checked by reviewing the matrix.

Based on the structure of the hierarchical FEP matrix, we developed a database system (CASCADE: Computer Assisted Scenario Controlling And Development System; see Figure 3) for storage and application of the information related to FEPs. The CASCADE system consists of 4 main windows. The windows and associated information have links that coincide with the structure of the hierarchical FEP matrix.

3.2   *Screening of FEPs for assessment calculations*

FEPs that correspond to one of the following four criteria are screened out to clarify the scope for the subsequent analyses:

(1) FEPs which are judged not to have a significant impact on the performance of the geological disposal system, provided an appropriate disposal site is selected;

(2) FEPs which are judged not to have a significant impact on the performance of the geological disposal system, provided the repository is adequately designed;

(3) FEPs with a low likelihood of occurrence;

(4) FEPs which do not correspond to the above criteria, but whose impact on the geological disposal system can be shown to be insignificant.

The following two classifications of scenarios are referred to in the AEC Guidelines:

- Scenarios in which the human environment may be affected due to the physical isolation of the waste being compromised (isolation failure scenario);

- Scenarios in which radionuclides may be transported to the biosphere by flowing groundwater (groundwater scenario).

Judicious site selection can avoid isolation failure scenarios and it is therefore sensible to focus on the groundwater scenario in the H12 consequence analysis. Studies concerning to the stability of the geological environment in Japan concluded that there are geological environments in Japan which are likely to remain stable and contain no natural resources likely to be of interest to future generations. For human activities, legal controls (e.g. limitation of land use), warnings by the setting of markers and by maintaining written records, will also reduce the possibility of human intrusion. By means of the above countermeasures, some geologic stability and human intrusion FEPs can be screened out. It is concluded that isolation failure or a significant impact due to sudden natural phenomena and human activity can be avoided by appropriate site selection and repository design and thus these are screened out according to criteria (1) to (3) above. However, the transport of radionuclides in groundwater is assumed to be inevitable, and thus the safety of the multi-barrier system is evaluated quantitatively for groundwater scenarios, in accord with the AEC Guidelines.

Shaded FEPs in Table 2 have been screened out by one of the above four criteria. FEPs which are not excluded in this step are considered in a quantitative or qualitative manner in the development of groundwater scenarios and in definition of calculation cases.

3.3 *Introduction of a "bottom-up" approach into scenario development*

To define the groundwater scenario and the corresponding calculation cases, it is more appropriate to group together FEPs, that share common expected safety functions, potential detrimental/favorable factors or perturbation factors, rather than work with the individual FEPs. This approach provides a practical advantage in minimizing the work to analyze the effect of the functions and/or the factors on the system performance. Understanding/judgement of these groups forms the basis for deciding scenario and calculation cases based on the linkage to the body of scientific expertise for individual FEPs and their interactions. The group of FEPs is consequently treated as an item of system understanding and various information used in scenario analysis can be recorded in one unit.

3.4 *Development of groundwater scenario*

Based on the concept of geological disposal in Japan, it is reasonable to adopt the following assumptions in defining a starting point for exploring the range of groundwater scenarios:

- The current conditions of the geological environment remain unchanged indefinitely;

- The initial conditions of the EBS are guaranteed to meet the expected functions;

- The current conditions of the surface environment remain unchanged indefinitely.

A groundwater scenario developed based on the above assumptions is known as the *normal evolution scenario*.

After screening out the FEPs according to a set of well-defined criteria and defining the scope of the normal evolution scenario, an influence diagram was constructed to describe influences among the relevant FEPs (see Figure 4). This forms the basis for defining scenarios and calculation cases. An additional feature of the methodology as applied in H12 is that it focuses on the part of the influence diagram containing FEPs which correspond to the expected safety functions of the system. To cover the wide scope of the scenario analysis in H12, the influence diagram relevant to the safety functions is regarded as the intersection of all the scenarios. To define a "Reference Case", that is a baseline among the consequence analyses in H12, model assumptions are developed for the processes relevant to the safety functions of a geological environment and the corresponding repository design. Then these assumptions are mapped onto a flow chart of the assessment models.

Then other calculation cases are developed to investigate the sensitivity of the system performance by considering alternative geological environments, options for repository and EBS designs, alternative models including potential detrimental/favorable processes and parameter ranges.

Finally, a series of alternative scenarios, referred to as *perturbation scenarios*, are developed to illustrate possible impacts of external perturbation factors (natural phenomena, future human activities and initial deficiencies of repository components) on the expected system performance under the normal evolution scenario. The objective of defining these scenarios is to investigate the sensitivity of the long-term safety to the evolution of the geological environment and changes to the expected safety functions caused by these factors. For each perturbation scenario, changes are made to the model assumptions and data used in the Reference Case reflecting possible effects due to external perturbations.

4.   Classification and Definition of Calculation Cases

Calculation cases for the groundwater scenario are established based on the following groups according to variations and uncertainties considered in the safety assessment. Figure 5 summarizes the classification of calculation cases and Figure 6 shows the structure of the consequence analysis in H12.

- **Reference Case**

    The Reference Case has been defined as a baseline for a number of calculation cases in H12. Model assumptions *(Reference-Case conceptual model)* were developed for all the processes relevant to the expected safety functions (see Table 1) given a single geological environment and corresponding repository design. In developing the *Reference-Case conceptual model*, the approach has been to adopt realistic descriptions to the relevant phenomena where possible. However, where realistic approaches were found to be difficult to apply because of uncertainties arising from insufficient understanding of the relevant phenomenon, conservative assumptions have been made. Similarly, the data for the models *(Reference-Case data)* was selected to be realistically supported by available data according to current understanding of the processes or features being represented. However, where available data were not sufficient to provide a realistic dataset, conservative values were used.

    - **Parameter level classification**

    A series of calculations *(data variation cases)* were carried out to bound the impact of parameter uncertainty and to investigate the sensitivity structure. These cases considered data uncertainties originating from heterogeneity of the system, lack of understanding of phenomena, experimental errors and/or various interpretation of the experimental results. For many parameters relating to the EBS performance where data used in the Reference Case are already deemed conservative, further conservatism for these data is not taken into account. However, for the parameters corresponding to nuclide transport in the host rock around the repository, conservative values and/or ranges were assumed based on the data, e.g. obtained from tests and measurements near the ground surface where physical and chemical disturbances to the rock are likely to have taken place, and sensitivity of the barrier performance to these parameters were also investigated.

- **Model level classification**

    A one-to-one mapping from the FEPs in the Reference-Case model assumptions and the Reference-Case data is assumed in the central thread of calculations. However, there are often a few alternative conceptual models and associated mathematical formulations. Furthermore, there are processes not included in the Reference Case that may increase or decrease the safety functions. To understand these model uncertainties, a set of calculation cases corresponding to the model options (*alternative model cases*) was developed.

- **System level classification**

  One important feature of H12 is that different geological environments in Japan and associated repository/EBS design options are taken into account as *alternative geological environment cases* and *alternative design cases*, respectively. The geological environment, design, model and data in the Reference Case are reviewed against these system alternatives and revised as required in a consistent manner.

- **Scenario level classification**

  To illustrate possible impacts of external perturbations, a series of calculation cases are defined based on the perturbation scenarios. In H12, the following external perturbations are considered and illustrative calculation cases are defined:

  - Natural phenomena: uplift/erosion, climate/sea-level change;

  - Initial deficiencies: incomplete seal of overpack;

  - Future human activities: well development, drilling activity.

The effects of these phenomena and events are taken into account in calculation cases as changes of parameters that are important to the safety functions of the geological disposal system.

As shown in Figure 6, the above calculations are performed to investigate the sensitivity of the performance of each barrier with respect to the variations and uncertainties.

According to the classification of calculation cases shown in Figure 5, they are defined by the following procedure:

- First, Reference-Case conceptual models and data are defined considering features and processes relevant to the expected safety functions in a geological disposal system.

- Then, alternative data are taken into account to investigate the potential impact of uncertainty in data used in the Reference Case.

- Then, alternative models are taken into account to investigate the potential impact of uncertainty in the models used in the Reference Case.

- Potential favorable factors or potential detrimental factors, which are not considered in the Reference Case, are described as changes of model and/or data from the Reference Case.

- The features of alternative geological disposal systems are considered as changes of model and/or data from the Reference Case.

- The impact of potential perturbation factors on geological conditions and/or the expected safety functions are described as changes of models and data from the Reference Case according to perturbation scenarios.

These modifications from the Reference-Case conceptual models and data are linked to illustrated effects of factors on system performance (see Table 1). Then they are labeled by the classification of calculation cases (alternative geological environment cases, alternative design cases, alternative model cases and data variation cases) or by the name of the perturbation scenario. For each calculation case, this procedure is designed to increase the transparency of the relationship to the sensitivity of specific factors and alternatives.

Based on the results of the sensitivity analysis mentioned above, a set of calculation cases to illustrate the total system performance is defined. These are primarily focused on alternative geological environments (rock type, groundwater type and hydraulic condition) in Japan. This is consistent with the scope of H12 in which the wide variety of geological environments in Japan must be considered. In the total system performance analysis, inconsistent combinations among the variations and uncertainties are excluded and those having similar impacts on the long-term safety are grouped together.

5.   *Concluding Remarks*

In scenario analysis for the safety assessment in H12, comprehensive FEP list, various scenarios and calculation cases were developed in a systematic manner. Procedures adopted in the scenario analysis have features as follows:

- Development of a comprehensive FEP list in a structured fashion (hierarchical FEP matrix) relevant to safety of geological disposal system,

- Introduction of a top-down approach to integrate the result of a bottom-up approach (FEPs and their interactions) as scenarios and calculation cases in a comprehensive manner,

- Expansion of the scope of scenario analysis to avoid inconsistency and loosing traceability at the interface between scenarios and calculation cases, and

- Development of computor system to manage all process of scenario analysis.

By application of this procedure, 6 scenarios (one normal evolution scenario and five perturbation scenarios), 100 sensitivity analysis cases and 32 total system performance analysis cases were successfully developed for the H12 safety assessment.

References

The Advisory Committee on Nuclear Fuel Cycle Backend Policy, the Atomic Energy Commission of Japan (1997): Guidelines on Research and Development Relating to Geological Disposal of High-level Radioactive Waste in Japan.

Hodgkinson, D.P. and Sumerling, T.J. (1990): A Review of Approaches to Scenario Analysis for Repository Safety Assessment, Proc. Int. Symp. Safety Assessment of Radioactive Waste Repositories, pp.333-350, OECD/NEA, Paris.

OECD/NEA (1991): Review of Safety Assessment Methods, A Report of the Performance Assessment Advisory Group of the Radioactive Waste Management Committee, OECD Nuclear Energy Agency.

OECD/NEA (1992): Systematic Approaches to Scenario Development: A Report of the NEA Working Group on the Identification and Selection of Scenarios for Performance Assessment of Radioactive Waste Disposal.

OECD/NEA (1997): Safety Assessment of Radioactive Waste Repositories - Systematic Approaches to Scenario Development – An International Database of Features, Events and Processes. Draft Report (24/6/1997) of the NEA Working Group on Development of a Database of Features, Events and Processes Relevant to the Assessment of Post-Closure Safety of Radioactive Waste Repositories.

Table 1. Expected safety functions, potential detrimental factors and potential perturbation factors

Expected Safety Functions (System Performance)	Related FEP (see Table 2)
Faborable groundwater chemistry (e.g. reducing conditon)	H-4.2/H-4.3
Small groundwater flux	H-2.3
Mechanical stability	H-3.2
Negligible effect of repository components	D-2.2/D-2.3/D-3.2/D-3.3/D-4.2/D-4.3
Physical isolation from human and his environment	H-6.3
Confinement of vitrified waste	Op-3.2/Op-3.3/Op-4.2/Op-4.3/Op-4.4/Op-4.5/Op-4.6/Op-4.7 B-3.2, G-5.1/G-1.4/G-1.2, Op-1.2, B-1.2, D-1.2, H-1.2
Mitigation of radionuclide dissolution	G-3.2/G-3.3/G-4.2/G-4.3/G-4.8/G-5.1/G-6.2.1
Low permeability of buffer material	B-2.2/B-3.3, D-2.2, H-2.3/H-2.2
Swelling property and ductility of buffer material	B-2.2/B-3.2/B-3.3, D-3.2, H-3.2
Chemical buffering	B-4.2/B-4.3, Op-4.3, D-4.2, H-4.2
Low solubility in porewater in buffer material	G-4.2/G-6.2.2, B-4.2/B-6.3.4, Op-4.2/Op-6.3.4
Slow mass transport in buffer material	B-4.2/B-6.2/B-6.3.2, Op-4.2/Op-6.2/Op-6.3.2, H-6.3.1
Radionuclide retardation in buffer material	B-4.2/B-6.3.3, Op-4.2/Op-6.3.3
Filtration of colloid, microbial and organic matters in buffer material	B-6.2/B-4.7, G-4.7, Op-4.9
Radionuclide retardation in host rock	H-6.2/H-4.2/H-2.3/H-6.3.1/H-6.3.2/H-6.3.3
Radionuclide dispersion and dilution in host rock	H-6.2/H-2.3/H-6.3.1
Radiological decay	G-5.1, Op-5.1, B-5.1, H-5.1
Potentially Detrimental Factors to System Performance	**Related FEP (see Table 2)**
Volumetric expansion due to overpack corrosion	Op-3.4/Op-4.5, B-3.4/B-3.5/B-6.2/B-3.2, D-3.2, H-3.2/H-2.3
Extrusion of buffer matrial	B-3.5/B-6.2, Op-3.4, D-2.3, H-2.3
Degradation of repository components	D-4.8/D-4.3/D-4.2/D-2.3
Organic matters in host rock	H-4.6/H-6.3.3
Colloid formation and migration in host rock	H-6.3.5/H-4.7, B-4.7, D-4.7
Deformation of host rock	H-3.3/H-2.3/H-6.2
Deficiencies of repository components	Op-7.1
Potential Perturbation Factors to System Performance	**Related FEP (see Table 2)**
Natural phenomena	G/Op/B/D/H-7 (Uplift/erosion, Climatic/sea-level change)
Human activities	G/Op/B/D/H-7 (Well drilling, Exploratory drilling)

Table 2. Hierarchical FEP Matrix

(Shaded box means that the FEP was excluded from safety assessment calculations following discussion at the FEP Classification stage)

	G. Glass	Op. Overpack	B. Buffer	D. Plug/Grout, Tunnel-support, Backfill	H. Host Rock (Including EDZ & Major Fault)
1.Thermal	G-1.1 Thermal Properties G-1.2 Temperature of Glass G-1.3 Thermal Expansion of Glass G-1.4 Decay Heat Generation	Op-1.1 Thermal Properties of OP/CP Op-1.2 Temperature of OP/CP Op-1.3 Thermal Expansion of OP/CP	B-1.1 Thermal Properties of Buffer B-1.2 Temperature of Buffer B-1.3 Thermal Expansion of Buffer	D-1.1 Thermal Properties of Materials D-1.2 Temperature of Materials D-1.3 Thermal Expansion of Materials	H-1.1 Thermal Properties of Host Rock H-1.2 Temperature of Host Rock H-1.3 Thermal Expansion of Host Rock
2.Hydrological			B-2.1 Hydrological Properties of Buffer B-2.2 Saturation of Buffer B-2.3 Hydraulic Flow in Buffer	D-2.1 Hydrological Properties of Materials D-2.2 Saturation of Materials D-2.3 Hydraulic Flow in Materials	H-2.1 Hydrological Properties of Host Rock H-2.2 Recharge to Host Rock H-2.3 Hydraulic Flow in Host Rock
3.Mechanical	G-3.1 Mechanical Properties G-3.2 Mechanical Stress G-3.3 Glass Cracking	Op-3.1 Mechanical Properties Op-3.2 Mechanical Stress Op-3.3 Overpack Breaching Op-3.4 Volumetric Expansion due to Corrosion Op-3.5 Overpack Sinking	B-3.1 Mechanical Properties of Buffer B-3.2 Mechanical Stress of Buffer B-3.3 Swelling of Buffer B-3.4 Deformation of Buffer B-3.5 Extrusion of Buffer	D-3.1 Mechanical Properties of Materials D-3.2 Mechanical Stress of Materials D-3.3 Swelling of Materials D-3.4 Deformation of Materials D-3.5 Extrusion of Materials	H-3.1 Mechanical Properties of Host Rock H-3.2 Mechanical Stress of Host Rock H-3.3 Deformation of Host Rock

4.Chemical	G-4.1 Chemical Properties of Glass
	G-4.2 Porewater Chemistry
	G-4.3 Glass Dissolution
	G-4.4 Gas Generation and Effects
	G-4.5 Microbial Activity
	G-4.6 Organics
	G-4.7 Colloid Formation
	G-4.8 Glass Alteration
		Op-4.1 Chemical Properties of OP/CP
		Op-4.2 Porewater Chemistry
		Op-4.3 Interaction of OP/CP with Porewater
		Op-4.4 Corrosion
		  Op-4.4.1 Uniform Corrosion
		  Op-4.4.2 Pitting Corrosion
		  Op-4.4.3 Crevice Corrosion
		  Op-4.4.4 Stress Corrosion Cracking
		Op-4.5 Formation of Corrosion Products
		Op-4.6 Gas Generation
		Op-4.7 Microbial Activity
		Op-4.8 Organics
		Op-4.9 Colloid Formation
			B-4.1 Chemical Properties of Buffer
			B-4.2 Porewater Chemistry
			B-4.3 Interaction of Buffer with Porewater
			B-4.4 Gas Generation/ Effect
			B-4.5 Microbial Activity
			B-4.6 Organics
			B-4.7 Colloid Formation
			B-4.8 Chemical Alteration of Buffer
			B-4.9 Salt Accumulation
				D-4.1 Chemical Properties of Materials
				D-4.2 Groundwater Chemistry
				D-4.3 Interaction of Materials with Porewater
				D-4.4 Gas Generation/ Effect
				D-4.5 Microbial Activity
				D-4.6 Organics
				D-4.7 Colloid Formation
				D-4.8 Chemical Alteration of Materials
					H-4.1 Chemical Properties of Host Rock
					H-4.2 Groundwater Chemistry
					H-4.3 Interaction of Host Rock with Porewater
					H-4.4 Gas Generation/ Effect
					H-4.5 Microbial Activity
					H-4.6 Organics
					H-4.7 Colloid Formation
					H-4.8 Chemical Alteration of Host Rock (eg. Fracture Mineralisation)

5.Radiological	G-5.1 Radioactive Decay and Ingrowth G-5.2 Radiolysis G-5.3 Radiation Damage	Op-5.1 Radioactive Decay and Ingrowth Op-5.2 Radiolysis of Porewater Op-5.3 Radiation Damage	B-5.1 Radioactive Decay and Ingrowth B-5.2 Radiolysis of Porewater B-5.3 Radiation Damage	D-5.1 Radioactive Decay and Ingrowth D-5.2 Radiolysis of Groundwater D-5.3 Radiation Damage	H-5.1 Radioactive Decay and Ingrowth H-5.2 Radiolysis of Groundwater H-5.3 Radiation Damage of Host Rocks

6.Mass Transport	G-6.1 Mass Transport Properties of Glass
	G-6.2 Geometry and Pore Structure
	G-6.3 Radionuclide Release from Glass
	  G-6.3.1 Congruent Dissolution
	  G-6.3.2 Precipitation / Dissolution
		Op-6.1 Mass Transport Properties of OP/CP
		Op-6.2 Geometry and Pore Structure
		Op-6.3 Radionuclide Migration in CP
		  Op-6.3.1 Advection/Dispersion
		  Op-6.3.2 Diffusion
		  Op-6.3.3 Sorption
		  Op-6.3.4 Precipitation / Dissolution
		  Op-6.3.5 Colloid Migration
		  Op-6.3.6 Gas Driven/Mediated Transport
			B-6.1 Mass Transport Properties of Buffer
			B-6.2 Geometry and Pore Structure
			B-6.3 Radionuclide Migration in Buffer
			  B-6.3.1 Advection/Dispersion
			  B-6.3.2 Diffusion
			  B-6.3.3 Sorption
			  B-6.3.4 Precipitation / Dissolution
			  B-6.3.5 Colloid Migration
			  B-6.3.6 Gas Driven/Mediated Transport
				D-6.1 Mass Transport Properties of Materials
				D-6.2 Geometry and Pore Structure
				D-6.3 Radionuclide Migration
				  D-6.3.1 Advection/Dispersion
				  D-6.3.2 Diffusion
				  D-6.3.3 Sorption
				  D-6.3.4 Precipitation / Dissolution
				  D-6.3.5 Colloid Migration
				  D-6.3.6 Gas Driven/Mediated Transport
					H-6.1 Mass Transport Properties of Host rock
					H-6.2 Geometry and Pore/Fracture Structure
					H-6.3 Radionuclide Migration in Host Rock
					  H-6.3.1 Advection/Dispersion
					  H-6.3.2 Diffusion
					  H-6.3.3 Sorption
					  H-6.3.4 Precipitation / Dissolution
					  H-6.3.5 Colloid Migration
					  H-6.3.6 Gas Driven/Mediated Transport
					H-6.4 Radionuclide Accumulation (leading to Criticality)

7.Perturbation	G-7.1 Glass Defects and Poor QC in Fabrication	Op-7.1 Overpack Defects and Poor QC in Fabrication	B-7.1 Buffer Defects and Poor QC in Fabrication B-7.2 Inadequate Buffer Emplacement	D-7.1 Defects and Poor QC in Fabrication D-7.2 Inadequate backfill / Compaction or Inadequate Emplacement of Plug, Grout, Tunnel-support	H-7.1 Borehole Seal Failure and Degradation
	Natural Phenomena (Earthquake/Faulting, Uplift/Erosion, Volcanic Activity, Climatic/Sea-level Change, Meteorite Impact, Flooding, etc.)				
	Human Activity (Exploratory/Exploitation drilling, Resource Mining, Underground Construction/Tunneling)				

OP:
CP: Corrosion

Not

Figure 1. Procedure for scenario analysis

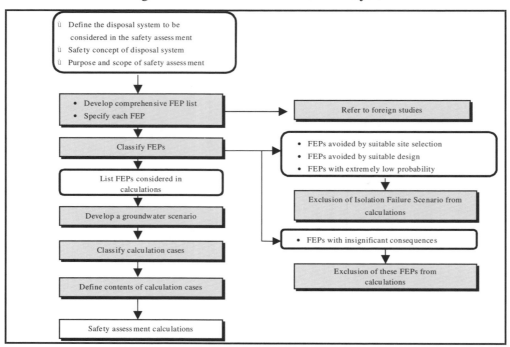

Figure 2. An overview of the hierarchical FEP matrix

	Glass	Overpack	Buffer	Plug/Grout Support, Backfill	Host Rock
Thermal	G-1	Op-1	B-1	D-1	H-1
Hydrological	G-2	Op-2	B-2	D-2	H-2
Mechanical	G-3	Op-3	B-3	D-3	H-3
Chemical	G-4		B-4	D-4	H-4
Radiological	G-5	Op-5	B-5	D-5	H-5
Mass Transport	G-6	Op-6	B-6	D-6	H-6
Pertubation	G-7	Op-7	B-7	D-7	H-7

Natural Phenomena (Earthquake/Faulting, Volcanic Activity, Uplift/Erosions, Climatic/Sea-level Change, Meteorite Imapct, Flooding, etc)

Human Activities (Exploratory/Exploitation Drilling, Resource Mining, Underground Construction/Tunnering, Landuse Development, etc.)

Op-4.1	Chemical Property of OP/CP Material
Op-4.2	Porewater Chemistry
Op-4.3	Interaction of OP/CP Material and Porewater
Op-4.5	Formation of Corrosion Products
Op-4.6	Gas Generation
Op-4.7	Microbial Activity
Op-4.8	Organics
Op-4.9	Colloid Formation from CP

NOTE) OP: Overpack, CP: Corrosion

Op-4.4.1	Uniform Corrosion
Op-4.4.2	Pitting Corrosion
Op-4.4.3	Crevice Corrosion
Op-4.4.4	Stress Corrosion Cracking

Figure 3. **A schematic view of information link in the CASCADE system**

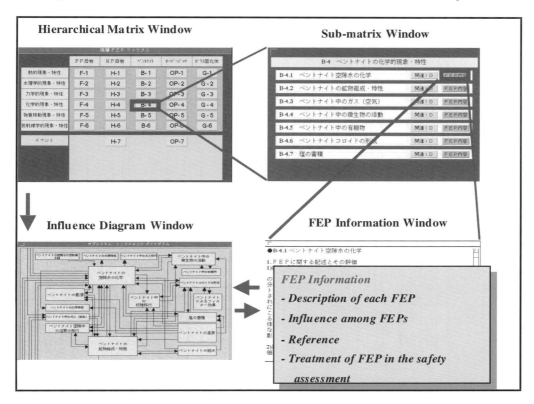

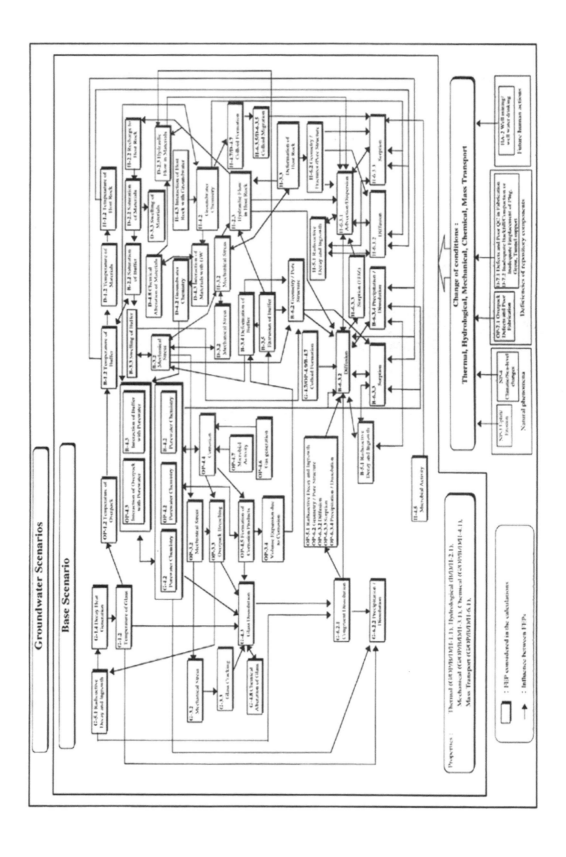

Figure 4. Influence diagram for groundwater scenario

Figure 5. **Classification of scenarios and calculation cases**

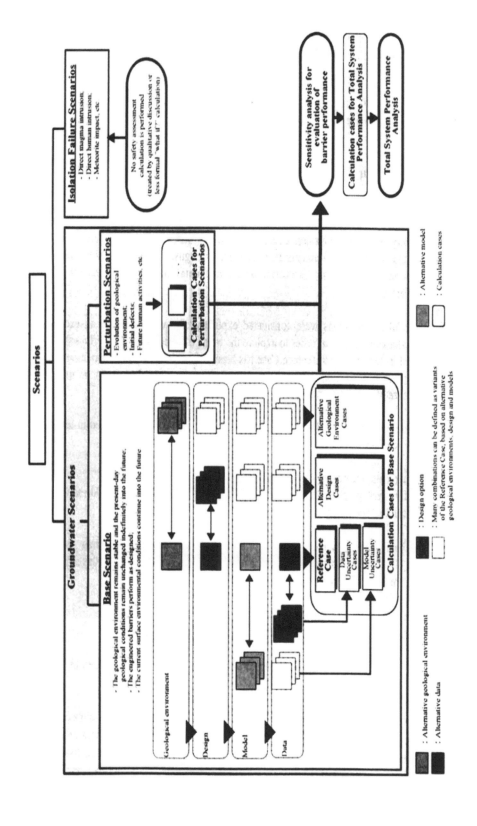

239

Figure 6. **Structure of safety assessment calculations**

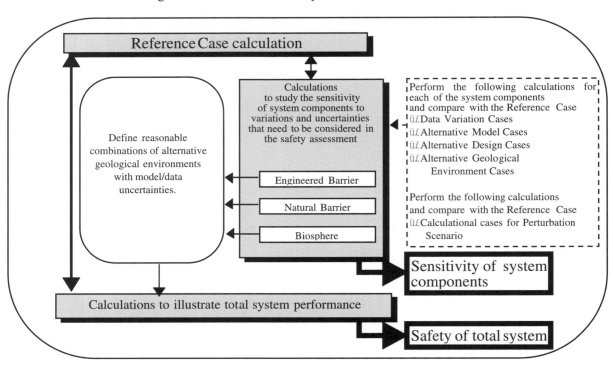

The NEA wishes to express its gratitude to the Government of Japan
for facilitating the production of this report.

本報告書の作成に関し、日本政府の協力に謝意を表する。

ALSO AVAILABLE

NEA Publications of General Interest

1999 Annual Report (2000)   *Free: available on Web.*

NEA News
ISSN 1605-9581   Yearly subscription: FF 240 US$ 45 DM 75 £ 26 ¥ 4 800

Geologic Disposal of Radioactive Waste in Perspective (2000)
ISBN 92-64-18425-2   Price: FF 130 US$ 20 DM 39 £ 12 ¥ 2 050

Radiation in Perspective – Applications, Risks and Protection (1997)
ISBN 92-64-15483-3   Price: FF 135 US$ 27 DM 40 £ 17 ¥ 2 850

Radioactive Waste Management in Perspective (1996)
ISBN 92-64-14692-X   Price: FF 310 US$ 63 DM 89 £ 44

Radioactive Waste Management

Using Thermodynamic Sorption Models for Guiding Radioelement Distribution Coefficient (KD) Investigations – A Status Report (2001)
ISBN 92-64-18679-4   Price: € 50 US$ 45 £ 31 ¥ 5 050

Gas Generation and Migration in Radioactive Waste Disposal – Safety-relevant Issues (2001)
ISBN 92-64-18672-7   Price: € 45 US$ 39 £ 27 ¥ 4 300

Confidence in Models of Radionuclide Transport for Site-specific Assessment (2001)
ISBN 92-64-18620-4   Price: € 96 US$ 84 £ 58 ¥ 9 100

Nuclear Waste Bulletin – Update on Waste Management Policies and Programmes, No. 14, 2000 Edition (2001)   ISBN 92-64-18461-9   *Free: paper or Web.*

Geological Disposal of Radioactive Waste – Review of Developments in the Last Decade (1999)
ISBN 92-64-17194-0   Price: FF 190 US$ 31 DM 57 £ 19 ¥ 3 300

Water-conducting Features in Radionuclide Migration (1999)
ISBN 92-64-17124-X   Price: FF 600 US$ 96 DM 180 £ 60 ¥ 11 600

Features, Events and Processes (FEPs) for Geologic Disposal of Radioactive Waste
An International Database (2000)
ISBN 92-64-18514-3   Price: FF 150 US$ 24 DM 45 £ 15 ¥ 2 900

Porewater Extraction from Argillaceous Rocks for Geochemical Characterisation (2000)
ISBN 92-64-17181-9   Price: FF 380 US$ 60 DM 113 £ 37 ¥ 6 350

Regulatory Reviews of Assessments of Deep Geological Repositories – Lessons Learnt (2000)
ISBN 92-64-05886-9   Price: FF 210 US$ 32 DM 63 £ 20 ¥ 3 400

Strategic Areas in Radioactive Waste Management – The Viewpoint and Work Orientations of the NEA Radioactive Waste Management Committee (2000)   *Free: paper or Web.*

Stakeholder Confidence and Radioactive Waste Disposal (2000)
ISBN 92-64-18277-2   *Free: paper or Web.*

Progress Towards Geologic Disposal of Radioactive Waste: Where Do We Stand? (1999)
                                                        Free: paper or Web.

Confidence in the Long-term Safety of Deep Geological Repositories – Its Development and Communication (1999)   *Free: paper or Web.*

Order form on reverse side.

ORDER FORM

OECD Nuclear Energy Agency, 12 boulevard des Iles, F-92130 Issy-les-Moulineaux, France
Tel. 33 (0)1 45 24 10 10, Fax 33 (0)1 45 24 11 10, E-mail: nea@nea.fr, Internet: www.nea.fr

Qty	Title	ISBN	Price	Amount
			Total	

❑ Payment enclosed (cheque or money order payable to OECD Publications).

Charge my credit card   ❑ VISA   ❑ Mastercard   ❑ Eurocard   ❑ American Express

(N.B.: You will be charged in French francs).

Card No.	Expiration date	Signature
Name		
Address	Country	
Telephone	Fax	
E-mail		

OECD PUBLICATIONS, 2, rue André-Pascal, 75775 PARIS CEDEX 16
PRINTED IN FRANCE
(66 2001 12 1 P) ISBN 92-64-18722-7 – No. 51993 2001